THE
National ⚾ Pastime

Short But Wondrous Summers
Baseball in the North Star State

Edited by Daniel R. Levitt

Published by
The Society for American Baseball Research

THE NATIONAL PASTIME

Editor: Daniel R. Levitt
Design and Production: Lisa Hochstein
Cover Design: Lisa Hochstein
Fact Checker: Clifford Blau

Front cover: Photos courtesy of the Minnesota Twins,
the Minnesota Historical Society, Getty Images and Rex Hamann.

Published by:
The Society for American Baseball Research, Inc.
4455 E. Camelback Road, Ste. D-140
Phoenix, AZ 85018

Phone: (800) 969-7227 or (602) 343-6455
Web: www.sabr.org
Twitter: @sabr
Facebook: Society for American Baseball Research

Copyright © 2012
The Society for American Baseball Research
Printed in the United States of America

ISBN 978-1-933599-22-9

Contents

Foreword

I have been kidded that by plugging away for so long before finally making it to the majors, I have made it harder to convince other prospects with little chance at the majors to quit baseball and get on with the rest of their lives. But for me, I wouldn't have traded it for anything. As Dan noted when he asked me to write this forward, I have been intimately involved with many aspects of Minnesota baseball. I grew up playing at the youth and then high school level. I played at the University of Minnesota and had a cup of coffee with the Twins. And in what may have been the highlight of my career, I came back to face them in what many consider the greatest World Series of all time.

I spent my first years of any sort of organized athletics in Marshall, a small town in Southwestern Minnesota. Growing up with my older brother Jeff gave me an opportunity to play with the bigger kids. When I was eight or nine I hung around his youth baseball team, acting as an informal batboy. When his teammates missed games because they were on vacation or sick, I would fill in, and since I was pretty good for my age I found I could hold my own when given the chance.

I was nine when my family moved to Edina, outside of Minneapolis, where sports were much more regulated. I could no longer play up with my brother's team and was stuck playing a year of cub softball. But the area had well-organized youth baseball, and over the next couple of years I played on some elite teams and at some of the best facilities in the region. At Edina East High School I made the varsity team at third base as a sophomore in 1977, a memorable year in which we made it all the way to the state championship game before losing to St. Peter.

After graduation I hoped to follow in the footsteps of Steve Ramler, another Edina player two years older than me who had gone to Oral Roberts University, but the baseball coach didn't think I was good enough. Fortunately, University of Minnesota baseball coach George Thomas did. After the first day of practice he called me into his office and asked if I'd ever been a catcher. When I told him I hadn't, Thomas said it was time I learned and that starting tomorrow, I was a catcher. No question, that moment made a big difference in my getting to the majors. My sophomore year I played with all three of New Ulm's Steinbach brothers, including Terry, who went on to play many years in the majors.

The New York Mets drafted me in the seventh round after my junior year when I was named a first team All-American. I slowly worked my up through the Mets system, but after seven years I had plateaued at Triple-A. I was now a minor league free agent. Rather than retire, I signed a minor league contract with the Twins for 1989. The Twins called me up in June when Dan Gladden was injured, and in my first appearance I caught for Juan Berenguer. A couple of days later I had my first hit when I laced a Bryan Harvey pitch off the top of the left field Plexiglas. Angels left fielder Chili Davis played the carom perfectly, holding me to a single. Kirby Puckett, whom I knew from my days in the minors, liked to razz me that I hit the longest single in the history of the Metrodome.

Unfortunately, I only stayed in the big leagues for a short stint, and after the season the Twins released me. I still thought I could play major league baseball, however, and signed with the Atlanta Braves. My persistence was finally about to run into some good luck. Because spring training in 1990 was delayed due to a short lockout, teams were allowed to carry 27-man rosters through April 30. I started the season in the minors, but was called up almost immediately to be the team's third catcher. When I finally had a chance to catch a couple of weeks into the season, Tom Glavine was the pitcher. Glavine liked working with me and asked manager Russ Nixon to allow me catch him going forward. Because I was also hitting well I soon became the team's regular catcher and even made the All-Star team.

The next season, 1991, was my most enjoyable in baseball. Every player's dream is to play in the World Series, and here I was, not only in it, but playing against my hometown Minnesota Twins. I caught every inning in that seven-game series, but unfortunately we came out at the short end in one of baseball's most famous Game Sevens.

I was able to be a part of Minnesota's baseball tradition at nearly all levels. From youth baseball to the World Series, I experienced some of the best moments the sport has to offer. I remain involved today, working with young baseball players hoping for a chance to play at a higher level. As long as there are young people who love the game and are willing to work at it, Minnesota should have many more kids following in my footsteps.

– Greg Olson

Introduction

Summers in Minnesota are short but wonderfully pleasant. During the short season Minnesotans spend much of their time outside, and baseball has long been an important part of their summer schedule. Even before the inception of statehood in 1858, Minnesota's residents played and watched baseball. In this volume of *The National Pastime* you will find the story of baseball in Minnesota: from the town of Nininger organizing a team in August 1857 to the Twins under general manager Terry Ryan.

Organized professional baseball leagues first came to Minnesota in the mid-1870s. Various professional leagues then struggled to gain a permanent foothold until the American Association—one step below the majors—was organized in the early 1900s. The Minneapolis Millers and St. Paul Saints captured the interest of Twin Cities baseball fans for nearly 60 years, and their streetcar-connected holiday twin bills—a game in the morning in one city and the afternoon in the other—highlighted the rivalry between the two cities and their teams. Finally, in 1961 the state had only one team to root for at the highest level when the Washington Senators moved to the Twin Cities and became the Minnesota Twins. Popular and successful throughout the 1960s, the team finally rewarded its fans with World Championships in 1987 and 1991.

Of course, there was much more to baseball in Minnesota than the majors and top minor leagues. The Northern League generated a strong following in several of Minnesota's outstate cities. The University of Minnesota can boast a terrific baseball tradition, as can a number of smaller public and private colleges. For many years black players struggled for opportunities to play, occasionally working their way onto some integrated teams outside of Organized Baseball. Women, also, found opportunities to play the game. Inside, you'll find these stories, too.

One of the pleasures of working on this book was getting to work with some of area's foremost baseball historians, as the authors of the articles were universally timely, courteous, and helpful. In many ways this publication is a product of the Halsey Hall chapter, one of SABR's most active and involved—although I may be a bit biased. Bob Tholkes, Minnesota's expert on early baseball, reviewed a number of articles and otherwise helped edit and improve this volume. Another nineteenth and early twentieth century historian who knows more about baseball in Northern Minnesota than anyone else I know, Rich Arpi, reviewed several articles. Twins blogger and noted authority John Bonnes reviewed several, as did Mark Armour, chair of SABR's biography project and a terrific writer and historian, even if not from Minnesota. Lastly, I need to thank Stew Thornley, Minnesota's preeminent baseball historian, for taking the time to review the vast majority of the articles in this volume and offer his insights and support.

Along with a terrific lineup of articles, you will find a great assortment of interesting and unique images and photographs. Foremost thanks go to the Minnesota Twins, the Minnesota Historical Society, and the *Star Tribune* for letting us dig through their archives and allowing us to use their photos. Others who helped with images and photos include Fred Buckland, who graciously allowed us to use some of his postcards, Joel Rippel, the National Baseball Hall of Fame, several of the colleges and universities mentioned in the book, and many of the authors who contributed photographs for their articles. In addition, Dave Jensen was a big help in finding photos and tracking down permissions.

From the national SABR team, Cecilia Tan was a great help, letting me bounce my many questions off her and offering guidance and support. Fact-checker Cliff Blau proved tremendously valuable; his ability to rapidly turn around articles and correct errors on every subject was truly astounding.

The book you are holding tells the story of baseball in Minnesota, from the grand scope to the fascinating vignette. Turn the page and dig in.

— Daniel R. Levitt

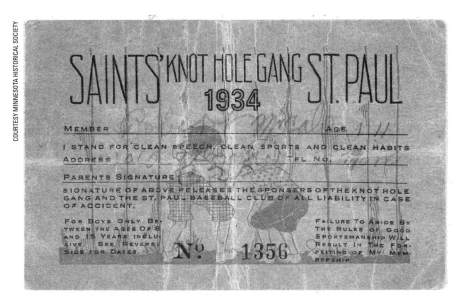

St. Paul Saints knothole card.

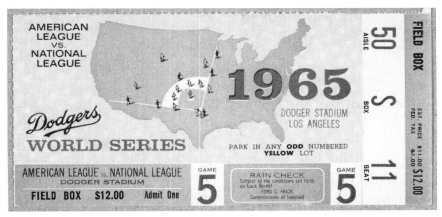

1965 World Series ticket.

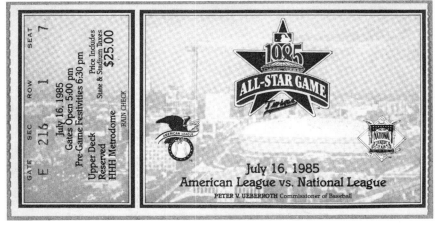

1985 All-Star Game ticket.

The Rise of Baseball in Minnesota

Cecil O. Monroe, excerpted by Bob Tholkes

The Halsey Hall Chapter of SABR welcomes the opportunity to honor the work of pre-SABR baseball history pioneer Cecil O. Monroe by including the following excerpt in our SABR 42 convention publication. Cecil O. Monroe was born in 1901 in South Dakota. According to his son, Donald Monroe, Cecil was a longtime devotee of baseball history as well as a fan, both of the local Aberdeen Pheasants and of the American Association Minneapolis Millers and St. Paul Saints, taking his family to their games during summers spent pursuing postgraduate education at the University of Minnesota. During one (or more) of those summers he used the extensive collection of Minnesota historic newspapers at the Minnesota Historical Society in St. Paul to research The Rise of Baseball in Minnesota, *which the Society published in the* Minnesota History Quarterly *in June, 1938. Cecil O. Monroe died in Yankton, South Dakota, in 1965.*

Following the demobilization of the armies in 1865, there came a rapid and widespread development of baseball clubs. Minnesota pioneers, however, were familiar with the game even before the war. In August 1857, for example, the citizens of Nininger decided to organize a baseball club. The editor of the Nininger newspaper hoped the venture would stimulate the young men of neighboring towns to organize clubs so that "matches and return matches" could be played for "assembled thousands."[1]

In St. Paul, a baseball organization claimed the attention of newspapers as early as the summer of 1859. The club showed a lack of vigor in 1860, and late in the summer William Wilson "requested all members" to hold an organization meeting. The result was the formation of the Olympic club, which took part in a baseball game on September 11, 1860. During the next few years, events of more significance absorbed the attention and energy of citizens.[2]

In 1865 intercity baseball competition began. In the issue of May 17 the *Saint Paul Press* announced that the North Star club of St. Paul was scheduled to play a game with the Excelsior club of Fort Snelling. The game was played before a large crowd and the North Star club won by the overwhelming score of 38 to 14.[3]

The North Star boys challenged the sportsmen of Hastings to "match play." The first game was played at Hastings on July 1. The Vermillion club of Hastings had been organized the "day preceding the match" and its members "had never played together before." The Vermillion club played the second and final game of the match at St. Paul in September, the North Stars winning by a score of 49 to 16.[4]

In 1865 the North Star club showed consistent activity. Although it was inactive the next year, baseball prospered in St. Paul. On April 14, 1866, "all interested in forming a Base Ball Club"[5] were called upon to meet at the grounds of the North Star. By July 27 two clubs had been organized, the Olympic and the Saxon. The first game between the rival clubs was won by the Olympic nine by a score of 20 to 18. The rivalry between the two teams was especially keen because the Saxon club represented Lower Town and Olympic, Upper Town. The second game, a smashing victory for the Olympics, was played late in August. This team also won the final game on October 29 and became the city champions.[6]

In the fall of 1866 the Champion club of Winona was organized, and a club was reported in Red Wing. At the end of 1866 baseball had a firm hold in St. Paul, a good beginning in Hastings, and a start in both Winona and Red Wing. The stage was set for the banner year of 1867.[7]

During the first week of April, 1867, "old members" and all others interested were requested to meet in Munger's Hall in St. Paul to reorganize the North Star club.[8] The first match game of the season was played with the Minneapolis club on May 27, and thirty-five members of the North Star club went to the neighboring city for the occasion. The results were most gratifying for the visitors, who won the game by a score of 56 to 26.[9] A second game with the Minneapolis nine was played in St. Paul, and the North Star club was again victorious by a score of 47 to 29.[10]

In less than a week after the second triumph over

the Minneapolis nine, the North Star club challenged the Crescent club of Red Wing. For six innings the game was evenly contested, but the St. Paul boys batted hard in the closing innings to win by a score of 52 to 34.[11]

The North Star club continued to arouse interest in the great game of baseball by going to Mankato in July. Since the Frontier club had been organized only a short time, it was no match for a nine "so well disciplined as the North Star," whose members were hailed as the "Champions of the State."[12] It is clear that much of the credit for the popularity of baseball in Minnesota in 1867 should go to the North Star club. For an amateur organization it was excellently directed. It held meetings regularly each month during the season, and issued many special calls. The first nine was selected from the membership, which totaled fifty-seven names. Regular practice and social games between the first and second nines gave the members a chance to prove their skill.

Many other Minnesota towns had baseball clubs in 1867. The Lake City Union Base Ball Club was organized on July 10. The Gopher State club (Rochester) played at Owatonna on July 29 and 30. A team from St. Peter was beaten by the Frontier club of Mankato before five hundred spectators.[13]

Many other clubs organized in 1867 apparently did not participate in intercity matches. The St. Croix club was formed at Stillwater sometime during July. According to the Goodhue County Republican a club was organized at Cannon Falls. The Minnehaha club of Northfield and a club at Faribault were in the field and helped to organize the Minnesota State Association of Base Ball Players, as did clubs from Dundas and St. Cloud.[14] The formation of this association was the outstanding feature of Minnesota baseball history in 1867. The *St. Paul Press* of August 20 printed a call for a "Base Ball Players' Convention." All newspapers in Minnesota were urged to reprint this notice, which was signed by the presidents of the baseball clubs at St. Paul, Owatonna, Hastings, Minneapolis, Red Wing, Northfield, Winona, Faribault, and Mankato. The North Star club of St. Paul was the leading spirit in the movement to create a state organization.

The convention was held as scheduled. The committee on credentials seated delegates from the Gopher club of Owatonna, the Crescent club of Red Wing, the Faribault club, the Minnehaha club of Northfield, the Adriatic club of Dundas, the North Star and Saxon clubs of St. Paul, the Arctic club of St. Cloud, the National club of Lake City, and the Minneapolis and High School clubs of Minneapolis. The convention ignored the delegates and active ballplayers in electing as president General Henry H. Sibley, who was famed not only as a soldier and statesman, but also as a sportsman. The convention undertook to select a location for the first state tournament, for which Minneapolis, Faribault, and St. Paul were bidding. A committee of five, with General Sibley as chairman, was appointed to conduct the tournament after St. Paul was chosen.[15]

Only five clubs entered the tournament—a cause for bitter disappointment. They were the Arctic club of St. Cloud, the Vermillion club of Hastings, the North Star and Saxon clubs of St. Paul, and the St. Croix club of Stillwater.[16] For the first-class championship, the North Stars played the Vermillions after the latter had disposed of St. Cloud by a score of 100 to 44. The final game attracted a large crowd, including so many boys that it seemed as if "all the schools in the city had made a special holiday." The umpire was H. S. Seymour of the Niagara club of Buffalo, New York. The summary of the game in the St. Paul Press indicates an interesting contest.[17]

The championship prize, a silver ball, was, of course, presented to the captain of the North Star team, W. Wilson.

Regulations for future match play for the championship trophy, published in

COURTESY NORTHFIELD HISTORICAL SOCIETY

The first baseball game between St. Olaf College and Carleton College, on the St. Olaf College campus, 1887.

the *St. Paul Press* of October 8, 1867, defined the manner of challenging and of paying fees and expenses. To obtain the silver ball a team must win two out of three games, all players on the competing nines must have been members of the club in good standing for thirty days prior to the match, and the Base Ball Players' Book of Reference published in 1867 by J. C. Haney and company was made the basis for settling disputes not covered by rules of the state association. The mere creation of rules, however, did not smooth all the bumps in the path of championship play; in fact, they seemed to make new difficulties. Bickering, accusations of unfairness, and sometimes disputes so bitter as to interrupt a game, now arose.

Following victories over teams from Faribault, Hastings, and Hudson, Wisconsin, in the spring of 1868, the Minnehaha club of Northfield challenged the North Star club to defend its title. A controversy over the thirty-day eligibility clause threatened to wreck the match. When the teams arrived on the playing field on July 17, the North Star club was planning to use a certain William Miller of Stillwater as pitcher. The St. Paul boys admitted that Miller had pitched for the St. Croix team, but insisted that he "was now coming to St. Paul to live," and therefore should be allowed to play. Another quarrel arose when the game was stopped by rain in the eighth inning, with the score 78 to 38 in favor of the Minnehaha nine. After considerable argument, the North Stars finally conceded the game to the Minnehaha nine, but pointed out the legality of the St. Paul claims by several references to Haney's rules. On August 14 the Minnehaha team claimed the championship trophy by defeating the North Stars 40 to 38.[19]

The Northfield team was given only a month in which to enjoy its victory over its St. Paul rivals before it was challenged by the St. Croix club of Stillwater. The first game was played on September 23 at Northfield. Possibly the absence of three regular players had something to do with the defeat of the Northfield team, for it won a second game at Stillwater by a score of 58 to 47. The decisive game of the series was played at Hastings, where Captain Olin of the North Stars and Hersey of the Lake City club were umpires. This game produced the best baseball played in Minnesota prior to 1869, with proof that pitching is essential to a successful team. If the score is acceptable evidence, both pitchers were good. Miller of the St. Croix did especially fine work, but the Minnehaha pitcher lost his effectiveness in the eighth inning. Up to that time each team had made only eight runs, but the St. Croix nine made seven runs in the eighth and

Table 1. 1867 Title Game Box Score

North Star	Outs	Runs	Vermillion	Outs	Runs
Olin, pitcher	4	5	Greiner, catcher	4	3
W. Wilson, catcher	4	5	Van Inervan, third baseman	4	4
Paine, first baseman	1	6	Norton, pitcher	1	5
C. Wilson, shortstop	5	3	Crozier, second baseman	3	4
Tostevin, second baseman	3	3	Kinzie, left fielder	5	1
H. Wilson, left fielder	2	5	Jones, shortstop	4	3
Oakes, center fielder	2	6	Twitchell, center fielder	2	5
P. Wilson, third baseman	3	5	Etheridge, first baseman	2	5
Noyes, right fielder	2	5	Torrence, right fielder	2	5
	—	—		—	—
Totals	27[18]	43	**Totals**	27	35

Innings	1	2	3	4	5	6	7	8	9	Totals
North Star	0	0	10	12	10	8	0	1	2	43
Vermillion	1	2	1	5	1	6	5	1	3	35

Home runs	Tostevin 1; Crozier 1
Fly catches	North Star 10; Vermillion 9
Passed balls	North Star 6; Vermillion 14
Struck out	North Star 3; Vermillion 2
Bases on called balls	North Star 4; Vermillion 4
Time of game	2 hours and 25 minutes

two in the ninth innings, and the Minnehahas were able to score five times. In fact, all the playing was especially good for players of limited experience.[20]

The St. Croix club held the title and had possession of the silver ball until July 1869, when the Lake City Union nine captured the trophy. The final game of the match was played in St. Paul, where the Saxon club immediately challenged the victorious nine. The Saxons won the championship and were called upon to defend it by the Crescent club of Red Wing. For some unknown reason the Crescents failed to appear in St. Paul for the first game, and the Saxons won the second game by the close score of 25 to 21.[21]

Until the Gopher State club of Rochester met the Saxons, the championship play of 1869 had been peaceful. The champions and the Gopher State team agreed to play for the silver ball at the state fair in Rochester. At the end of the seventh inning, with the Rochester nine leading, the Saxons "placed a fielder behind their catcher." An argument followed, but the Saxons refused to remove their "illegal" fielder. Immediately upon resumption of play a foul fly was caught by the second catcher, and the umpire declared the batter out. After the subsequent wrangle, the Saxons refused to continue the game, and the umpire was forced to declare a victory for the Gopher State team. The next morning, when the teams met again, two referees were chosen to settle disputes which the umpire might not be able to adjust. With the score a tie, the Saxons announced they had to leave immediately for the depot, and no amount of argument could change their decision. As a result the umpire declared the Gopher State club the winner and the rightful owner of the silver ball. The Saxon club refused to surrender the trophy and it must have been sustained in that act by the state association, for in the following summer the Union nine of Minneapolis won the championship from the St. Paul team, and retained the title during the remainder of the year.[22]

There were signs that the quality of the game was improving in Minnesota. By 1869 margins between the scores of the winning and losing teams were becoming smaller—an indication that playing ability was more evenly distributed than in 1867. In the championship game of 1867, fourteen "passed balls" were charged against Greiner of the Vermillion club, who was considered the best catcher of the tournament. Each catcher had only one passed ball in the final game of the championship match of the following year. The reduction in scoring shows that pitching skill was improving. Probably the best of the early Minnesota games was that between the Union club of Chester and the Independent nine of Lake City in 1870. The score was tied at fourteen at the end of nine innings, and the Unions finally won in the twelfth with the score 17 to 15. The game was played in "one hour and fifty minutes."[23]

As sporting events became more popular on holidays, especially on July 4, baseball became a feature attraction. The Owatonna and Rochester nines played on July 4, 1867. On July 4, 1868, two Minnesota teams played at Hudson, Wisconsin. Lake City promoted a baseball tournament on the same day, in which teams from Stillwater, Red Wing, and St. Paul participated with two nines from Lake City. In 1869 the Rochester team traveled to Winona on Independence Day. The Saxons of St. Paul played a championship game with the Union nine of Minneapolis on July 4, 1871.[24]

Eventually cash prizes were substituted for trophies. At Red Wing in October 1867, a "citizens' purse" of twenty dollars was offered for "visiting clubs outside the county," and on July 4, 1867, at Lake City the winning team received twenty-five dollars. In October 1868, Hudson, Wisconsin, invited the Saxons of St. Paul and the St. Croix club of Stillwater to compete for "a purse of fifty dollars."[25]

Although there was no professionalism in Minnesota baseball in the sixties, there were some signs pointing in that direction. The first was the effort of the North Star club to obtain the services of the pitcher of the St. Croix team. A Minneapolis paper of 1869 recommended procuring the services of an expert "and paying him wages…whether in instructing the club or in playing matches."[26]

Intercity contests, a state association, and the first state tournament with its championship play marked the beginning of a sport that has had remarkable growth in Minnesota. As early as 1867 a Minnesota editor remarked that "The game of Base Ball has become so much the style that nearly every village and hamlet has its club, and to be a member of the first nine is now looked upon as being nearly as honorable a position as a seat in the Legislature."[27]

*   *   *

Concentrating on telling the story of the origin and spread of inter-club play in Minnesota, Monroe omits—or may have overlooked, since he lists an Olympic Club as founded in 1860—the group which may fairly be called the state's Knickerbockers, the Olympic Club of St. Paul. Formed in December 1858 to organize the efforts of its members to engage in "manly exercise," as a popular contemporary phrase put it, the club played several intrasquad matches in the summer of 1859, choosing sides for each date or playing married men vs. bachelors, a popular format in early baseball. One St. Paul newspaper, the *Daily Minnesotian*, the city's Republican Party organ, covered the group's activities, including box scores of the games. It may have helped that a co-founder and the club's first captain, Samuel P. Jennison, was prominent in Republican circles. ∎

Notes

The author benefited, as latter-day researchers into the formative years of Minnesota baseball continue to benefit, from the Minnesota Historical Society's mission of collecting in-state newspapers, a mission included in its 1857 charter. For the 1860s, a period in which baseball activity was wholly among in-state clubs, these newspapers, in 2010 as in 1938, are the sole contemporaneous sources for the story of the game's rise in Minnesota. One, the *Winona Republican*, is now available online.

1. *Emigrant Aid Journal of Minnesota*, August 1, 15, September 12, 1857.
2. *Pioneer and Democrat* (St. Paul), July 30, 1859, August 11, September 11, 1860; *St. Paul Press*, March 31, 1864.
3. *St. Paul Press,* May 13, 14, 19, 1865.
4. *St. Paul Press*, July 2, September 21, 1865.
5. *St. Paul Press*, April 14, 1866.
6. *St. Paul Press*, July 27, August 22–23, August 28-29, October 30, 1866.
7. *St. Paul Press*, October 13, November 5, 1866; *Goodhue County Republican* (Red Wing), April 12, 1867; *Wilkes' Spirit of the Times* 14: 262 (June 23, 1866).
8. *St. Paul Press*, April 6, 1867.
9. *St. Paul Press*, May 27, 1867.
10. *St. Paul Press*, June 15, 1867.
11. *St. Paul Press*, June 16, 23, 1867; *Goodhue County Republican*, June 21, 28, 1867.
12. *St. Paul Press*, July 12, 1867.
13. *Lake City Leader*, July 13, August 16, 1867; *Goodhue County Republican*, July 26, August 2, 1867; *St. Paul Press*, August 1, 16, 1867.
14. *Goodhue County Republican*, August 2, 1867; *St. Paul Press* June 20, July 13, 30, August 22, 1867.
15. *St. Paul Press*, September 5, 1867. The constitution and by-laws of the association were also published in this issue.
16. *St. Paul Press*, September 24, 1867.
17. *St. Paul Press*, September 28, 1867.
18. This column actually totals only 26.
19. *Northfield Recorder*, July 24, August 21, 1868; *St. Paul Press*, July 18, August 16, 1868; *St. Paul Pioneer*, July 18, 21, 1868.
20. *Northfield Recorder*, September 11, 1868; *Northfield Enterprise*, September 25, October 16, 30, 1868; *St. Paul Press*, September 23, 24, October 10, 1868; *Stillwater Republican*, October 27, 1868.
21. *St. Paul Pioneer*, July 25, August 8, 1869; *Lake City Leader*, July 2, 23, August 6, 13, 1869; *Saint Paul Dispatch*, July 24, August 27, September 3, 6, 1869.
22. *Staint Paul Dispatch*, October 2, 4, 1869; *Rochester Post*, October 2, 1869; *Minneapolis Tribune*, June 11, 12, 1870.
23. *Lake City Leader*, July 1, 1870.
24. *St. Paul Press*, July 7, 1867; July 7, 1868; *Goodhue County Republican*, July 3, 1868; *Northfield Recorder*, July 10, 1868; *Lake City Leader*, July 14, 1868; *Rochester Post*, July 10, 1869; *Minneapolis Tribune*, July 4, 1871.
25. *Goodhue County Republican*, October 11, 1867; *St. Paul Press*, October 16, 18, 1868; Leader, July 9, 1869.
26. *Minneapolis Tribune*, April 9, 1869.
27. *Lake City Leader*, August 23, 1867.

Professional Base Ball Debuts In Minnesota

The St. Paul Red Caps, Minneapolis Brown Stockings, And Winona Clippers Of 1875–1877

Rich Arpi

Base ball clubs from various Minnesota cities began playing match games with each other in the mid-1860s. The first games were rather cordial events between clubs of gentlemen; within a few years they became spirited games for the silver ball, awarded to the base ball champions of Minnesota. The North Star Base Ball Club of St. Paul won the silver ball at the first state tournament, which it hosted in 1867. By 1870 the Silver Stars of Northfield were acclaimed the state champion. Under the rules at the time a nine needed to beat the Silver Stars twice to capture the state championship. It is unclear whether any team accomplished this feat and the possession of the silver ball remains unknown.[1]

In the early 1870s, St. Paul's dominant team was the Metropolitan Base Ball Club. In June 1875, four prominent members of the Metropolitans, unhappy with practice policies and playing time, quit the team and joined the newly formed Red Caps. The weakened Metropolitans then promptly lost several games to the Red Caps, who became St. Paul's preeminent team. On July 5, the Red Caps beat the Minneapolis White Shirts 35–13, before 2,000 fans at the Lyndale grounds in south Minneapolis. Several weeks later, the *St. Paul Dispatch*, sensing a public demand for higher quality baseball, remarked on a mistake-prone game involving the White Shirts, "from this point each seemed to strive to outdo the other in muffing, overthrowing and general lack of skill in ball tossing. We trust that both nines will practice more before they attempt to play in public again."[2]

Six weeks later, on August 20, the White Shirts (now renamed as the Minneapolis Westerns) traveled to St. Paul for a rematch with the Red Caps. They acquitted themselves much better, falling only by two runs, 18–16. By this time, however, another club, the Minneapolis Unions, had cornered many of Minneapolis's best players and challenged the Red Caps for state honors. At the first game between the two squads, played on the Lyndale grounds in Minneapolis before 500 fans on August 30, the Red Caps won and took home a purse of $50. At a second game,

played in St. Paul on September 11, the Red Caps again prevailed, 25–9. On September 3 the Unions traveled to Northfield to help the Silver Stars inaugurate their new ballpark before a crowd of 400. They fell 34–10 to the host club but gushed over the hospitality of the Northfield club, which furnished them with dinner at Northfield's finest hotel and escorted them to and from the ballpark in fine carriages. Later in the month the Unions beat the St. Croix club of Stillwater 45-39 and the Crescent club of Hastings 21–15 at the state fair baseball tournament. A formal dance, featuring all the baseball players, was the featured evening entertainment at the tournament. To conclude the event, the Unions were scheduled to meet the Red Caps in the final game of the tournament, but rain prevented the match. For the rescheduled game in early October, the Unions did not show up, apparently having disbanded for the season.[3]

Meanwhile, another Minnesota club, the Winona Clippers, was playing solid baseball and supporters began clamoring for a match with the Red Caps. As proof of their prowess, on September 8 the Clippers defeated the Silver Stars, 8–1, in a game the *St. Paul Dispatch* wrote would rival professional games played out east. For their victory the Clippers earned a silver bat and a $100 purse, but were charged with playing two professional players. One, W.W. Fisher, a black second baseman and pitcher, apparently recruited from the Chicago Uniques, was subjected to racial taunting by some of the Northfield players. They pinned some "n.....baby" badges on their shirts in hopes of provoking Fisher. Negotiations for a game between St. Paul and Winona apparently stalled because the Red Caps refused to play if Winona used Fisher. The Red Caps claimed its objection was not racial but based on Fisher's being a professional. St. Paul eventually dropped their objection and a game was scheduled as a "bonanza" game to be played at the state fair (i.e. not part of the regular baseball tournament) for $100 and bragging rights as the state's strongest baseball club. The game turned out to be quite a remarkable affair with plenty of money changing hands on bets of all kinds. The score was tied after nine innings at 17. When the Red Caps scored five runs in the tenth inning, victory seemed assured, but the Clippers stormed back with seven runs of their own, winning the match, 24–22.

In the return match at Winona on October 16 the Red Caps gained some revenge, edging the Clippers, 8–7. Winona completed its season 13–5 and St. Paul finished 9–3. Since each team won one game against the other, no clear champion was crowned. After the game, rumors spread that Frank Smith and Fisher had sold out to gamblers and performed at less than their best against the Red Caps. Smith coerced Fisher into signing a confession, and Fisher was run out of town, never to be heard from again. Smith left town as well, although he appeared several times in Minnesota as a player with the Janesville [Wisconsin] Mutuals.[4]

In addition to some fine matches between St. Paul, Minneapolis, Winona, and Northfield, the 1875 season should be remembered for the establishment of the Minnesota Association of Base Ball Players. Representatives from the Red Caps, Clippers, Silver Stars, and Waseca Champions ball clubs met in Northfield in late August to establish this organization, which despite its name, was an organization of the state's baseball clubs. To be admitted, clubs needed to have at least 18 members and after they paid their $10 dues were entitled to send two delegates to the annual convention. Money raised via dues would fund the organization and pay for a championship pennant, inscribed with the words "Champions, the club's name and year," which the club could fly permanently. The season would run from March 1 to November 1 and each member was required to play at least two games against every other member to be eligible for the pennant.[5]

The April 24, 1876, issue of the St. Paul Dispatch complained that a man named Harry Arundel from Philadelphia, slated to spend the summer in Winona, ostensibly for his health, was in reality a ringer

> "A small base ballist...one of the lower town infant nine...whose head had been filled with base ball to such a degree that he was useless for anything else, was interviewed on the subject by his mother, in the wood shed last night, with a piece of shingle. He afterwards said, mournfully, that his mother was a professional, for she made more 'base hits' on him in one inning than the Brown Stockings did in the last three games with the Red Caps."
>
> – St. Paul Dispatch, May 22, 1877

brought to town to strengthen the ballclub. The Clippers also recruited several other professional players from Chicago and Milwaukee in hopes of becoming Minnesota's top baseball team. Knowing Winona's preference for professionals, the paper concluded that the Winona management must believe, "it's as well to be hung for stealing a sheep as a lamb." The Dispatch maintained that the Red Caps, on the other hand, were comprised entirely of residents of St. Paul who play for the "love of it and not for the almighty dollar." Nonetheless, the paper maintained the Red Caps would try their best against the "invalid ball tossers" of Winona.

Like most clubs at the time, the Red Caps scheduled their games from week to week as the season progressed, and thus had long stretches of inactivity between games early in the season followed by a flurry of games in August and September as interest grew. For the season Winona won 14 of 20 games and split its four games with the Red Caps. Since the Clippers outscored the Red Caps 33 to 27 in their four matches, the Clippers declared themselves the champions of Minnesota.

Testifying to baseball's growing popularity, on June 21, the Red Caps christened their new grounds, named Red Cap Park, with a game against the St. Croix Base Ball Club of Stillwater. The park, located across the river and south of downtown, cost $800 to construct and featured a ten-foot-high fence enclosing a field 500 feet long by 360 feet wide. It had an amphitheater which seated 1,000 persons, a ticket office, and dressing rooms. The diamond had its sod removed and was scraped and rolled until it was hard and smooth. Room was also reserved for those who wished to view the games from their carriages along the foul lines and outfield. Concession stands sold cigars, fruit, and liquid refreshments. No liquor or pool selling (betting) was allowed. Game days were announced with a large flag flying from the center field pole.[6] For the season the Red Caps had a record of 21–14–1. Against the strongest Midwest competition, however, including teams from Detroit, Chicago, and Milwaukee, the Red Caps lost all six games.

Not surprisingly the Red Caps concluded, as did the St. Paul Dispatch, that they too needed professional talent to compete. Consequently, near the end of the season the Red Caps picked up several professional players, including Charles Wilson "Dory" Dean, of the Cincinnati National League club. Dean was available because during the 1876 season, his only one in the major leagues, he recorded one of the lowest winning percentages in history, .133 (4–26). A stellar all-around athlete, after his baseball career, Dean became a fine tennis player.[7]

For 1876, Minneapolis was late assembling its premier squad, now known as the Blue Stockings, finally opening at home against the Northfield Silver Stars on July 18. For the opener they inaugurated a new ball grounds at the corner of Twentieth Avenue South and Eighth Street, thereafter known as Blue Stocking Park. A board fence enclosed a lot of 500 feet by 475 feet and a roofed grandstand held seats for 300 people.[8] Later in the season, after losing a game 9–0 to the Aetna Baseball Club of Detroit that featured a battery of pitcher William Bohn and catcher William "Sunny" Hoffman, Minneapolis's management realized that they needed to acquire better players (and pay them) to compete at the level to which they aspired. Accordingly, they entered immediate negotiations with the Detroit battery and lured them both in time for a game against the Marshalltown, Iowa club on September 15. To further bolster their club, in early October the Blue Stockings acquired Harry Arundel, James O'Day, and William Phillips from the recently disbanded Winona Clippers. The Blue Stockings finished the season with ten wins, ten losses, and one tie.

Just how far Minnesota's best still had to improve to join the nation's elite became apparent when the National League's Chicago White Stockings (today known as the Cubs) featuring early baseball legends Al Spalding and Cap Anson and fresh off winning the National League's inaugural pennant toured Minnesota in mid-October. In two games Chicago toyed with Minneapolis, beating the locals 26–1 and 26–2. That same week the White Stockings also played the Red Caps in St. Paul, beating the St. Paul nine 19–1

> "These flannel-clad heroes have been at times a source of much joy to many of our citizens, while at other times they have been the moving cause of more profanity than was warranted by the circumstances. To the citizens of St. Paul there is a great and abiding joy (aside from the actual closing of the season) to be derived from the season's work. That is, we have at one bound (as it were) taken place among the great cities of the union in the maintenance of a full fledged professional ball club, for it has come to this, that water works, paid fire departments, common councils, gas, and a robust municipal debt availeth nothing towards a city's reputation if it lacks nine hired ball whackers."
>
> — *St. Paul Pioneer Press, October 3, 1877*

and 11–4. St. Paul took particular pleasure in the latter game, maintaining that limiting the White Stockings to only 11 runs proved St. Paul was the strongest team in the state. Enticed by a guaranteed purse of $100, the White Stockings finished their Minnesota trip on October 19 with a game against the St. Croix club in Stillwater. The result, not unexpectedly, was an 18–3 victory for the Windy City nine.[9]

St. Paul, Minneapolis, and Winona all entered the 1877 season with designs on competing with the best professional teams in the country, excepting only the National League. St. Paul and Minneapolis joined the League Alliance, a loose confederation of 13 clubs allied with the National League (meaning they would respect each other's contracts). The League Alliance featured clubs from Syracuse, Memphis, Indianapolis, Milwaukee, Chicago, Fall River and Lowell, Massachusetts, but should not be considered a league as we understand the concept today. Clubs were independent entities that scheduled their own games, both within the Alliance and with other clubs. In fact, getting ahead of our story a little, in 1878 two strong Alliance clubs, Milwaukee and Indianapolis, defected to the National League as the Alliance collapsed.

For that first Alliance season, both St. Paul and Minneapolis scheduled as many games as possible. Though not quite arranging as many games as they hoped for, St. Paul doubled its matches to 72. On June 19 the Red Caps embarked on a 13-game road trip that lasted until July 4, taking the team to Winona, Milwaukee, Janesville, Chicago, Indianapolis, Evansville, and Memphis. Upon returning, the Red Caps again faced the Chicago White Stockings at Red Cap Park on July 9 and 11. The first game was a close 2–0 loss, but the second turned into an 18–1 blowout in favor of the National Leaguers. The season wound up with 22 consecutive games against Minneapolis because Winona had folded in late August and the other League Alliance teams could not be induced to travel to Minnesota.

The Red Caps used 20 players during the 1877 season, mostly imported professionals. Several local players, with experience on the 1875 and 1876 Red Caps, filled in for a few games. The core of the team was nine imported players: Joe Ellick from Cincinnati, Ed Gault from Milwaukee, catcher Emil Gross from Chicago, William Henry "Little Mack" McClellan from Chicago, Sumner Ely from Girard, Pennsylvania, Art Allison from Philadelphia, Harry Salisbury of Providence, Rhode Island, field captain Joseph W. Miller from Cincinnati, who had experience with three clubs in the National Association and spent 1876 with Indianapolis, and William Bohn, pilfered from the

Minneapolis club. All except Gault, Ely, and Bohn had or would in the future play at the highest level of base ball in the country (The National Association, National League, or American Association). The Red Caps dressed entirely in white, including their shoes; a red cap with a white band and a narrow belt with a red edging added color.[10]

When the Memphis team disbanded in mid-July, the Red Caps telegraphed star outfielder Oscar Walker, asking for his terms. "Seventy-five dollars per month and a train ticket to St. Paul," he replied. Later that month after a series with the Manchester, New Hampshire club the Manchesters induced Walker to jump to their squad. The Red Caps cried foul and spread the word that teams should not play Manchester if Walker appeared in their lineup. This became the first and most celebrated case of contract jumping, or a "levanting base ballist," as Walker was dubbed, faced by the League Alliance. At the National League meeting in December, the league upheld the Red Caps contract with Walker and his subsequent expulsion for jumping his contract. Walker claimed he had never signed a contract with St. Paul and was thus free to go to Manchester, but the league ruled his acceptance via telegrams was evidence of a contract. Walker served a year suspension, but later played a few years in the major leagues.[11]

The pitching matchups between star hurlers William Bohn and Harry Salisbury provided one of the more interesting features of the 1877 season. Unfortunately the Minneapolis and St. Paul papers didn't provide full coverage with box scores for games at the end of the season, so pitching lines for the season are incomplete and may never be known. The two faced each other at least 16 times in 1877 and it could have been as many as 29 (my guess is around 24–25). Moreover, they switched teams in August, Salisbury going to Minneapolis and Bohn to St. Paul.

In League Alliance games the St. Paul Red Caps finished 29–21–3, winning the most games against league competition.[12] Although Indianapolis had a better winning percentage at 23–11, the Spalding Guide for 1878 awarded St. Paul the League Alliance pennant. Versus the other Minnesota clubs, the Red Caps won six of ten games; splitting eight with Winona, and beating the St. Croix club and a picked nine of former Red Caps players in an alumni game. Against Minneapolis, the Red Caps most common opponent, St. Paul won 19 of 36 (three games ended in ties). Overall, they finished 39–30–3.[13]

Minneapolis started the 1877 season with high hopes, including plans for games in Chicago, Indianapolis, Detroit, and several cities in Canada as well

as home games against some of the strongest independent teams in the country. While none of these anticipated road games ever occurred, the team did take a ten-day trip through Wisconsin and increased its schedule to 60 games. Their slightly updated attire consisted of a white uniform, brown stockings and belt, and caps of a different color for each player. Because of their new stockings the team would now be known as the Brown Stockings, though their home field was still referred to as Blue Stocking Park. In early June owner F.W. Chase sold the club to the Minneapolis Base Ball Association, a stock company of at least 72 individuals, for $350. The new owners immediately began raising money by selling shares at $10 each.[14]

Shortly thereafter the team departed on its long road trip to Winona and four cities in Wisconsin. The Minneapolis club did quite well on this trip, winning seven out of ten games, despite some wet weather. By mid-August, however, the club was running into financial difficulty. When the stock sale failed to bring in sufficient funds, the team paid off its players and disbanded on August 15. Three players found other positions immediately: Charlie Eden signed with the Chicago White Stockings of the National League; Billy Bohn signed with the cross-town St. Paul Red Caps; first baseman William Phillips latched on with Winona. The rest of the players re-formed the club on a co-operative basis and continued playing. The team hardly missed a beat, taking the field on August 17 with replacements for the departed players. The final 22 consecutive games against the St. Paul Red Caps sapped the interest of both fans and newspaper editors alike. Despite the August re-organization, the Brown Stockings finished with a creditable record of 31–26–3.[15]

Initially the Winona Clippers were unsure if they wanted to field a professional team for 1877, but finally decided to do so and compete against St. Paul and Minneapolis. They hired three professional players from the Nameless Club of Brooklyn to start the season and in June brought in George Baker from the St. Louis Alerts. The club struggled to remain competitive; at one point in June they were outscored 35–0 over five games against the Red Caps and Brown Stockings. With their record sitting at 4–11 in mid-July, the Clippers acquired five more professional players from the recently defunct Erie, Pennsylvania club. Thus bolstered, the club finished strong, winning 11 of 15 to end up with a .500 record at 15–15.

Rochester was also represented by a baseball club in 1877. Called the Gopher States Baseball Club, the organizers created a stock company in early June and sold 100 shares at $5.00 each. The club used the proceeds to hire four local men from the St. Paul Red Caps displaced when that team upgraded its roster. Not part of the League Alliance, the 1878 Spalding Guide placed Rochester among the handful of clubs for which no records existed. In fact, Rochester opened the season with a win against the St. Charles White Caps on June 26 and finished its season on August 10 with a 6–4 win over the Winona Clippers. In between those dates, they had trouble scheduling anybody but Winona to whom they dropped six consecutive games.[16]

The 1876 and 1877 seasons, while entertaining to many fans of the Twin Cities, Winona, and Rochester, quickly exposed management to the realities of running a professional base ball team. The 1877 season, which opened with high hopes and much promise in the spring, finished with hardly a whimper and little press coverage. Management underestimated how difficult it would be to run a professional base ball club so far from the eastern population centers. It was much more difficult than anticipated to induce strong eastern clubs to travel to Minnesota without financial guarantees. In fact, this problem was not just a minor league issue; two National League clubs, New York and Philadelphia, were expelled after the 1876 season for not completing their schedules with the western clubs.

The losses sustained by Minnesota's professional clubs in 1877 soured the state's baseball entrepreneurs on the sport as a profitable enterprise. Not until 1884 when teams from St. Paul, Minneapolis, and Stillwater competed in the Northwestern League did Minnesota have teams in an organized baseball league. Having learned painful lessons in the 1870s, the new magnates established a league that had a defined schedule, a geographical focus, recognized each other's contracts, and recruited baseball men who would run the clubs as a business and not as a part-time leisure activity. ∎

Notes

1. Stew Thornley, *Baseball in Minnesota: The Definitive History*, (St. Paul: Minnesota Historical Society Press, 2006), 10–11. *Northfield Standard*, various issues 1873–1874.
2. *St. Paul Dispatch*, July 6, 1875 and July 24, 1875.
3. *Minneapolis Daily Tribune*, various issues between June and October 1875; particularly August 26 and September 5.
4. Steve Hoffbeck, editor, *Swinging for the Fences: Black Baseball in Minnesota*, (St. Paul: Minnesota Historical Society Press, 2005), 3–10 and *Winona Daily Republican*, June–October 1875.
5. *Northfield Standard*, September 9, 1875.
6. *St. Paul Dispatch*, June 20, 1876.
7. David Nemec, *The Great Encyclopedia of Nineteenth Century Major League Baseball*. Second Edition, (Tuscaloosa: University of Alabama Press, 2006), 113.
8. *St. Paul Dispatch*, July 22, 1876.
9. *Stillwater Lumberman*, October 20, 1876.
10. *St. Paul Dispatch*, March 14, 1877.
11. *New York Clipper*, August 25 and September 8, 1877; *St. Paul Dispatch*, August 7, 1877 and December 7, 1877; *St. Paul Pioneer Press*, August 3, 1877 and September 23, 1877.
12. The *Spalding Guide* and the *Minor League Encyclopedia* show St. Paul's record in the League Alliance as 28–21. My research indicated that St. Paul finished the with a record of 39–30–3; this total of 72 games ties to the highest games played listed for several of the Red Caps players as listed in the *Spalding Guide*. In my game by game account I determined that 10 wins and 9 losses were against clubs outside the League Alliance; subtracting these games results in a League Alliance record of 29–21–3, a discrepancy of one win and three ties. I believe that the extra win was against Janesville, Wisconsin. The game in question occurred on May 25, when Janesville left the field in the seventh inning with the score tied 0–0, and the game was forfeited to St. Paul. The ties were all against Minneapolis and do not count in the standings.
13. *Spalding's Official Baseball Guide* for 1878, (Chicago: A.G. Spalding & Bro., 1878), 22–39. Several papers including the *St. Paul Dispatch* have been used to compile the record for the St. Paul Red Caps.
14. *Minneapolis Tribune*, April 17, 1877 and May 1, 1877.
15. *St. Paul Pioneer Press*, August 17, 1877.
16. *Rochester Record Union*, July 14, 1876, August 11, 1876, September 8, 1876, October 6, 1876.

Rube and His Bears

A Short History of the Virginia Ore Diggers and the Team's Time in the Northern League

Rich Arpi

My home town of Virginia, Minnesota, on the Mesabi Iron Range, is best known for its iron ore and as the home of the Virginia and Rainy Lake Lumber Company, for a time the largest white pine sawmill in the world. Sadly, growing up I had no knowledge of Virginia's rich baseball past. It was not until I got into graduate school and should have been working on other more important projects that I stumbled upon the existence of the Virginia Ore Diggers, to this day the Iron Range's only franchise in Organized Baseball. The appendix in Robert Objoski's, *Bush League* (MacMillan, 1975), which lists towns in North America that have fielded professional baseball teams, is responsible for sending me on this baseball odyssey.

Towns in northern Minnesota, Wisconsin, Michigan, North Dakota, and Manitoba had featured minor league ball for ten years or so before Virginia decided to enter the professional ranks. Teams from Winnipeg (Manitoba), Fargo (North Dakota), Grand Forks (North Dakota), Crookston (Minnesota), Duluth (Minnesota), and Superior (Wisconsin) competed in the Class D Northern League (1902–1905, 1908), and the Class C Minnesota-Wisconsin League (1909–1912). Mesabi Range towns, established only in the early 1890s after iron ore was discovered, fielded town teams almost immediately. Rivalries quickly developed among the Range towns of Eveleth, Virginia, and Hibbing and they often imported professional players to give them an edge. Frank Isbell, later of the 1906 Champion White Sox, pitched in Virginia in 1896.

Virginia, sixty miles northwest of Duluth, was not yet ready to compete professionally with the larger towns. First, the town needed to find a building material more permanent than wood. Virginia had burned to the ground in both 1893 and 1900. By 1912, though, the city had been rebuilt with brick and stone and was a prosperous burg of 15,000 residents. The high school featured a swimming pool and a first class stage, and the city had paved streets with lighting and a municipal steam power plant. Virginia had turned from a frontier town into a first-class city almost overnight. In the spring of 1912 a group of Virginia businessmen felt they could take the next step by fielding a professional baseball team. They entered into talks with representatives from several other regional cities to establish the Central International League. When it became apparent the league would have only six teams, Virginia (along with Fargo) dropped out. The league operated as a four-club circuit, with Duluth easily beating out Superior, Winnipeg, and Grand Forks for the pennant.

For 1913 a stronger eight-team, Class C minor league, taking the name Northern League, was proposed. It would include the four 1912 Central International League cities, Winona of the defunct Minnesota-Wisconsin League, a franchise for both Minneapolis and St. Paul, and one additional city. Hibbing, the largest city on the Iron Range, was a logical choice, but that town's team, the Colts, preferred to remain independent. Virginia lobbied hard for admittance to the league, arguing they would be a perfect half-way point between Duluth-Superior, Winnipeg and Fargo and that the population within 10 miles of Virginia was enough to sustain a franchise. Also, a recently constructed interurban railway line could bring fans in from 30 miles away.

The Minneapolis Northern League team was owned by Mike and Joe Cantillon, owners of the American Association Minneapolis Millers. They would use the Northern League team, known as the Bronchos, but often referred to as "Little Millers" as a place to stockpile players not quite ready for the Millers or on injury rehab. Similarly, in St. Paul, George Lennon, owner of the St. Paul Saints, also owned the St. Paul Colts or "Little Saints" of the Northern League. He sold the team to H.P. Conrad early in the season but still followed the league closely in search of talent for his American Association club. For playing venues, the Twin Cities' Northern League franchises would use the Millers' Nicollet Park and the Saints' Lexington Park, respectively as their home fields. The American Association, fearful of strong competition, allowed the lower classification Northern League to enter the Twin Cities as a one year experiment.

PROCLAMATION

Whereas, the Northern League Baseball season starts in Virginia May 4th, I hereby request that all business places close from the hours of 2:15 to 4 p. m., so that the people of Virginia may show the owners of the team and players that we appreciate what they are doing for our city.

I would especially ask that all offices close so that no office boy need spring the old gag that he has to go to his grandmother's funeral in order to get away to see the first game of the great national sport.

MICHAEL BOYLAN,

Virginia, Minnesota, May 3rd, 1916.　　Mayor.

Virginia Mayor Michael Boylan's proclamation saves lives...or at least delays some funerals (*Virginia Daily Enterprise*, May 3, 1916).

After being admitted to the league, Virginia management had only a few weeks to organize the team, putting them at a distinct disadvantage with respect to the other teams. Five of the clubs had existed the year before and thus had experienced baseball men in charge and some holdover players. Virginia, however, was starting from scratch. They dithered over a manager for two months, finally deciding on an ex-major league ball player, Spike Shannon, who had played for the St. Paul Saints and John McGraw's New York Giants. As player-manager, Shannon was also expected to recruit players. He did the best he could in the time he had and felt he had uncovered some talent on the sandlots of Chicago and the Twin Cities.

As an omen of things to come, opening day was postponed not once but twice in Virginia. April 23 was scheduled as the start of the season, but rain prevented play that day and the next. Friday, April 25, witnessed the opening of the season and the third parade in three

days. The game itself, a 5–2 loss to Winnipeg, was shortened to eight innings so the Canadian club could catch its train. After a poor start at home (1-6) Virginia spent almost the entire month of May on the road. Twenty-four games including a series with every other team (two with Superior) were scheduled between May 2 and May 25, of which only 20 were played due to weather conditions. The Ore Diggers went 5–15 on this trip and found themselves in last place with a 6–21 record.

On May 17 in Superior, the Ore Diggers won a game 1–0 despite getting only one hit. The run was scored on a hit batsman, a sacrifice, and a double. Virginia pitcher Frank Schimons, allowed only four hits in recording his only victory of the year. On May 23, Carter Wilson of Grand Forks no-hit the Ore Diggers, one of five no-hitters in the league that year.

Despite their poor record, Virginia was involved in some interesting games and had some notable players. On May 31 they beat Winona 21–4 and on June 9 they blasted the Colts in St. Paul 23–2. These were among the highest run totals for any one team in the league that year. Unfortunately, those 44 runs scored in two games represented almost ten percent of their entire season run total of 453.

On July 17 in a home game against Minneapolis a special ground rule was enacted. Since the outfield was full of water, any ball hit on the fly into the outfield and not caught was a ground rule double. Heine Berger, the Minneapolis third baseman, hit a ball just behind second base. Apparently the ball was not hit deep enough to be declared a ground rule double. Virginia fielders lost the ball in the mud while Berger circled the bases with a home run. Minneapolis Millers shortstop Andy Oyler has been credited with a similar play in a number of publications, described as the world's shortest home run since he apparently hit it into a puddle in front of the plate. The Oyler story comes with no date or place and his known home runs (there weren't many) do not match up, so this documented play involving another Minneapolis infielder maybe the true source of the tale.

Shannon had clearly overestimated the talent he had picked up on the sandlots, and not surprisingly he didn't survive the season. On July 1, he was released as player-manager after compiling a record of 15–46–1. He was replaced by Bobby "Braggio" Roth, acquired from the Kansas City Blues of the American Association. In 31 games for Virginia, Roth batted .347 (35 for 101) and stole 10 bases after batting .235 in 54 games for Kansas City.[1] He managed the club for two weeks (6–9) before being replaced by infielder Ed Stewart,

Virginia team photo, 1914 (*Duluth News Tribune*, May 24, 1914).

who led the club to a forgettable 9–32 finish. In 1914 Roth began his eight year major league career as an outfielder and third baseman, and Spike Shannon became an umpire in the Federal League.

Virginia had particular trouble with doubleheaders in 1913. Although none were originally scheduled, rainouts resulted in the club playing 16. The team won only four of those 32 games. They swept one, split two, and lost both ends 13 times. Three times Virginia played doubleheaders back to back: June 28–29 in Duluth, August 16–17 in Winnipeg and La Crosse, and August 19–20 in Minneapolis. They lost all 12. Three times they were shutout in both ends of a doubleheader.

Virginia finished 30–87 and held down last place the entire season, except for one day, June 14, when they were one-half game in front of St. Paul. The Colts won the next day, while the Ore Diggers lost, pushing Virginia back into last place.

Interestingly, the home opener marked the only appearance of the Winnipeg club in Virginia during the 1913 season. In July, in search of larger crowds and paydays, series scheduled in second-division cities were transferred to first-division cities. As a result, the next 14 games between Virginia and Winnipeg were played in Winnipeg with the "Peggers" winning 13 of

those games. As the best-drawing city in the league, Winnipeg was allowed to play 24 more home games than road games. At the other end of the scale, Virginia and Minneapolis, both second-division clubs, played 20 and 17 more road than home games. Only Winona, the league champion, had a winning road record.

Although the *Reach Guide* lists only 17 players as having played for the Ore Diggers in 1913, in fact 54 different players saw action. League policy limited team rosters to only 14 or 15 men at any one time, resulting in a constant turnover of players. Only four players played in more than 70 games: shortstop Mike Breyette led with 105 games played; first baseman Art Couture played in 102 games; catcher Harry Brammell in 91; and outfielder Jimmy Collins in 80 games.[2] The desperate Ore Diggers signed some local players, chiefly stars of the amateur Trolley League, for a short tryout. Most lasted only one game while others lasted a week or so.

Tony Faeth was the Ore Diggers' best pitcher in 1913. The St. Paul resident went 9–18 for Virginia and 0–1 for La Crosse. Faeth began the season with Virginia, was suspended a month for indifferent play, pitched one game for La Crosse, and was reacquired by the Ore Diggers. In subsequent years he pitched in the American Association for the St. Paul Saints (his best year being 15–4 in 1924) and he saw some major league service with the Cleveland Indians in 1919–1920 (43.1 innings pitched with a 0–0 record).

The most famous Ore Digger, by far, was Hall of Famer George Edward "Rube" Waddell, best remembered as a stalwart left-hander for Connie Mack's Philadelphia A's of the early twentieth century. He was also one of the more eccentric and erratic players ever to play the game, often wandering off to chase fire engines or go fishing. His single season strikeout record of 349 in 1904 lasted as the American League record until 1973 when Nolan Ryan (383) broke it. In 1911 and 1912 Waddell pitched for Pongo Joe Cantillon's Minneapolis Millers going 20–17 and 12–6 respectively. Cantillon kept a close eye on Waddell and took him on numerous hunting and fishing trips, which Waddell enjoyed almost as much as baseball. Cantillon must have suspected something was wrong with Waddell when he optioned Rube to the Northern League Minneapolis team rather than keep him with the Millers.

With the Bronchos, Waddell appeared in four games, his best game being a three-hit shutout with 11 strikeouts coming on May 2 against Grand Forks. Soon thereafter Waddell tired of Cantillon's watchful eye and threatened to quit the game. He had offers from a club in Marshall, Minnesota, clubs out east, and every other Northern League team.

On May 18 Waddell opted for the Ore Diggers, one of the worst teams in the country, largely because of the great fishing reports from nearby Lake Vermillion. For Virginia, of course, he was an immediate gate attraction. Hopes that his pitching would lift them out of the cellar did not come to pass, however. While Waddell pitched some good games for the Ore Diggers, he was inconsistent. He lost two games 2–1 (one in 12 innings) and another two games by one run. In his other starts, though, he was knocked around badly. Overall, in 14 games for Virginia he finished with a 1–8 record and two saves (retroactively calculated).[3]

Waddell's best game as an Ore Digger was on June 28 in Duluth where he pitched 11 ⅓ innings, gave up nine hits, two runs, and one walk, and struck out 12. He lost 2–1, however, as Duluth pitcher Pecky Rhodes hurled 12 innings with 17 strikeouts. Rhodes also pitched a shutout in the seven inning second game, allowing just two hits and striking out four.

Beset by poor performances, tough luck, and ill health (particularly bouts of pneumonia and pleurisy), Waddell went AWOL after his July 20 appearance for the Ore Diggers, his last in professional baseball. While injuries, illness, and alcoholism shortened Waddell's career and life, he made fans everywhere, even forest inhabitants.

While the story in the sidebar below makes a cute, heart-warming tale the real story is a bit different. The *Minneapolis Journal* on April 2, 1914 reported that there were four bears in Virginia's Olcott Park that Waddell played with on a more or less daily basis (hopefully one at a time, but one never knows) and that Waddell named them after John McGraw, Christy Mathewson, Ty Cobb, and Tillie Shafer. The bears died one at a time after Waddell left Virginia but probably not from a broken heart. Park officials believed that the candy and popcorn children (and some adults) fed the bears wreaked havoc with the animals' digestive systems and were responsible for their demise. It was just a coincidence that one of the bears died the same day as Waddell.

Around the rest of the league in 1913, Winona's quartet of pitchers, Ralph Bell (28–6), Bill Snow (19–7), Louis Meyers (15–11), and Hiram Toraason (14–10), led them to the pennant. Bell's stellar record raised some notice, but his major league career, consisting of three games with the White Sox was behind him. Rube Schauer (20–10) of Superior was the league's other twenty-game winner. He was sold directly to the New York Giants in June for $7,500. He reported to New York at the end of the Northern League season in August and lasted five years in the major leagues, finishing with a record of 10–29.

The 1913 season was a season of streaks. It was a five team race until mid-July. Superior won 14 straight games going into an August 5 series at Winona to pull within one-half game of the first place Pirates. Winona swept the three game series, which started their own 14 game winning streak, with Superior going 9–5 during this same time period. Winona now had a 5½ game lead, which they lengthened to 7½ games by the end of the season. Another long winning streak was recorded by Grand Forks which won ten games in a row between July 19 and July 28. At the other extreme,

Virginia had a 14-game losing streak (with one tie) between June 21 and July 12 and 12 straight losses from April 28 to May 10. The season for Minneapolis was ruined when they lost 17 of 18 games between July 19 and August 4.

In the Twin Cities the experiment of having four professional teams turned out badly for the Northern League franchises. As early as June it was rumored that the St. Paul Colts were heading elsewhere. Finally on July 23 the franchise was officially transferred to La Crosse, Wisconsin. The Colts were on the road at the time and did not play their first game in La Crosse until August 5. They did not fare well there, either, completing the season 12–24 as La Crosse—after going 28–54 as St. Paul —and finished in seventh place. The Minneapolis Bronchos elected to ride out the season in Minneapolis but never garnered much fan support or created their own identity. The Millers, who won 97 games and finished second were clearly the favorites of the 1913 Twin Cities baseball public. The minor league Northern League would never again attempt to invade the Twin Cities baseball market.[4]

Despite the troubles of the Twin Cities franchises, the rest of the Northern League was solid and the only franchise shifts for 1914 involved those two clubs. The La Crosse Colts were moved to the Canadian sister cities of Fort William and Port Arthur, (later merged under the name Thunder Bay in 1970). Minneapolis team owners, Joe and Mike Cantillon, transferred the franchise to Fargo-Moorhead, but retained ex-big leaguer Bob Unglaub as manager. On the field Virginia was remarkably improved and finished in fifth place with a record of 55–68. Bob Wright and Harry Matts joined 1913 holdover Tony Faeth on the pitching staff. Outfielders Fred Greisch, Max Brokaw, and Joe Weidell and infielders John Sundheim, Bill Fortman, Art Couture, and John Kernan led the hitting attack.

The Duluth White Sox, under Darby O'Brien, who would manage the club from 1910–1916, won the pennant by 1½ games over Winnipeg. Duluth outfielder Hank Brackett and infielder Jimmy Collins, each with 72 stolen bases, helped the White Sox steal 303 bases and run away with the pennant. Duluth's George Cunningham led the league's pitchers with 23 wins.

The Northern League saw another franchise shift before the start of the 1915 season, when Winona was replaced by a third Canadian team, the St. Boniface Bonnies. Two other clubs did not finish the season: Superior and Grand Forks bowed out on July 5 with records of 20–26 and 21–28, respectively. Virginia finished sixth, 1½ games off their 1914 pace at 53–69. Shortstop John Sundheim led the league with 38 stolen

Prizes promised to Virginia players (*Virginia Daily Enterprise*, May 3, 1916).

bases and a trio of Ore Digger pitchers—Bob Wright, Ray Sorenson, and Tony Faeth—finished in the top seven in innings pitched. Wright contributed 19 wins.

Fargo-Moorhead, with a trio of outstanding pitchers, Ralph Bell (22–13), Roy Patterson (21–5), and George Dumont (20–10), breezed to the pennant by 9½ games. St. Boniface, with Hack Miller leading in hits, Billy Lane in triples, and Charles Boardman in strikeouts finished second. Fort William had the top four home run hitters in the league and finished third. Duluth boasted a trio of outfielders who hit over .300 but finished in fourth place. Kenzie Kirkham led the league in batting with a .344 average and in doubles with 31. Outfield teammates Williams and Altman batted .324 and .314, respectively.

The Northern League opened in 1916 as a six team circuit because St. Boniface and Grand Forks elected not to field a team. In early July the Canadian backers of the Fort William franchise, unwilling to fund the club's losses, simply quit, leaving the club in limbo. The other league owners had no interest in bankrolling the team and let it fold, leaving the league with an unwieldy five teams. One other team would have to be dropped from the league.

League owners decided either Virginia or Fargo-Moorhead would be the team contracted. Virginia drew the black ball and was kicked out of the league on July 10, even though the Virginia owners and fans wanted to continue. They felt cheated because the Ore Diggers had just won 11 of their last 16 games and were playing possibly their best baseball in their four year history. While looming labor unrest on the Range (both mining and lumber strikes were in the near future) made the future of the franchise problematic at best, league owners didn't know this in July 1916. As it turned out, the Northern League itself did not exist much longer due to World War I and other factors. After Virginia (28–32) and Fort William (22–39) were dropped on July 10, the league continued with four clubs in a split-season second half. Fargo-Moorhead finished two games ahead of Winnipeg in the second half, while Winnipeg had a comfortable lead in the first half and finished 2½ games ahead in the combined standings. The playoff series ended suddenly when a riot broke out during the fifth game. For the season, Hank Miller of Winnipeg led in batting (.335), hits, doubles, homers, and total bases. Teammate Warren Adams finished second in batting (.331), and led in runs scored and stolen bases. Teammate Harry "Red" Donovan, at 21–6, led the league's pitchers.

In 1917, Duluth and Superior were replaced by Minot, North Dakota and Warren, Minnesota, but the four team circuit disbanded on July 4, with Fargo comfortably in front by 11 games. The Northern League did not reappear in the Upper Midwest until 1933. But no Iron Range town ever again fielded a team in Organized Baseball. ■

Notes

1. The SABR minor league database does not currently have Roth's statistics with Virginia; I compiled them from newspaper box scores.
2. The games-played data for Brammell and Collins differs from some other sources; the totals in the text are based on my review of newspaper box scores.
3. When a player played for two or more clubs in the same league, some reference guides apparently combined the players statistics under the last team he played for in that particular year. For example, *Daguerreotypes*, published by *The Sporting News* and updated from time to time and the 1914 *Reach Guide List* Waddell's 1913 statistics under Virginia as 15 games and a 3–9 record. My research with the newspaper box scores shows Waddell pitched 4 games for the Minneapolis Bronchos (2–1 record) and 14 games for Virginia (1–8 record).The discrepancy between 15 and 18 games pitched is probably a typographical error.
4. In 1993, the St. Paul Saints, of the newly established six team independent Northern League began play. The success of the Saints and the Northern League that year encouraged others and led to a boom of independent leagues across the country.

Sources

Foster, John B., editor. Charles D. White, compiler. *Spalding's Official Base Ball Record*, 1916. New York: American Sports Publishing Company, 185–188 (1915 season statistics).

Foster, John B., editor. Charles D. White, compiler. *Spalding's Official Base Ball Record*, 1917. New York: American Sports Publishing Company, 190–193 (1916 season statistics).

Johnson, Lloyd and Miles Wolff, editors. *The Encyclopedia of Minor League Baseball*. Second Edition. Durham, North Carolina: Baseball America, Inc., 1997.

Richter, Francis C., editor. *The Reach Official American League Baseball Guide for 1914*. Philadelphia: A.J. Reach Company, 1914; 459–466 (1913 season statistics).

Richter, Francis C., editor. *The Reach Official American League Baseball Guide for 1915*. Philadelphia: A. J. Reach Company, 1915; 273–276 (1914 season statistics).

NEWSPAPERS: *Minneapolis Tribune*, 1913–1916, *Daily Virginian* (Virginia, Minnesota), 1896, 1913–1916, *Duluth News Tribune*, 1913–1916: I relied on the *Daily Virginian*, *Duluth News Tribune*, and *Minneapolis Tribune* to compile the game accounts, box scores, game results, and standings day by day of the Northern League for the four years Virginia was a league member, 1913–1916. When I was finished I was able to determine home and road records, doubleheader results, winning and losing streaks for the 1913 season, and many other facts about the 1913 season. Work continues on the 1914–1916 seasons. I also used *The Sporting News* for multiple years.

Perry Werden's Record-Setting 1895 Season and the 1890s Minneapolis Millers

Joel Rippel

It took some time for professional baseball to take hold in Minneapolis. Ultimately, a feisty first baseman with the unintimidating nickname of "Peach Pie Perry" made a record-setting contribution to get professional baseball over the hump in Minneapolis.

Organized professional baseball first arrived in Minnesota in 1877 when Minneapolis, St. Paul, and Winona sported entries in the League Alliance. Minneapolis fielded an independent professional team in 1878, but the city's next venture into professional baseball was not until 1884 with an entry in the North-western League. For the next 10 years, a baseball fan in Minneapolis needed patience. After just one season, there was no professional baseball in Minnesota in 1885. The Northwestern League returned to Minnesota in 1886 and 1887. In 1888, the Northwestern League was reorganized as the Western Association. The Minneapolis Millers didn't finish the season, playing their last game on August 18. The franchise was sold and finished the season in Davenport, Iowa.

Minneapolis returned with an entry in the Western Association in 1889. After two uneventful seasons in 1889 and 1890, the Minneapolis team folded on August 20, 1891. In 1892, the league was renamed the Western League, but again the Millers failed to complete the season, disbanding on July 15. The Millers, however, at least outlasted the St. Paul entry, which moved to Fort Wayne, Indiana on May 25 before dissolving on July 7.

Neither Minneapolis nor St. Paul fielded a team in the Western League in 1893, which, reduced to only four teams, disbanded on June 30. Despite the worsening economic depression—caused by a financial crisis that began in February 1893—a new Western League and another team in Minneapolis was organized for 1894. For the first time since 1889, the league's season was successfully completed without any franchise movement or interruption. Ban Johnson, a former Cincinnati sportswriter and the league's new president, stabilized the league, while Perry Werden (known as "Peach Pie Perry" as a youth but also called "Moose"), would help solidify baseball in Minneapolis. Werden,

who made his professional debut at the age of 22 in 1884 as a pitcher for St. Louis of the Union Association, had spent 1893 with St. Louis in the National League. Although he hit only .276 with one home run, Werden's league-leading 29 triples indicated he could hit with power.

In Minneapolis Werden played his home games at compact Athletic Park, an enclosed sports ground on land just a block from where Target Field is now. The 6-foot-2, 220-pound, right-handed hitting Werden took advantage of his tiny ballpark, barely 250 feet down the lines, to hit .417 and slug a professional baseball record 43 home runs (37 at home) as the Millers finished the 1894 season fourth with a 63–62 record.[1] The Sioux City Cornhuskers won the league title, and following the season, Charles Comiskey purchased the future Chicago White Sox franchise and relocated it to St. Paul.

On January 16, 1895, the *Minneapolis Tribune* reported that team management "claims to have signed Perry Werden, the great first baseman, who was the star favorite of the Minneapolis team last year." But the newspaper cautioned that the league reportedly had adopted a salary cap, "prohibiting any club from paying any one man over $200 per month for his services," and then noted, "if this is true it is hard to see how Werden could have been secured, as it was understood that the big man received more than that last year."

Two months later, on March 16, the *Minneapolis Tribune* reported, "[team official] Jack Bennett, who attended the league meeting in Milwaukee told the *Tribune*, 'Perry Werden will be with us this year and has probably been signed at about $175 per month. This is not a large salary and he is well worth it if he can control his temper and keep out of trouble.'"

The Sporting News, in its March 16 edition, raised the issue of doctored baseballs;

At the board of director meetings in Milwaukee, the [Western League] directors also acted upon the charge of 'ringing' in softballs by the management of the Minneapolis club at Minneapolis last season. It was voted that every ball used by the Minneapolis club must bear the stamp of the president of the league otherwise the Minneapolis club would be liable to forfeiture of the game.

The Millers tuned up for the 1895 season with seven exhibition games. They opened with a 32–4 victory over the University of Minnesota before playing four games against the newly-formed Page Fence Giants. The Giants, a black professional team named for the Page Woven Wire Fence Company of Adrian, Michigan, were led by player-manager Bud Fowler. Fowler, the earliest documented African American to play in Organized Baseball, had played for Stillwater (Minnesota) of the Northwestern League in 1884.

Minneapolis Millers team photo, 1896. Werden is top row, second from left.

Led by Werden, the Millers swept the four games from the Giants, outscoring them, 77–15. Werden was 12-for-21 with three doubles and four home runs. In other relevant preseason action, the Millers and their cross-town rivals, the St. Paul Apostles, owned by Charles Comiskey, split two exhibition games before the eight-team league, which included Detroit, Grand Rapids (Michigan), Indianapolis, Kansas City, Milwaukee and Toledo) opened its season on May 1.

When the bell rang, the Millers and Werden came out swinging. The Millers opened their season in Milwaukee, winning 4–3 before 6,000 fans in Milwaukee's new ballpark. The Millers went on to sweep the three-game series from the Brewers as Werden went 8-for-13, including his first home run of the season on May 3 in the series finale. The club moved on to Kansas City, where the first game of the series was rained out. The Millers won the next two games, 12–8 and 14–1, as Werden went 5-for-9 and hit a home run in each game.

The Millers returned to Minneapolis for their home opener on May 8. Werden hit another home run as the Millers outslugged Kansas City, 18–10, before a crowd of 4,000 on an unseasonably warm spring day that reached 85 degrees.

On May 9, the Millers suffered their first loss of the season, 11–5 to Milwaukee. After a rainout, the Millers scored seven runs in the ninth inning to rally for a 21–19 victory over Milwaukee. Werden led the attack by going 5-for-7 with two home runs. Werden went 3-for-4 with a home run the next day as the Millers defeated Kansas City, 10–5, at Minnehaha Driving Park, their "Sunday" home. Werden followed this up with a

3-for-3 day in a 13–12 loss to Milwaukee, just the Millers' second loss in 10 games. After 10 games, Werden was hitting .553 (26-for-47).

Up next was the first meeting of the season between the Millers and Apostles. The *Minneapolis Tribune* wrote that the "fur would fly" between the two teams but the first two games of the series were rained out before the Millers won in Minneapolis, 8–5, on May 16. The Millers went on to take two of the next three from the Apostles.

But it would not last. On May 21, the first-place Millers (11–3) embarked on a road trip which would see them slump, losing eight of 11 games. As they fell down the standings, the team's and their fans frustration with the league's umpiring grew. On June 5, the Millers outslugged Toledo, 18–15, even though Werden was ejected early in the game, because, the *Minneapolis Tribune* reported, he "worked his mouth too hard for the umpire." On June 16, the team announced that "ample police protection" would be provided to "ensure order at the game" because stones and verbal abuse heaped on the umpire "would no longer be tolerated."

Meanwhile, Millers hitters continued to abuse opposing pitchers. Three days later, the Millers scored 11 runs in the third inning (to rally from a 9–2 deficit) but, despite two home runs and a 4-for-5 day from Werden, the squad couldn't hold on in a 21–20 loss to Kansas City. The *Minneapolis Tribune* reported, "Umpire Sheridan gave Minneapolis just about the worst deal it has received on balls and strikes and on one hit by third which was foul by two feet."

After an off day on June 20, the Millers opened a series in Milwaukee and resumed their feud with Sheridan. Milwaukee won the game, 8–6, but Werden again provided the fireworks. The *Minneapolis Tribune* said Sheridan warned Werden and the Millers before the game that he "wouldn't tolerate their overbearing methods." Werden ignored the warning and immediately voiced his displeasure. Sheridan fined him five dollars for his pre-game outburst, which only served to make Werden angrier. As the game progressed, Werden continued to voice his opinions with the umpire. In the fifth inning, Sheridan fined Werden $50 and ejected him, requiring two police officers to escort him off the field. In the game's overall chaos, Sheridan had also fined two other Millers and one Milwaukee player.

The Brewers went on to win the next two days to sweep the three-game series and drop the slumping Millers into seventh place. Minneapolis, which had opened the season 8–1, was now only 21–23. Things didn't improve in Kansas City where the Millers dropped two of three. As the season deteriorated, frustration with the league's umpiring spilled beyond the players, and team secretary-president Tom Murphy was suspended indefinitely for throwing stones at an umpire.

On June 29 at Athletic Park, the Millers and Apostles opened a six-game series with one of the more memorable games of the season. Werden went 5-for-7 with three home runs, but the Apostles outlasted the Millers, 22–21. Werden homered twice during the Millers' 11-run eighth inning. The next day, a crowd of 6,500 gathered at the Apostles' "Sunday" ballpark in West St. Paul to see the Millers win 10–6, just their third victory in 11 games.

Werden finished 3-for-5 in each of the next two games but the Apostles won both, 9–5, and 14–11. The Millers won 22–12 on July 3 as Werden went 3-for-6, but the Apostles swept a holiday twinbill on July 4, winning 21–5 in the morning game at St. Paul's Aurora Park (scoring 13 in the second inning) and 14–8 in the afternoon game in Minneapolis. Werden went hitless in the afternoon game—the last time for seven weeks that he would go without a hit.

Werden began his hitting streak on an 11-game road trip that saw the Millers slump continue. When they won 12–11 in Grand Rapids, the *Minneapolis Tribune* headline read, "Millers take one. They actually win a game of baseball." The Millers lost four of their next five. A 15–2 loss in Detroit on July 11 prompted the Minneapolis Tribune to write, "Better come home. Millers have forgotten how to play baseball." The front office remained in turmoil as well. When they returned to Minneapolis, the team was greeted by the news that the

league had forced Murphy out as the team president.

On the field, the Millers were glad to be home. Werden went 3-for-5 with two home runs in a 20–5 victory over Detroit. The next day, he went 4-for-5 with a home run as the Millers outslugged Indianapolis, 16–12. On July 22, Werden continued his barrage, going 4-for-4 with two home runs in a 17–8 loss to Indianapolis. The next day, he slugged four home runs (with a single in a 5-for-5 performance) and drove in nine runs. On July 27, Werden hit a two-run home run in the Millers' 19–7 victory over Grand Rapids—a victory that would start a nine-game winning streak. During the streak, the Millers scored 134 runs as Werden went 24-for-49.

Werden's hitting streak finally came to an end after 40 games on August 20. Kansas City pitcher Charlie Hastings held Werden to 0-for-3 and limited the Millers to one hit (by Billy Hulen) in a 5–0 victory. During the streak, which started on July 6 and went unmentioned in newspaper reports, Werden batted .477 (94-for-197) with 18 home runs.

The Millers opened September with a 19–6 victory in Grand Rapids as Werden resumed his hot hitting, going 4-for-6 with two doubles and two home runs. On Saturday, September 14, the Millers and Apostles each played a game as part of a doubleheader at the State Fairgrounds in St. Paul. The Millers outslugged Terre Haute (where the Toledo club moved on June 30), 16–13, while the Apostles rallied from an 8–3 deficit for a 10–8 victory over Detroit. A crowd of at least 10,000 watched the two games played on a makeshift field the *St. Paul Sunday Globe* described as "a stretch of undulating prairie and precipitous bluff." The newspaper added, "The outfielders played in a ravine, and no part of them below the neck was visible from the plate. The pitchers pitched up hill and the runners in making the circuit of bases ran down hill and then ran up again. The diamond was built on sand hills, and it was difficult to gauge a fly on account of the high wind, which blew a gale from the east."

Unfortunately for the Twin Cities' ball clubs, by this point the pennant race was effectively over. The *St. Paul Sunday Globe* noted on September 15 that, with one week remaining the season, Indianapolis had clinched the league title (Indianapolis was 77–40 while second-place St. Paul was 70–49). On a positive note, the paper added that the season had been a financial success with six of the eight teams in the black financially (only seventh-place Terre Haute and eighth-place Grand Rapids lost money).

The Millers and Werden continued to pound the ball as the season wound down. On September 17 Werden had one of the Millers' five home runs in a

COURTESY MINNESOTA HISTORICAL SOCIETY

Athletic Park.

25–15 victory over Grand Rapids. The home run was his 44th of the season, breaking his record of 43 set the previous season. On September 19, Werden went 5-for-6 and hit his 45th home run of the season in a 20–10 victory over Grand Rapids. His 45 home runs would stand as the record in Organized Baseball until Babe Ruth hit 54 for the New York Yankees in 1920.

Werden, who hit safely in the Millers' final 18 games of the season, also led the league in batting average at .428 and tied for the lead in hits with St. Paul's Bill George at 241. Despite Werden's heroics at the plate, the Millers finished in fourth place with a 64–59 record.

In 1896, the Millers and Werden were forced to find a new home. About a month into the season the Millers received notice that they were being evicted from Athletic Park, their home since 1889, because the landlord intended to redevelop the valuable downtown property. On Saturday, May 23, the Millers played their final game at Athletic Park, defeating Columbus (which had replaced Terre Haute), 15–7. The next day the Millers were rained out and then left on a road trip, not knowing where they would play when they returned to Minneapolis.

For their new home a site just south of downtown Minneapolis was chosen and a ballpark—eventually named Nicollet Park—was constructed in less than four weeks. On June 19, the Millers made their debut in their new home—a 13–6 victory over Milwaukee before 4,000 fans.

The Millers were a hit in their new ballpark. In August, the Millers won 30 of 31 games in one stretch, which included winning streaks of 11 and 19 games interrupted only by a loss to Kansas City. The hot Millers captured their first league title, finishing 89–47, nine games ahead of second-place Indianapolis.

Werden led the league in home runs for the third consecutive season, but his total of 18 (equaled by teammate William "Pop" Schriver) was a huge drop off from the previous season. In fact, Werden hit seven of his home runs in the 17 games at Athletic Park before the move.

In 1897 Werden was given another shot at the big leagues with Louisville in the National League. He turned in a pretty good year, hitting .301 with five home runs, but returned to Minneapolis for 1898. He missed the 1898 season because of a broken leg, but came back to bat .346 in 1899. Werden made his final professional appearance in 1908 with Indianapolis at the age of 43. In 24 seasons in professional baseball, he had 2,897 hits, 195 home runs and 500 recorded stolen bases (as then defined) (four times he stole more than 50). But the exclamation point on Perry Werden's long and productive baseball career was his record-setting 1895 season in which he set a long-standing home run mark and hit in 40 consecutive games. ∎

Notes

1. Stew Thornley, "Athletic Park (Minneapolis)," Society for American Baseball Research Biography Project (www.bioproject.sabr.org).

Sources

Johnson, Lloyd and Miles Wolff, ed. *Encyclopedia of Minor League Baseball*, 3rd edition. Durham, NC: Baseball America Inc., 2007.

Johnson, Lloyd, Ed. *The Minor League Register*. Durham, NC: Baseball America Inc., 1994.

Peterson, Todd. *Early Black Baseball in Minnesota*. Jefferson, NC: McFarland & Company, Inc., 2010.

Podoll, Brian A. *The Minor League Milwaukee Brewers 1859–1952*. Jefferson, NC: McFarland & Company, Inc., 2003.

Thornley, Stew. *On To Nicollet. The Glory and Fame of the Minneapolis Millers*. Minneapolis, MN.: Nodin Press, 1988.

NEWSPAPERS: *Minneapolis Journal, Minneapolis Tribune, The Sporting News, St. Paul Globe, St. Paul Pioneer Press, Terre Haute Express*.

Baseball's Twin Towers in the Twin Cities

The Minneapolis Millers and the St. Paul Saints in the American Association, 1902–1960

Rex Hamann

THE RIVALRY TAKES ROOT

After spending the better part of the 1890s hosting entries in the Western League, the cities of Minneapolis and St. Paul became part of the newly formed American Association when the league organized in Chicago in November 1901. The independent circuit would compete with the American and National Leagues, placing clubs in cities closely mirroring that of the old Western League. On April 23, 1902, the Minneapolis Millers and St. Paul Saints opened their season as members of the fledgling league on the road against the Columbus (Ohio) Senators and Toledo Mud Hens, respectively. The Millers stepped off the train to a shutout, 5–0, while the Mud Hens handed the Saints a narrow defeat, 8–7.

The two teams came home to their neighboring cities on the Mississippi River just weeks later and began a long legacy of baseball in the high minors. In their May 10, 1902, home openers, the Millers crushed the Louisville Colonels, 9–4, at Nicollet Park, while the Saints initiated the Indianapolis Indians, 4–0, behind right-hander Charlie Chech (pronounced "Check") who struck out nine at expansive Lexington Park, then on the western outskirts of St. Paul. Neither Twin Cities team went on to glory that first year, but a new and lasting era of professional baseball was born.

Known at various times in the city's history as the "Apostles," the newly christened "Saints" landed in third place (72–66) in 1902 under Massachusetts-born player-manager Mike Kelley. The club sported a cast of players previously with St. Paul's Class-A Western League franchise, including future Hall of Famer Miller Huggins at second base. The 1902 Millers were in a more developmental stage. Posting a team batting average of .244, 24 points below the league average, Minneapolis finished the season with a 54–86 record under player-manager Walt Wilmot, who hailed from Plover, Wisconsin.

The Twin Cities' new American Association entries continued a tradition of inter-city rivalry that extended from the days of the old Northwestern League in the 1880s, and their American Association battles would become legendary over a period of six decades. The cross-town holiday twinbills, with screaming trolley cars packed to the gills, raucous carnival-style barkers on street corners, grandstands and bleachers filled to the brim, overflow crowds, popular Sunday bouts, and perennially well-matched teams, brought out local revelers on a robust scale. These teams and their fans put what was then an isolated Midwestern locale securely onto the baseball map until the Millers and Saints played their final games in 1960, departing the scene to make way for the Minnesota Twins.

ST. PAUL SAINTS: 1903 AND 1904

Riding the 25-year-old Chech, who won 24 and lost nine, the Saints won the 1903 pennant with 88 wins and 46 losses. The Saints' style of play on the home grounds changed drastically in mid-July. From the wide-open spaces of Lexington Park (at the corner of University and Lexington in St. Paul), the club moved to the diminutive Downtown Park (aka "Pill Box"), located near the city center. Perhaps the most unusual feature of the facility was the lack of foul territory around the entire perimeter of the playing field. The first game was played at the brand new venue July 20, 1903, against the Minneapolis Millers and resulted in a convincing win for the Saints, 11–2, at a time when they were battling with Milwaukee for the league lead. Despite the move, the Saints stayed hot, winning their first 14 home games after the switch.

St. Paul hitters out-paced the opposition with a .281 batting average, but where the Saints really did their damage was on the basepaths. With 267 steals, the club led the league courtesy of three rabbits with at least 40 each: second-baseman Miller Huggins (48), outfielder Jimmy Jackson (42) and outfielder Spike Shannon (41). "Little Phil" Geier was the Association's top batter at .361.

The Saints kept their hands on the league crown in 1904 on the strength of two righties: Chech (27–8) and Perry Sessions (27–10). They now had a full season in which to swat two-baggers in Downtown Park, and they led the league with 270. Again Mike Kelley was at

Nicollet Park at capacity, 1904.

the helm, and again the Saints ran rampant, racking up 237 steals, 54 more than second-ranked Milwaukee. Jimmy Jackson exceeded his old form by amassing 59 swipes for the Association lead. The 5-foot-6, 165-lb. Pennsylvanian also excelled at the plate, hitting .335 and swatting league-highs with 13 home runs and 39 doubles. Jackson's productivity placed him among the league's elite, ranking third in both slugging percentage (.480) and total bases (278). The speedy right-fielder was the perfect number-two hitter and an indispensable weapon in the Saints' arsenal during the pennant chase of 1904.

With a record of 95–52, the "Kellyites" (as they were often dubbed in the local press) won the pennant by eight games over the Columbus Senators. In a post-season series between St. Paul and the Eastern League champion Buffalo Bisons managed by George Stallings, Buffalo beat the Saints, two games to one.

MINNEAPOLIS MILLERS: 1910–1912

It wasn't until 1909 that either team had much hope of bringing another flag to the Twin Cities. Under Bill Clymer the Columbus Senators became kings of the AA by capturing the league crown from 1905–07, the first three-peat in league history. In 1909, Minneapolis and the Milwaukee Brewers battled for the top spot all season long, but a late surge by the Louisville Colonels shoved them both aside.

The Millers began their ascent in 1910. Managed by another Wisconsin native, "Pongo Joe" Cantillon, Minneapolis carried out the league's second three-peat and in the process won a cumulative total of 311 victories against 187 defeats. Minneapolis finished the season with 107 wins and 61 losses.

The 1910 season was the Millers' most successful in club history. After losing to the Kansas City Blues in the season opener at cozy Nicollet Park, the Millers split the four-game series. With a record of 16–9 by mid-May, they asserted their strength with a seven-game home winning streak, then losing only sparingly. Through June 25 the Millers never lost more than two straight games. With steady work and good fortune, they did not lose a homestand all season.

Potent offense characterized the club. The Millers led the league in batting with a .272 mark; the league batting average was a paltry .243. With 79 triples Cantillon's men set a standing club record (which the Millers tied in 1922). The lead performer on a cast of offensive stars was 29-year-old Californian Gavvy "Cactus" Cravath who paced the league in hits (200), doubles (41), home runs (14), and batting average (.326). Cravath would later star for the National League's Philadelphia Phillies. Center fielder Otis Clymer, the Millers' perennial leadoff man, rang up 30 doubles and stole 38 bases while scoring 109 runs in addition to his top-notch fielding.

Fielding was another club hallmark. Two Miller infielders led the league with the leather: second baseman Jimmy Williams and third baseman Hobe Ferris, both players with considerable prior major league experience.

Chicago-born right-hander "Long Tom" Hughes was the staff ace for the Millers in 1910. After showing signs of a tired arm while with the American League's Washington Senators, Hughes became a Miller in 1909. But with new life in his lame arm, he shattered all expectations by nailing down 31 wins against 12 losses. This "shot in the arm" performance propelled him back to Washington to pitch for the Senators for three more years. Unlike many other pitchers of the era, he overcame his arm problems to continue pitching at a high level well into his 40s.

Even without Hughes for 1911, the team barely lost a beat. The league's leader in wins, Roy Patterson (24–10), and former Philadelphia Athletics star Rube Waddell (20–17) combined for 44 of the club's 99 wins. Waddell struck out 185 batters. But even with their record of 99–66, the Millers finished only 4½ games in front of Dan Shay's Kansas City Blues.

Six regular position players batted over .300 for the 1911 Millers. At the forefront was Cravath who went on a tear the likes of which the Association had never seen. He led the league in batting (.363), hits (221), doubles (53), and home runs with 29, upsetting the previous record of 18 set in 1907 by John Frank "Buck" Freeman, another Minneapolis outfielder. Cravath's remarkable .637 slugging percentage topped the league's runner-up by more than 130 points.

In 1911 the combined strength of the Millers' base-stealing and the recently introduced juiced ball resulted in an offensive surge. The Millers topped the league with a .301 mark, surpassing the .300 level for the first time in league history, and led the circuit in runs scored. From 1910 to 1911, the league batting average went from .243 to .268, while total runs jumped from 5,055 in 1910 to 6,169, a 22% increase. The following season the American Association returned to the customary "dead" ball and the numbers subsided.

Ushering in a new age, the 1912 American Association was reclassified as a Double-A league, granting it higher status relative to several other leagues in the high minors. With Cantillon again in command, the Millers captured the flag with a record of 105–60.

In terms of wins and losses, the 1912 Millers were comparable with the 1910 team, but there was one big difference: the 1912 team amassed 292 stolen bases, the highest total in the six-decade expanse of American Association history. Shortstop Dave "Filipino" Altizer's 68 swipes set a new Association record, one which stood until 1921. Right-hander Fred Olmstead won 28 games to lead AA pitchers and struck out 131. Outfielder Claude Rossman swatted 32 doubles and topped the club with a .322 batting average.

Local fans appreciated the Millers' strong showing, as attendance at Nicollet Park led the league. Logistics may have played a part in the club's strong draw as the park, at West 31st and Nicollet Avenues, was located adjacent to a street car terminal, allowing fans unparalleled access from a variety of points in the city.

MINNEAPOLIS MILLERS: 1915

Milwaukee captured the crown from 1913–14, its first championships in the American Association. Then in a remarkable turn of events, both St. Paul and Minneapolis came out of nowhere to become contenders in the most competitive and dramatic season the two clubs ever played against one another.

On Wednesday, May 19, a just-turned-20-year-old southpaw named Harry Clayton Harper took the hill for the Millers at Nicollet Park against the Saints and reeled off a no-hitter. The gem would become the only Millers vs. Saints no-no ever in the American Association. Despite the no-hitter, the Millers continued to struggle, and it seemed both teams were having trouble getting out of their own way.

By mid-June the Millers were mired deeply in the second division, spending the entire second-half of the month dipping in and out of seventh-place. They were struggling, but there were still some live embers buried deeply within the Miller woolens.

Just as the summer was about to kick off, things began to heat up for both teams. During the last half of June, St. Paul won 10 of 15 games under Mike Kelley, resulting in an appreciable rise in the standings. The Millers were beginning to capture their stride as well, as Cantillon's crew used the period from June 15–30 as a platform for future success. By month's end they found themselves in sixth place, punctuating their resurgence by sweeping a doubleheader against Kansas City on June 30.

The Saints were now competing for the top spot in the American Association. Kelley's men had bridged a wide river, winning 23 of 27 games during their homestand stretching between June 26 and July 21. It was a sign the planned ownership change was the right move for the team. Long-time club owner George Lennon gave up the reins to a group of St. Paul businessmen who saw the recent successful run of the team translate into a bigger payday at the gate.

Just as the Saints' string of 13 wins was ending, the Millers started a streak of their own. Facing a pair of second-division teams, the Columbus Senators and Cleveland Spiders (the Toledo Mud Hens had moved to Cleveland as a tactic against a potential Federal League invasion in that city) at Nicollet Park, Minneapolis began to surge. After the Senators took the first meeting July 16, Millers pitchers tossed four consecutive shutouts.

The Millers winning ways continued until July 27 when they lost a close one in an 11-inning battle at Kansas City's Association Park in the second game of a twin bill. But the Cantillon nine finally took over first place on August 22, after sweeping twin tilts against Cleveland at Nicollet Park. Defeating the Spiders, 4–3, in the second game pushed the Millers' record to 71–50 for their tenth straight win.

Baseball Game at Lexington Park, 1916.

It was part of a 13-game string dating back to August 14—and it all started in St. Paul. From that point their largest lead over the Saints was four games on September 1. The Saints kept nipping at their heels until the close of the season on September 19 when Minneapolis finished atop the Association with a thread-like 1½ game lead over their down-river rival.

ST. PAUL SAINTS: 1919 TO 1924

The Saints and Millers both finished in the first division in 1916, but were not considered contenders. The following season, St. Paul was competitive until the end, finishing just 2½ games behind Jack Hendricks' Indianapolis Indians. As World War I took its toll on the nation, the 1918 American Association season was mandated complete through the games already complete on July 21 at which point the Saints and Millers finished sixth and seventh, respectively.

But in 1919 the Saints rose from the lull. Finishing 94–60, Mike Kelley's men used speed and pitching to grab the American Association flag for the first time in 15 years. Outfielder Elmer Miller was a one-man wrecking crew, posting league highs in total bases (302), slugging percentage (.497), triples (16), and home runs (15).

First-baseman Leo "Lee" Dressen was another impact player that year, leading the club in five offensive categories. A table-setter, Dressen drew 94 walks and stole a league-leading 46 bases. As the American Association's only player ever to lead the circuit in steals in three seasons (1917, 1919–20), Dressen was an impressive lead-off batter.

Catcher Eugene "Bubbles" Hargrave was solid defensively, but his hitting was vital. He led the club in

doubles (35) and had a team-second 233 total bases. While it wasn't a sustained relationship, the Saints also employed a 24-year-old outfielder by the name of George Halas to fill in for 39 games and do some hitting, which he did, to the tune of a .274 batting average. On the hill, two 20-game winners graced the St. Paul roster, lefty Dick Niehaus (23–13, .639) and Dan "Rusty" Griner (21–14, .600).

The 1920 Saints went on a barnstorming tour of sorts—across the American Association—again with Kelley managing. Three 20-game winners provided the boost as St. Paul won 115 games with only 49 losses. Compiling more wins than any other team in American Association history and posting the league's best winning percentage ever at .701 the Saints had the season wrapped up early, winding up with a 28½ game lead over the second-place Louisville Colonels.

Heading the charge off the hill was right-hander Charley "Sea Lion" Hall (real name Carlos Clolo) with a league-leading 27 wins against only eight losses. On August 26 against the Columbus Senators, Hall allowed no runs and no hits at St. Paul's Lexington Park for a historic 6–0 win. In his third year with the Saints, lefty John Merritt had 21 wins against only 10 losses. Righty Rees "Steamboat" Williams racked up 20 wins for the second time as a Saint, losing only six—nearly matching Hall's league-high .771 winning percentage.

The Saints also boasted a potent offensive attack in 1920. They established a new Association record with 1,679 hits, scoring 961 runs, 142 more than the runner-up. Third baseman "Goldie" Rapp essentially shared the batting crown with teammate Bubbles Hargrave (who had 62 fewer at-bats), hitting .335 with 37 doubles. Hargrave banged out a club-high 22 long balls

The St. Paul Saints of the late teens and early 1920s were some of the greatest minor league teams of all time.

while leading the club in total bases (292—tied with second-year Saint Elmer Miller) and slugging. Joe Riggert, a St. Paul stalwart in the outfield for 12 seasons (1912–24, excluding 1914), led the league in triples.

At the time, the American Association pennant winner played the champion of the International League in what was billed as the Little World Series (renamed the Junior World Series in 1932). For the 1920 minor league crown, the Saints faced the Baltimore Orioles, another dynasty made up of a number of future big league stars. Despite their stellar season, the Saints could not defeat their East Coast opponent, losing the best of nine series five games to one.

In 1921 St. Paul took a tumble, landing in sixth-place. But in 1922, Mike Kelley and the Saints were right back in the fray. In decisive fashion, St. Paul nailed down the American Association pennant, beating their cross-river rival by 15 games. Returnees included second baseman Marty Berghammer, outfielders Bruno Haas and Joe Riggert, and pitchers Charley Hall and John Merritt. Outfielder Walt "Cuckoo" Christensen led the club in runs (117) and bases on balls (97).

The pitching staff was led by Tom Sheehan (26-12), Charley Hall (22–8), and John Cleave "Rube" Benton (22–11), who had been banished to the minors in 1921 for his gambling associations and unsavory reputation. Sheehan's 3.01 ERA was tops in the league, and his 26 wins, 53 appearances and 332 innings of work led the circuit as well. But the Saints fell again to the Baltimore Orioles in the Little World Series, five games to two.

In the 1923 campaign, despite a stellar record of 111–57, the Saints finished second, two games behind the Kansas City Blues. St. Paul's pitching was led by their ace, Sheehan, who was back with a vengeance, winning 31 games. Three other 20-plus game winners boosted the club's chances. It was Mike Kelley's final year managing St. Paul. For a generation of Twin Cities residents, it was the end of an era as 1923 was the last season when both Pongo Joe Cantillon and Kelley managed the Millers and Saints. The dramatic headline for 1924: the Saints' Kelley replaces Millers manager Cantillon!

In 1924 the Saints returned to the summit with their new manager, Nick Allen, a former catcher. Johnny Neun, the Saints new first baseman, stole 55 bases to lead the league, and "Cuckoo" Christensen scored 145 runs to top the circuit. That season also saw the emergence of third baseman Chuck Dressen who batted .347 and led the club in doubles (41), home runs (18), and RBI (151), the latter figure pacing the league. Dressen's club leadership in slugging (.534) and total bases (327—a new record for the St. Paul club) repre-

Willie Mays on base during his short stint as a Miller in 1951.

sented a powerful contribution to the Saints' lineup. For this final year of dominance the Saints set a team attendance record with 242,258 fans, a total that would not be surpassed until 1938. In the Little World Series the Saints finally came out on top. Allen's men faced Jack Dunn's Baltimore Orioles for the third time in five years, this time taking the 10-game series five games to four.

THE MILLERS AND SAINTS: 1925–1930
In 1925 the Saints and Millers finished back-to-back for the first time since 1922, in slots three and four, respectively, Kelley's Millers landing five games behind Allen's Saints. In 1926 the Saints and Millers were again "twins" in the season's final standings, St. Paul in sixth, the Minneapolis well behind in seventh. Interestingly, by the time the 1927 standings were sorted out, the Millers and Saints finished one on top of the other for the third straight year. From 1925–27 St. Paul led Minneapolis in each instance. The back-to-back pattern happened during one other stretch: 1914–16— when the Millers led each time.

Under Nick Allen in 1927 the Saints finished in fourth-place (90–78), 11 games behind Casey Stengel's surprising Toledo Mud Hens. Minneapolis landed in fifth under Kelley (88–80), just two games behind St. Paul. Millers' shortstop Frank Emmer won the

American Association home run derby that season with 32, the first time a shortstop won the honor in the Association. Over in St. Paul, a budding shortstop named Leo Durocher was cutting his teeth on American Association diamonds at the age of 21.

The Millers just missed in 1928, finishing 2½ games behind the Indianapolis Indians. The Saints, under new manager Bubbles Hargrave, renewed their trend of first-division finishes in 1929 (102–64), their first season with over 100 wins since 1923, but finished 8½ games behind Dutch Zwilling and his Kansas City Blues. The Saints maintained their momentum in 1930, but narrowly missed another pennant as the Louisville Colonels nabbed first-place by 2½ games.

ST. PAUL SAINTS: 1931

The Saints returned to the top in 1931 under their former pitcher, Al "Lefty" Leifield, who led them to 104 wins and 63 losses. The league temporarily returned to a 168-game schedule and the Saints worked it to their advantage by building a 14-game lead over Kansas City. Among the batting leaders were second baseman Jack Saltzgaver, pitcher-turned-outfielder Oscar Roettger, and outfielder George "Kiddo" Davis. Walter "Huck" Betts, a 34-year-old right-hander, held court with a 22–13 record, leading the staff with 285 innings and an ERA of 3.60. Right-hander William Jennings Bryan "Slim" Harriss may have had his best season as a pro, with 20 wins against 11 losses.

As entrants in the Little World Series that year the Saints faced off against the Rochester Red Wings who were led by future Hall of Fame manager Billy Southworth. Both teams scored 37 runs during the match-up, and the two teams' batting average and ERA nearly equalled one another. But after being shutout in the first game, Southworth's squad won four straight and prevailed five games to three.

MINNEAPOLIS MILLERS: 1932 TO 1935

The Saints fell to seventh-place the following year, but the Millers were there to take their place. With a record of 100 wins and 68 losses, Minneapolis captured the 1932 flag under the leadership of veteran Owen "Donie" Bush. Mike Kelley had finally stepped down from his managerial duties but remained active in club affairs. Thirty-three-year-old first baseman Joe "Unser Choe" Hauser came to the Millers from the Baltimore Orioles and showed the Flour City just how high he could rise. Swatting 49 home runs gave him the home run crown by a margin of 19. The Millers benefited from having a left-handed power hitter like Hauser with the short right field at Nicollet Park. The Millers'

188 home runs set an AA record, and nearly 80% were hit at home. Left fielder Joe Mowry, age 24, amassed 384 total bases and led the Association in games (168), at-bats (739), runs (175), and hits (257).

The Millers' 1932 pitching staff was anchored by Wilfred "Rosy" Ryan who led the AA with 22 wins while posting an ERA of 4.45. Arguably, 37-year-old Jesse Petty, the "Silver Fox," was the Millers' most efficient workhorse, appearing in 52 games and 236 innings. Perhaps the biggest story of the Miller mound crew was Rube Benton, who, at the age of 42, went 18–7. The Millers bowed to the International League's Newark Bears in their initial foray into Junior World Series territory, four games to two.

An impressive performance by the Columbus Red Birds (101-51) in 1933 left Minneapolis in the dust by 15½ games. Under one-year skipper, and future Hall of Famer, Dave Bancroft, the Millers led the league with a team batting average of .303, but they couldn't surpass Columbus despite the home run heroics of Hauser who set a new league record with a staggering 69 home runs in a 154-game schedule.

Donie Bush returned to the Millers in 1934, just in time to lead them to another first place regular season finish. With a record of 85–64, Minneapolis surged on the bats of Hauser, outfielder Albert "Ab" Wright, and 38-year-old catcher William McKinley "Pinky" Hargrave (brother of Bubbles). Each Miller regular batted over .300, but Hargrave was the bountiful backstop, hitting .356, slugging .523, and compiling a club-fifth 286 total bases. Outfielder Russell "Buzz" Arlett, the former Pacific Coast League star, stood out as a Miller that season. The 35-year-old California native led the Association in home runs (41) while hitting .319.

Thirty-two-year-old righty Walt Tauscher, in his second season with Minneapolis, was the Millers' undisputed pitching leader with 21 wins against only seven losses, giving him the league's top winning percentage. Adding to the mound corps mix was Petty who finished 19–7 with a 96–40 strikeouts-to-walks ratio in 40 games at the age of 39.

The previous year the American Association had introduced an experimental playoff system based on an "Eastern vs. Western" format. In this second year of the new scheme, the Millers were defeated by second-place Columbus, four games to three.

The 1935 season was the first year the Millers affiliated with a major league organization, creating a working agreement with Cleveland Indians. In 1934, only one American Association club had anything beyond a loose working arrangement with a major league parent: Columbus was aligned with the St. Louis

Cardinals. But the trend was growing, and the Millers, along with three other teams, were caught up in the farm system wave.

The 1935 Minneapolis Millers maintained their AA reign. Again under Bush they went 91–53, finishing five games ahead of the Indianapolis Indians. With 191 home runs, the Millers blasted more balls out of Association ballparks than ever. As Hauser's home run totals were subsiding (from 33 in 1934, to 23 in 1935), two players surpassed him: outfielder Johnny Gill, who led the league with 43 while slugging .656, and Arlett who drove out 25. Gill seemed to come out of nowhere that year, appearing in only eight games as a Miller in 1934.

Right-hander Denny Galehouse was a welcome addition to the Miller pitching staff, posting a club-high 140 strikeouts in the 23-year-old's first, and last, season in Minneapolis. The Millers now owned seven American Association championships, but could not return to the Junior World Series that year because of a one-year hiatus in the post-season series.

ST. PAUL SAINTS: 1938

The Saints affiliated for the first time in 1936, creating working agreement with White Sox. After finishing second under new manager Gabby Street, the Saints had high hopes for the coming season. In 1937 they changed their affiliation to the Boston Bees, but the team struggled, resulting in a mid-season managerial replacement. The Saints hoped to reverse course by naming their perennial first baseman, Phil "Hook" Todt, the successor to Street. Todt, one of the most adept first basemen in the league, was in his sixth and final season with the club; it was his seventeenth year in pro ball. But Todt could not turn the club around, and St. Paul finished in seventh place.

In 1938 the Saints renewed their affiliation with the Chicago White Sox, and Foster "Babe" Ganzel took over as manager. Meanwhile, the Boston Red Sox farmed 19-year-old future Hall of Famer Ted Williams to the Millers.

Ganzel led St. Paul to the flag with a 90–61 record, six games ahead of Kansas City. Second baseman Ollie Bejma had a career year, leading Ganzel's men in batting average (.326), slugging percentage (.548), total bases (304), and home runs (25). Outfielder Malin "Bit" McCullough spurred the St. Paul offense with his league-topping 41 doubles and his club-best 14 triples.

Vic Frazier (17–7) and former Miller Ray Phelps (12–8), two right-handed veterans, had exceptional years on the mound. But the most remarkable pitching performance belonged to 32-year-old Art Herring, an-

other experienced righty. With three shutouts to his credit, Herring posted a 16–6 record and 3.74 ERA in 200 innings.

But in the Shaughnessy play-off system adopted in 1936 (involving the league's top four teams), Kansas City advanced to the Junior World Series after Bill Meyer's Blues eliminated St. Paul, four games to three, in the final round of the playoffs.

ST. PAUL SAINTS: 1949

St. Paul slogged through the 1940s, nailing down a first-division finish on only four occasions before capturing its ninth and final flag in 1949. A 36-year-old Walter "Smokey" Alston took the reins in 1948, finishing 86–68, a huge improvement over 1947. A Brooklyn Dodgers affiliate since 1944, St. Paul was an incubator for talent, and the odds were in their favor in 1949. First baseman Danny Ozark (.307), second-sacker Hank Schenz (.345), third baseman Danny O'Connell (.314), and outfielders Eric Tipton (.320) and Bob Addis (.346) topped the batting list. Ferrell "Andy" Anderson, the presiding St. Paul backstop, hit .303 while his back-up Sam Calderone hit .316.

The 1949 Saints specialized in manufacturing runs, spiced with a dash of power, and playing solid ball behind its pitchers. With 112 stolen bases, the Saints bested all Association rivals for the first time since 1928. In addition, their 121 home runs was runner-up to the Millers' league-high 202 long balls. On the mound, Phil Haugstad had a career year. With a record of 22–7, Haugstad posted a 2.85 ERA, 140 Ks, 17 complete games, and two shutouts, all club highs.

In the first round of the playoffs, St. Paul was defeated by Milwaukee, four games to three. The club also lost its manager after the season as the Dodgers organization sent Alston east to manage the Montreal Royals.

MINNEAPOLIS MILLERS: 1950

Fifteen seasons after their last pennant, the Millers were due. Prior to becoming an affiliate of the New York Giants in 1946, Minneapolis was a second-division team during the decade's first half. But in 1950, 36-year-old former catcher Tommy Heath, in his second year managing the club, pushed the team back into the top spot, finishing 90–64.

Heath's brand of ball hinged on defense. The Miller infield was the Association's envy with future NL All-Star second baseman Davey Williams, third baseman Ray "Dannie" Dandridge, and shortstop Bill Jennings.

Minneapolis also continued to capitalize on Nicollet Park's short fence in right, topping the league by a significant margin with 176 home runs, and the club led the circuit in runs for the second straight year. Bert Haas, the Millers' 36-year-old first baseman/outfielder, was Heath's leading man at the plate. He led the league in doubles (36) and topped his teammates in home runs (24), batting average (.318), and total bases (276). The 36-year-old Dandridge, a long-time former Negro Leagues star, was the Millers' first African American player. In his second season with Minneapolis Dandridge paced the American Association in hits (195) while showing off his endurance with a league-high 627 at-bats.

Perhaps Dandridge's real value to the Millers came defensively. With a .978 fielding average, he demonstrated his superiority over all other Association third-basemen. As a hot corner hero, Dandridge didn't just "flash the leather," rather, sparks came out of it.

On the mound, Hoyt "Old Sarge" Wilhelm, at age 27, was becoming a household name by putting his knuckleball to good use. The first reliever elected to the Hall of Fame, Wilhelm was in his first season as a Miller, winning 15 against 11 losses. Millard "Dixie" Howell, finished 14–2 with a pair of shutouts. Dave Barnhill (11–3) and Cuban Adrian Zabala (11–4) nearly matched Howell's performance.

The influence of television was making itself felt across the minor leagues, and attendance suffered dramatically in minor league cities across America. But fielding a winner helped Minneapolis stave off the television blues, and the club suffered little at the gate. In 1949, official league records indicate a Nicollet Park draw of 247,637; in 1950, the Millers drew 238,285— a reduction of only 3.8 percent.

In the first round of the league playoffs, the Columbus Red Birds knocked the Millers out of contention for the Junior World Series four games to two.

MINNEAPOLIS MILLERS: 1955–1960

During the 1950s the American Association went through a variety of changes. Franchise transfers and ownership changes characterized these times as teams tried to save themselves from economic hardship, much of it due to the advent of television. When Toledo left for Charleston (WV) at mid-season in 1952, the move represented the league's first major shift since the Toledo Mud Hens became the Cleveland Spiders in 1914. Unlike that temporary transfer, Toledo's move to Charleston was intended as permanent.

Against this backdrop the 1955 Millers achieved the ninth and final American Association regular season title for Minneapolis. In their final season at Nicollet Park, they finished on top with a record of 92–62, eight games over the Omaha Cardinals, one of four new fran-

chises in the Association. Leading the league with 18 complete games, Al "Red" Worthington was the staff ace, winning 19 against 10 losses under 37-year-old manager Bill Rigney, serving his second stint as skipper.

The Millers exploded for 241 long balls in 1955— the highest total in Association history—tipping their collective cap to the old barn at 31st and Nicollet Avenues, not with a bang, but with a resounding thunderclap. Among those providing the home run heroics were two experienced Miller outfielders: Bob "Archie" Lennon and George "Teddy" Wilson, each with 31 circuit clouts. Catcher Carl "Swats" Sawatski hit 27 four-baggers, while third-baseman Rance Pless had 26.

In the playoffs, the Millers swept both Denver and Omaha in four games to win the Governor's Cup, the top prize of the American Association champion. Minneapolis became the first American Association team to sweep both rounds of the playoffs since the inception of intra-league postseason play. Facing the Rochester Red Wings in the Junior World Series, the Millers overcame their .235 series batting average to capture the crown, four games to three. With 16 home runs during the seven-game series, Minneapolis achieved an all-time Junior World Series record.

In 1958 Minneapolis again made it to the Junior World Series. Finishing the regular season in third-place under Gene Mauch in his first year at the helm, the Millers defeated Wichita and Denver in the playoffs to earn the Governor's Cup. To seal the deal, Mauch's men swept Montreal, becoming only the second Association club to ever sweep a Junior World Series.

The Millers repeated as the Association's representative in the Junior World Series in 1959, whipping Omaha four tilts to two in the opening round of the playoffs. In the final playoff round, they skinned the Fort Worth Cats, four games to three. But this time the Junior World Series outcome was less favorable as the Havana Sugar Kings nipped the Millers four games to three in one of the closest battles in series history.

Minneapolis and St. Paul wrapped up their fifty-ninth season in the American Association by finishing fifth and fourth, respectively, in the standings, signaling an end to a long and dramatic history. In 1961 the Washington Senators moved to Minnesota and renamed their club the "Twins," a moniker suggesting a "coming together" of the two long-competitive rivals. Even today, the iconic Twins logo illustrating "Minnie and Paul" shaking hands across the Mississippi River lives on. Created by St. Paul artist Ray Barton for $15.00 in 1961, the symbolic emblem represents the region's storied baseball past in tribute to the Minneapolis Millers and the St. Paul Saints. ∎

SOURCES
Books

All-time Records and Highlights of the American Association, 1970.

Bailey, Bob. *History of the Junior World Series*. Lanham, MD: Scarecrow Press, 2004.

Barnard, Ernest S., ed. *Reach's Official American Association Base Ball Guide for 1903*. Philadelphia: A.J. Reach, 1903.

Benson, Michael. *Ballparks of North America*. Jefferson, NC: McFarland, 1989.

Dewey, Donald and Nicholas Acocella. *The New Biographical History of Baseball*. Chicago: Triumph Books, 2002.

French, Robert A. *Fifty Golden Years in the American Association of Professional Baseball Clubs, 1902–1951*. Minneapolis, MN: Syndicate Printing, 1951.

Johnson, Lloyd, Ed. *The Minor League Register*. Durham, NC: Baseball America, 1994.

Lin Weber, Ralph E. *The Toledo Baseball Guide of the Mud Hens*. Rossford, OH: Baseball Research Bureau, 1944.

Madden, W.C. and Patrick J. Stewart. *The Western League*. Jefferson, NC: McFarland, 2002.

Podoll, Brian. *The Minor League Milwaukee Brewers, 1859–1952*. Jefferson, NC: McFarland, 2004.

Reach's Official American Association Guide. Philadelphia: A.J. Reach, 1903.

Record Makers of the American Association. Minneapolis, MN, 1955.

Reddick, David B. and Kim M. Rogers. *The Magic of Indians' Baseball: 1887–1987*. Indians, Inc., 1988.

Thornley, Stew. *On to Nicollet, The Glory and Fame of the Minneapolis Millers*. Minneapolis: Nodin Press, 2000.

Wolff, Miles and Lloyd Johnson. *The Encyclopedia of Minor League Baseball*. Durham, NC: Baseball America, 1997.

Wright, Marshall. *The American Association*. Jefferson, NC: McFarland, 1997.

Periodicals

Minneapolis Journal, December 3, 1937.

Minneapolis Tribune, April 29, 1902; May 20, 1902; May 25, 1902; May 28, 1902; May 29, 1902; July 5, 1909; October 8, 1911.

St. Paul Pioneer Press, May 28, 1902; May 29, 1902; July 4, 1903; July 2, 1931.

Sporting Life, May 3, 1902; June 7, 1902.

The Sporting News, July 22, 1915; July 29, 1915.

Unpublished Files

Fink, Gary. 1932 American Association Pitching Records. ca. 2004.

Hamann, Rex. Unpublished database files: American Association Cumulative Team Battting, 1902–1962 American Association Nine-Inning No-Hitters, 1902–52.

American Association League Attendance Records, 1908–50. Unpublished file from the league offices of the American Association.

American Association Pitchers' Cumulative Records, 1902–52 American Association Team Batting Leaders, 1902–62.

Websites

www.almanacpark.blogspot.com
www.baseball-reference.com
bleacherreport.com/articles/382154-creator-of-minnesota-twins-logo-dies-at-age-80
maps.google.com/maps?q=Barton+County
minnesota.twins.mlb.com/min/history/minnesota_baseball_history.jsp
pro-football-reference.com
stewthornley.net/millers
usfamily.net/web/trombleyd/SaintsHistory02-19.htm

The St. Paul–New York Underground Railroad

Steve Steinberg

On New Year's Day, 1925, local newspapers announced that the St. Paul Saints of the American Association had been sold to Bob Connery, longtime New York Yankees scout. While Connery declared that he was severing all connections with the Yankees, the two teams were actually about to embark on a close relationship for the next few years.[1] A regular shuttle of players between the Yankees and the Saints would become a cornerstone of the New York team's player acquisition and development program. What was not announced on that New Year's Day—and would not become public knowledge until late 1929—was that that Yankees manager Miller Huggins was a silent partner, a one-third owner, of the Saints.

How much did the two teams and their owners (Connery and Huggins of St. Paul, and Jacob Ruppert of the Yankees) benefit from this relationship? To what extent did Jacob Ruppert and Yankees business manager Ed Barrow know of Huggins's financial interest in the Saints on those occasions when the Yankees' manager recommended the New Yorkers purchase players from St. Paul? There was no formal or ownership connection between the two teams—the Yankees, like many major league teams, had working relationships with minor league teams, but they would not embark on their own farm system until 1932. Yet as one newspaper noted in the summer of 1928, "Farm or no farm, the Saints have been delivering to the American League pace-setters."[2]

When Connery bought the Saints, they had just come off a successful 1924 season, winning the American Association pennant and then surprising the powerful Baltimore Orioles, International League champions, in the Little World Series, five games to four. John W. Norton, who had acquired the Saints ten years earlier from George Lennon, figured this was a good time to sell the ballclub. Reports stated that the sale price was between $175,000 and $200,000, the largest sum ever paid for an American Association club.[3] Ironically, back in early 1915, some papers reported that Miller Huggins was a minority partner in the Norton "syndicate" or was even trying to buy the Saints on his own.[4] Huggins was managing the St. Louis Cardinals at the time, and Organized Baseball was being hammered by competition from the Federal League, which was depressing the value of franchises.

Miller Huggins had a prior relationship with St. Paul from when he had played for the Saints in 1902 and 1903 under manager Mike Kelley.[5] Huggins developed a close friendship with his manager, which they had maintained over the years. Kelley would win five American Association pennants for the Saints (1903–1904, 1919–1920, and 1922), before moving across the river and buying the Minneapolis Millers after the 1923 season. Kelley's Saints rivaled the Baltimore Orioles as a minor league power, winning more than 100 games in three of his last four seasons.[6]

Huggins's other close friend was Bob Connery. Connery was born in 1880 and excelled at sandlot ball in St. Louis around the turn of the century. In 1903, he began his professional career with Des Moines in the Western League.[7] His 1967 obituary mentions that his playing career was curtailed by a car accident, and Connery then moved into managing. He became the skipper of Hartford in the Connecticut State League during the 1908 season, and the following year the Senators won the league pennant. Connery would remain the Hartford manager through the 1912 season.

When St. Louis Cardinals owner Helene Britton fired manager Roger Bresnahan after the 1912 season, Cardinals scouts Dick Kinsella and Bill Armour quit in support of Bresnahan. Britton hired Miller Huggins, the team's second baseman, as player-manager, and Bob Connery left Hartford to join the Cardinals as their scout.[8] With St. Louis, Connery gained fame for discovering and signing future Hall of Famer Rogers Hornsby, then a gangly youngster from Denison, Texas, for only $600 in 1915.[9] "Bob Connery, the present scout of the Yankees, deserves all the credit for discovering [Hornsby]," said Huggins several years later. "He saw him in action, watched him closely and kept following him until he had signed him for the St. Louis Cardinals."[10] Among his other signings for St. Louis were pitchers Bill Doak and Lee Meadows.[11]

Bob Connery was Miller Huggins's Cardinals and Yankees scout (1913–1924), as well as Huggins's closest friend. After the 1924 season, Connery wanted to travel less and move into ownership of a ball club. He bought the St. Paul Saints and was both the face of the franchise and the man who ran it. He maintained a close working relationship with his former employer, the New York Yankees.

When Miller Huggins became the manager of the New York Yankees in October 1917, he insisted on bringing along Connery as the team's scout. Yankees' owner Jacob Ruppert probably needed little persuasion: In his three years as co-owner of the club (with Tillinghast Huston), virtually none of the minor league and Federal League players the Yankees bought (signed by scouts Joe Kelley and Duke Farrell) had panned out.[12]

Among the future Hall of Famers Connery had a hand in signing for the Yankees were Earle Combs, Lou Gehrig, and George Halas (the last in the football Hall). Other signings included future stars Bob Meusel and George Pipgras. One Connery recommendation the Yankees regrettably ignored was pitcher Babe Adams, then making a comeback in the minors in 1917 and 1918.[13]

Connery operated behind the scenes and was rarely named in the press after he joined the Yankees. One of his rare mentions came in the spring of 1922. Carl Mays was "on the outs" with Yankees manager Miller Huggins and accused the skipper of being a mere "mouthpiece" for Connery, the team's real manager.[14]

Connery's reputation for fair and honest dealings was well known. "Bob's spoken word was every bit as good as his penmanship," wrote The Sporting News, "and small deals and those of moment could be closed over the coffee cup."[15] Connery was also described as "one of the most shadowy and least known figures in baseball."[16] A New York paper noted that Connery had been "a big man in the inner councils of the Yanks for several years."[17] By the end of 1924, besides the opportunity he saw in becoming the owner and president of a top-tier minor league team, Connery had tired of the peripatetic lifestyle of a scout and looked forward to settling down.

After he bought the Saints, Connery's statements on his new club's ownership and relationship with the Yankees were a maze of contradictions. He refused to name his partners; there were rumors he was one of three.[18] Only one of the others was mentioned in the press: St. Louis banker Leo Daly. Connery declared, "We shall not consider ourselves feeders to the big leagues."[19] Shortly after buying the Saints, he was quoted in the St. Paul Dispatch: "If the Yankees, at any time, want to purchase a St. Paul player, they will have to give our club what we want, just the same as any other club."[20]

Yet the very same day, the other St. Paul daily, the Press, reported that the Saints would make an "alliance" with the Yankees. It would make for an "unbeatable combination" because of the New York club's available money to buy players and willingness to send good young players to St. Paul.[21] Later that month, the Washington Post wrote that the Yankees would probably ship extra players and prospects to the Saints, "marked deliver to St. Paul club, care R.J. Connery." The article was entitled, "Yankees Plan to Use St. Paul as Pasture: Connery Offers to Use his Club to Develop Ivory for his Old Employer."[22]

The Yankees had a working relationship with Atlanta of the Southern Association, reported the New York Times, but wanted to connect with "the faster American Association," and "St. Paul may be that club."[23] Huggins and Connery actually had a St. Paul connection well before 1925. When they were with St. Louis, the Cardinals had options on players they had sent to the Saints.[24] Furthermore, in their early years with the Yankees, Huggins and Connery were already working with St. Paul. After the 1918 season, the Yankees sent outfielder Elmer Miller down to St. Paul and brought him back during the 1921 season. When the Yankees released George Halas in the summer of 1919, they sent him to St. Paul.

The very first action Connery took as owner and president of the Saints was to re-sign manager Nick Allen. Connery and Allen had been friends for years, the St. Paul Press reported.[25] The colorful Allen, "Roarin' Nick," had seen limited major league action as a catcher in the teens. He joined the Saints in 1921 and became their regular catcher. Three years later, as his playing career was winding down, he took over as the Saints' manager and led them to the 1924 American Association pennant.

The best prospect Connery had on the Saints was shortstop Mark Koenig. A number of major league teams had expressed interest in him, including the Yankees. Connery initially decided to hold onto Koenig for the season: Expecting a big year from the young-ster, Connery hoped to then sell him for at least $50,000.[26]

But the Yankees were getting desperate. The weakness of their middle infield became increasingly glaring as the 1925 season got underway, and they sank into the second division. Their aging shortstop, Everett Scott, had slowed dramatically, and their second baseman, Aaron Ward, though only 28, was experiencing a downtrend as well. In mid-May, newspapers were reporting that Barrow and Huggins were in St. Paul to finalize a deal for Koenig.[27] Koenig did

Table 1. Players Transferred Between St. Paul and New York

Walter Beall	StP/1927	NY-A/1924–27	
Ben Chapman	StP/1929	NY-A/1930–36	
Roy Chesterfield	StP/1928	DNP in Majors	
Pat Collins	StP/1925	NY-A/1926–28	9.3.25: Traded by St. Paul to NY-A for $20,000, Pee-Wee Wanninger (or $5,000) & one pitcher on option for 1926.
Dusty Cooke	StP/1929	NY-A/1930–32	
Nick "Tomato Face" Cullop	StP/1926	NY-A/1926	
Leo Durocher	StP/1927	NY-A/1925, 1928–29	
Curtis Fullerton	StP/1925	DNP for NY-A	10.9.25: drafted by NY-A, 3.23.26: Sent to Salt Lake City in Tony Lazzeri deal
Elias Funk	StP/1927–28	NY-A/1929	
Joe Giard	StP/1928–29	NY-A/1927	
John Grabowski	StP/1930	NY-A/1927–29	
Fred Heimach	StP/1927–28, 1934	NY-A/1928–29	8.6.28: Traded by StP to NY-A for $20,000 and player
Fred Hofmann	StP/1917, 1925–26	NY-A/1919–25	5.29.25: Traded by NY-A to StP with Oscar Roettger, Ernie Johnson & $50,000 for Mark Koenig
Ernie Johnson	DNP for StP	NY-A/1923–25	5.29.25: Sent to StP with Oscar Roettger, Fred Hofmann, and $50,000 in Mark Koenig deal
Hank Johnson	StP/1926	NY-A/1925-26, 1928–32	
Mark Koenig	StP/1921–22, 1924–25	NY-A/1925–30	5.29.25: Sent to NY-A for Fred Hofmann, Oscar Roettger, Ernie Johnson and $50,000
Cliff Markle	StP/1923-25	NY-A/1915–16, 1924	6.16.24: Traded by StP to NY-A for Oscar Roettger, 7.22.24: Purchased by StP from NY-A
Herb McQuaid	StP/1924–25, 1927–28	NY-A/1926	9.14.25: Traded by StP to NY-A for undisclosed players
Wilcy Moore	StP/1930	NY-A/1927-29, 1932–33	9.30.30: Drafted by Red Sox from StP
Ray Morehart	StP/1928–29	NY-A/1927	
Heinie Odom	StP/1925–27	NY-A/1925	
Ben Paschal	StP/1930–33	NY-A/1924-29	
George Pipgras	StP/1926	NY-A/1923–24, 1927–33	
Gene Robertson	StP/1927	NY-A/1928–29	8.8.27: Traded by StP to NY-A for $20,000 and player to be named
Oscar Roettger	StP/1924–31	NY-A/1923–24	6.16.24: Sent by NY-A to StP for Cliff Markle, 5.29.25: Traded by NY-A, with Fred Hofmann, Ernie Johnson and $50,000 to StP for Mark Koenig
Jack Saltzgaver	StP/1930–31	NY-A/1932, 1934–1937	6.27.31: Traded by StP with Johnny Murphy 2 players and cash to NY-A for Jimmy Reese
Al Shealy	StP/1927–1929	NY-A/1928	
Pee-Wee Wanninger	StP/1926–32	NY-A/1925	12.16.25: Sent by NY-A to StP as part of the 9.3.25: Pat Collins deal.
Jules Wera	StP/1924, 1926, 1928	NY-A/1927, 1929	12.21.26: Traded by StP to NY-A for $40,000 and 2 players

Note: (StP is the St. Paul Saints, and NY-A is the New York Americans, the Yankees. DNP=Did Not Play)

indeed join the Yankees that season, though not until September. Although he would have modest success with the Yankees in his four-plus seasons with them, including a sizzling 1927 World Series, Koenig never lived up to the huge purchase price.

As highlighted in table 1, the "underground railroad" between New York and St. Paul was very busy once Connery took over the Saints. "The Yankee reserve list is as crowded as a Lennox Avenue express in the rush hour," reported one paper.[28] The Yankees had not embarked on building a farm system as the St. Louis Cardinals were doing, but they had "strings" on a number of players beyond their active roster. Curiously, virtually all the ballplayers sold by St. Paul to the Yankees experienced only modest success—at best—in the majors. The same was true of almost all of the players New York sent down to St. Paul for seasoning.

Two things are striking about the steady stream of players between the two teams: The list is long, and it is devoid of stars. The Yankees spent well into six figures on St. Paul players—Dan Levitt writes that the amount was around $300,000—with very little return to show for this investment.[29]

It is fascinating that reports would surface from time to time—after Connery had left the Yankees—that he still had the final say on key Yankees' minor league acquisitions, and not only players they "farmed" out to St. Paul.[30] The most dramatic instance was the case of Tony Lazzeri. Before the Yankees finalized the deal to buy him, they used their influence with Connery to persuade him to travel to Salt Lake City and give his evaluation of the San Francisco prospect.[31] A year later, there were still reports that Connery had the final say on the Yankees' big minor league deals.[32] And when Joe McCarthy was hired as the Yankees' manager after the 1930 season, the press reported that he had already met with Bob Connery.[33]

Nick Allen's last year as the Saints' manager was 1928. In 1930, Connery hired his former Des Moines teammate from 25 years earlier, Lefty Leifield, as the Saints' manager.[34] A year later, Connery had his first American Association pennant, with Leifield at the helm.[35] The team then fell on hard times, both on the field and at the box office. Attendance in 1934 was only one-third what it had been in 1924, and it appeared that the team would move to Peoria.[36] After the 1934 season, Connery sold the Saints to a group of St. Paul investors, staying on as an advisor for the next two years.[37]

While there were indications from the start—soon confirmed by player transactions—that the Yankees were working closely with the Saints, there was virtu-

Miller Huggins occasionally expressed interest in owning and running a baseball franchise after retiring as a manager. He never did so, piloting the Yankees for more than a decade until his death in 1929. However, at the start of 1925, he became a silent investor in the St. Paul Saints, which his buddy Bob Connery was buying. The Yankees would acquire a number of players from the Saints, including shortstop Mark Koenig, over the next few years.

ally no mention that Miller Huggins owned a piece of the American Association franchise. He was a very silent partner, indeed, and remained so for the rest of his life.

Bob Connery was Miller Huggins's right-hand man for many years, though that hand "seldom appears on the surface."[38] Connery had such a low profile in New York that many New York City papers did not even mention his departure from the Yankees or his purchase of the Saints in early 1925. After he moved to St. Paul, Connery remained one of Huggins's closest friends. He was in the hospital room of the Yankees' skipper when he died on September 25, 1929, and accompanied the body on the train to Cincinnati.[39] Before the Yankees settled on Huggins's replacement, Connery was being "prominently mentioned" as his successor.[40]

After Huggins's death, his ownership stake in the Saints was mentioned casually and often, as if it had been public knowledge—which it had not been.[41] Two

Here is Miller Huggins's stock certificate, reflecting his owning a minority stake of 50 shares in the St. Paul Baseball Club. Note that the signature in the bottom right is that of "Robert J. Connery, President." Huggins's investment in the Saints was not publicized or widely known until after his death.

documents have surfaced in recent years which confirm Huggins's ownership stake in St. Paul. The first is a stock certificate signed on January 8, 1925, conveying fifty shares of stock (valued at $100 each, to be transferred on February 4, 1925) in the St. Paul Base Ball Club to Miller Huggins, signed by both Huggins and Bob Connery.[42]

The second document is a letter from Huggins to Connery, dated January 10, 1925, in which he outlined his investment in the Saints. "I think it best that I only take ⅓. Agree with you that it best we both have 40%, but conditions are such just at present writing, in a finance way with me, that I would have to sacrifice something that I can't afford to…I will send Norton a check for $12,500…Will send same to your office."[43]

Bob Connery spotted and signed some terrific talent for both the Cardinals and the Yankees. But he was unable to continue the delivery of top minor league talent after taking over St. Paul. Financially, however, the St. Paul-New York connection was a lucrative association for him and his St. Paul partners. When the Yankees bought a Saints' player recommended by Connery, Jacob Ruppert certainly knew that that Connery himself would benefit financially. Did Ruppert know that his manager, Miller Huggins, would also benefit financially? Shortly after Huggins's death, St. Paul sportswriter Dick Meade wrote, "It is well, though not widely, known that Miller Huggins is the owner of 25 per cent [sic] of the stock of the Saints."[44]

New York American sportswriter Bill Slocum offered a revealing look at how Huggins dealt with "the two hats" he wore, one as the Yankees manager and one as a Saints owner. In early August 1928, when the Yankees' big lead over the Philadelphia Athletics was slipping away, New York needed to shore up its pitching. Huggins liked St. Paul pitcher Fred Heimach, who had won 34 games for the Saints the past two seasons. A few other teams wanted Heimach too. Huggins "had to be loyal alike to his employer and his partner," wrote Slocum. He refused to recommend the deal. Instead, he called Ruppert and Barrow and asked them to send all available Yankees scouts to St. Paul to evaluate Heimach. Their reports were positive, and New York bought Heimach, who won a couple of crucial games down the stretch. "Huggins' high sense of propriety would not permit him to recommend a deal in which he might share financially, even with a pennant at stake," wrote Slocum.[45] ■

POSTSCRIPT: When the Yankees decided to build a farm system in 1932, business manager Ed Barrow recommended Bob Connery to head the operation. But owner Jacob Ruppert, dissatisfied with the Yankees' St. Paul connection, turned instead to George Weiss, who had run the New Haven and Baltimore minor league teams.[46]

Notes

1. *St. Paul Dispatch*, January 1, 1925.
2. *Charleston Gazette*, June 17, 1928.
3. *New York Evening Telegram*, January 2, 1925, and *St. Paul Press*, January 1, 1925. There have been no accounts of the source of Connery's financing, other than the money his partners invested.
4. *The Sporting News*, January 7, 1915, and August 19, 1915.
5. Huggins also played for St. Paul in 1901, when the team was in the Western League.
6. Kelley would not win a pennant at the helm of the Millers (1924–1931). He also was president of the club from 1932 to 1946, when the Millers won a number of pennants.
7. While many articles, including Connery's obituary, list 1903 as his first year in pro ball, Baseball-Reference.com lists Connery with only two years of minor-league play: 1904 with Des Moines (where he hit .219) and 1906 with Springfield (where he hit .199).
8. *St. Louis Post-Dispatch*, January 17, 1913, and *St. Louis Times*, March 6, 1913. Researcher Jim Hinman wrote that Connery credited Mike Kelley with getting him the position with the Cardinals. Hinman also stated that when Kelley bought the Minneapolis club, Connery and Huggins were going to invest with him. But they held off and instead bought the St. Paul club a year later. E-mail from Jim Hinman to the author on March 4, 2003.
9. That spring the Cardinals had split-squad exhibition games. Connery took the helm of the squad that travelled to Denison, where the young Hornsby caught his eye. "Uncovering Stars with Famed Scout Connery," *The Sporting News*, November 26, 1947.
10. *San Francisco Chronicle*, March 31, 1924.
11. SABR Encyclopedia, Scouts Database.
12. *The Sporting News*, November 15, 1917. Ironically, when Huggins began his major league career with Cincinnati, Kelley was his manager and the Reds' first baseman. There is no familial relationship between Mike and Joe Kelley. Joe Kelley stayed on as a Yankees' scout—no longer as head scout—through the 1923 season. *Washington Post*, January 20, 1925.
13. *The Sporting News*, April 7, 1921. The Pirates released Adams during the 1916 season, after he developed a sore shoulder. He made a strong comeback, with a 20–13 record in St. Joseph and Hutchinson of the Western League in 1917 and a 14–3 mark with Kansas City of the American Association the following year. Adams offered an additional attraction to the major-league team that brought him back: He was exempt from the military draft because he was over the age of 35. Adams returned to the Pirates late in the 1918 season, where he would win another 81 games, including 48 between 1919 and 1921.
14. *St. Louis Times*, April 6, 1922.
15. "Baseball Alphabet No Puzzle to Connery," *The Sporting News*, March 15, 1928.
16. *St. Paul Press*, January 1, 1925.
17. *New York Times*, January 20, 1925.
18. *St. Paul Dispatch*, December 31, 1924.
19. *San Antonio Daily Light*, January 1, 1925.
20. *St. Paul Dispatch*, January 20, 1925.
21. *St. Paul Press*, January 20, 1925.
22. *Washington Post*, January 20, 1925.
23. *New York Times*, January 20, 1925.
24. Stew Thornley, *Baseball in Minnesota: The Definitive History*. St. Paul: Minnesota Historical Society Press, 2006, 55.
25. *St. Paul Press*, January 1, 1925. It is not clear where and when their paths had crossed.
26. *St. Paul Dispatch*, January 16 and 28, 1925, and *St. Paul Press*, February 8, 1925. The *Dispatch* reported in late April that Connery had already turned down $50,000 for Koenig. Interestingly, Koenig's 1924 numbers were not that strong: He played in only 68 games and hit .267, with a slugging percentage of .333. In 1925, he hit .308 with a slugging percentage of .474.
27. *Bee* (Danville, VA), May 14, 1925.
28. *Washington Post*, January 20, 1925.
29. Daniel R. Levitt, *Ed Barrow: The Bulldog Who Built the Yankees' First Dynasty*. Lincoln: University of Nebraska Press, 2008, 277.
30. *Billings Gazette*, September 3, 1927.
31. *Atlanta Constitution*, July 30, 1927. In his Barrow biography, Dan Levitt says that Barrow practically ordered Connery to cross-check Lazzeri. New York sportswriter Dan Daniel wrote that Connery first turned the Yankees onto Lazzeri when he was still a Yankees scout. *New York Evening Telegram*, July 9, 1926. That would have been before Lazzeri's breakout season of 1925. In 1924, he spent the first half of the season in Salt Lake City; manager Duffy Lewis sent Lazzeri down to Lincoln of the Western League. His combined numbers that year were still impressive: a .307 batting average with 44 home runs. Connery strongly reaffirmed the Yankees' glowing reports on Lazzeri before they acquired him.
32. *Billings Gazette*, September 3, 1927.
33. *Chicago Daily Tribune*, October 14, 1930.
34. In 1904, Leifield won 16 games for Des Moines, and the following season he led the Western League in wins with 26. (Solly Hofman and Hans Lobert were also members of the Des Moines Prohibitionists in 1904.) Leifield joined the Pittsburgh Pirates late in 1905 and became a regular in their rotation, where he won 103 games in the next six seasons. He coached for a number of major league teams in the 1920s, before embarking on a career as a minor league manager.
35. The '31 Saints lost the Little World Series to the International League champions, Billy Southworth's Rochester Red Wings, five games to three.
36. Jim Hinman email to the author, March 4, 2003.
37. *Chicago Daily Tribune*, November 16, 1934, and *The Sporting News*, November 29, 1934. The latter article, "Fanning with Farrington," mentions that Connery might return to the Yankees in some capacity.
38. *St. Paul Press*, January 1, 1925.
39. *New York Times*, September 24, 1929, and undated UPI report.
40. *Winnipeg Free Press*, October 1, 1929.
41. Bozeman Bulger syndicated column, *Minnesota Standard*, September 29, 1929, and Bill Slocum, *New York American*, October 4, 1929.
42. The stock certificate appeared in auctions in recent years. It seems to contradict reports that Huggins's spinster sister was the actual owner of the one-third share. Thanks to Christine Putnam for a copy of the certificate.
43. Ken Willey, *Baseball's Golden Half-Century 1910–1959*. City of Industry, CA: Glenleaf Publishing, 2007.
44. Dick Meade, "Huggins Fights with Courage," September 25, 1929. Unsourced "Random Notes" column by Meade, Bill Loughman Collection of newspaper clippings. Whether Huggins at one time owned only 25% of the Saints cannot be known for certain, but a review of his estate disclosed that he had 33% at the time of his death.
45. Bill Slocum, "Miller Huggins, as I Knew Him," *New York American*, October 4, 1929. When the Yankees acquired Heimach on August 6, 1928, their 13½-game lead had shrunk to 3½ games.
46. Daniel R. Levitt, *Ed Barrow: The Bulldog Who Built the Yankees' First Dynasty*. Lincoln: University of Nebraska Press, 2008, 277.

The Saints–Millers Holiday Series

Joe O'Connell

On October 26, 1960, Calvin Griffith received permission to move his Washington Senators ballclub and bring major league baseball to Minnesota. As a result, in 1961 the cities of Minneapolis and St. Paul were joined in support of one team. Until the coming of the Twins, however, the two cities had been supporters of their own individual teams. The earliest recorded competition between a St. Paul and a Minneapolis team occurred on May 24, 1867, when the North Star Club of St. Paul played the Minneapolis Club. The St. Paul Pioneer Press reported that the game was played "on the prairie near the Fairgrounds." Before the contest the North Star Club was treated to a sumptuous dinner by their Minneapolis hosts. The North Stars unceremoniously repaid this hospitality by crushing Minneapolis, 56–26. The game was completed in a mere two hours and 20 minutes, despite the scoring of 82 runs. Afterward, the St. Paulites were again the guests of the Minneapolitans for a "fine supper." Both meals were served at the Nicollet House in Minneapolis.[1]

By the mid-1870s both cities were hosting professional teams, and for the rest of the nineteenth century Minneapolis and St. Paul fielded minor league teams on an on-again, off-again basis. In 1902 the rivalry took on a revitalized significance when the Apostles (as the St. Paul club was originally known) and the Millers began play in the new American Association.

One of the more interesting elements of this rivalry was the holiday twinbills scheduled between the clubs. On Decoration Day (later Memorial Day), the Fourth of July, and Labor Day, two games would be played: one in St. Paul and the other in Minneapolis. The cities would alternate which city hosted the morning and which the afternoon game. Don Zimmer, who spent over 50 years in the major leagues as a player, coach, and manager, and played for the Saints during parts of the 1952 and 1954 seasons, recalled, "the Saints-Millers strong rivalry was unusual for minor league baseball, probably due to the Dodgers-Giants rivalry at the major league level."[2] By the mid-1940s, Minneapolis was a Giants triple-A affiliate, and the Saints were a triple-A farm of the Dodgers.

The competition was also reflected in newspaper coverage of the teams. On May 31, 1920, at Lexington Park, the Saints home field, Huck Sawyer hit two home runs for the Millers in a Minneapolis victory. This prompted a St. Paul Pioneer Press sportswriter to accuse Sawyer of having "Babe Ruth delusions."[3]

Joe Hauser of the Millers went into the 1933 Labor Day twinbill against St. Paul with 62 home runs on the season, hoping to break his previous record of 63, attained three seasons earlier with Baltimore in the International League. During the morning game in St. Paul Hauser arrived at the plate in the seventh inning without a hit in three at bats. At the time the right-field fence stood atop an embankment 365 feet down the line, a long target for a left-handed batter such as Hauser. Nevertheless, he clobbered the ball over the right field fence and added one more in the ninth for number 64. He went on to finish the season with 69, which at the time established a new professional record.

Ted Williams joined the Millers in 1938. He was only 19 but went on to win the American Association Triple Crown. He also led the Association in runs

Minneapolis versus St. Paul at Lexington Park, 1926.

scored, total bases, and walks. Williams enjoyed only modest success, however, versus the Saints in the holiday twinbills. In the afternoon game on Memorial Day at Lexington Park, Williams had one of his best holiday games, going 2-for-3 with a home run and leading the Millers to a 2–1 victory. On July 4 Williams went 0-for-4 in the morning game as St. Paul defeated the Millers 8–1 before 8,056 fans, the record to that point. The afternoon game was postponed due to rain. In the Labor Day twinbill, Williams was 3-for-8, but St. Paul won both, 9–4 and 6–1.

Ab Wright's remarkable performance for the Millers marked the holiday twinbill of 1940. In the

Chuck Van Every, seated (and Clayton Montpetit, standing) in Midway Stadium after an altercation with Millers manager Gene Mauch.

Saints manager Walter Alston congratulates Roy Campanella after a home run during a Memorial Day twin bill versus the Millers.

morning game on July 4 at Nicollet Park in Minneapolis, Wright hit for 19 total bases: four home runs and a triple, with seven runs batted in. The Millers won the game 17–5 in front of a crowd estimated at 7,000.

Late in the 1945 season, St. Paul got a new shortstop, Bill Hart. He put up some exceptional numbers in just 38 games, batting .368 with 46 RBIs and 17 home runs. On Labor Day Hart hit four home runs at Lexington Park in a 6–1 victory over the Millers.

In 1948 Roy Campanella became the first black player in the American Association. On Memorial Day at Nicollet Park, Campanella, in his first Twin Cities appearance as a Saint, hit two home runs to lead St. Paul to an 11–6 victory over the Millers.

On Memorial Day, 1950, the Millers dominated their cross-town rivals. In the morning game at Lexington Park Minneapolis beat the Saints 10–4. During that game two Millers, second baseman Dave Williams and outfielder Joe Lafata, collided while chasing down a fly ball. No stretcher could be found, and consequently a door was used as a substitute. Fortunately, their injuries were not serious, and both played in the afternoon game at Nicollet Park. Williams showed no sign of injury as he hit two home runs and drove in eight to lead the Millers to a 28–9 victory, tying an American Association record for most runs scored by one team.

Twin Cities baseball fans were treated to a double slugfest on Memorial Day in 1955. In the morning contest Minneapolis defeated St. Paul, 14–12, at Nicollet Park, with the teams combining for eight home runs. Walt Moryn, Norm Larker, Jack Spears, and Charlie Thompson hit round trippers for the Saints, and Bob Lennon, Gail Harris, Eddie Bressoud, and Eric Rodin for Minneapolis. Millers manager Bill Rigney made more than a dozen trips to the mound during the game, which took 3:37 to complete, an unusually long time for that era. In the afternoon game at Lexington Park, the Saints rebounded with a 9–5 victory. The winning blow was a grand slam by St. Paul second baseman Roy Hartsfield. The two games took a combined seven hours to complete.

The rivalry was in strong evidence in 1956. Minneapolis Miller Dave Garcia, later a manager with the Cleveland Indians and California Angels, said that Millers manager Eddie Stanky offered to buy any Minneapolis pitcher who could defeat the

St. Paul native and *Peanuts* creator Charles Schultz remembered Ollie Bejma and the Saints in one of his comic strips (though Bejma was principally a second baseman).

Saints at Lexington Park a new suit. Two Miller pitchers accomplished the feat, enabling Mel Held and Phil Paine to collect new suits from Stanky.[4]

Scores of the holiday twinbills were also used for some quirky non-baseball related arrangements. Jim Hegerle of St. Paul and Joe Schmolze of Minneapolis, Minnesota boxers scheduled to meet for the state middleweight championship, both feared being the victim of a "hometown decision." It was decided that the scores of the Memorial Day twinbill would determine which town would host the bout. St. Paul defeated the Millers in both games, 5–1 and 11–8. Consequently the match was held at the St. Paul Auditorium. The location of the bout made no difference in the outcome, however, as Hegerle knocked out Schmolze.

In the 1959 Fourth of July morning game at Midway Stadium, a confrontation took place between Millers manager Gene Mauch and an overzealous Saints fan by the name of Chuck Van Avery. Van Avery habitually sat behind the visitors third-base dugout and harassed opponents using a portable loudspeaker. That morning he picked the wrong person to harass.

Miller infielder Johnny Goryl (who would play for the Saints the following season) said that Van Avery "was very critical of every move Gene made and made very personal remarks about Mauch."[5] During the game Mauch, who had played for the Saints in 1947 and would later manage the Twins, lost his temper and went into the stands after Van Avery. Fortunately, no blows were exchanged, as Mauch and Van Avery were kept apart and order was restored. Van Avery never used the loudspeaker again.

The 1960 season turned out to be the last year for both the St. Paul Saints and the Minneapolis Millers in American Association baseball. The long and bitterly contested rivalry ended after 59 years with the Saints slightly on top. For the record, the Saints won 679, the Millers 624, and the teams played to four ties. ∎

Notes

1. *St. Paul Pioneer Press*, May 25, 1867, 3.
2. Don Zimmer, interview with the author, May 25, 1981.
3. *St. Paul Pioneer Press*, May 31, 1920, 12.
4. Dave Garcia, interview with the author, August 28, 1982.
5. Johnny Goryl, interview with the author, August 28, 1982.

Ted's Year in Minneapolis

Bill Nowlin

Ted Williams wasn't happy about being sent to Minneapolis. He graduated from San Diego's Hoover High School, completed his second year with his hometown San Diego Padres, borrowed $200, and took the train cross country to Sarasota, Florida, where the Boston Red Sox held spring training in 1938.

There's a story that Bobby Doerr told Ted, "Wait'll you see [star first baseman Jimmie] Foxx hit." Ted supposedly replied, "Wait'll Foxx sees me hit!" Williams denied it in his autobiography, *My Turn At Bat*, but acknowledges, "I suppose it wouldn't have been unlike me." Ted was chagrined when he was assigned to Daytona Beach, the spring training home of the Minneapolis Millers, Boston's top minor-league affiliate. He'd come across as brash and cocky to manager Joe Cronin and been given some riding by his fellow outfielders, and he did admit to telling clubhouse man Johnny Orlando, "Tell them, I'll be back, and tell them I'm going to wind up making more money in this frigging game than all three of them put together."[1]

Cronin was probably wise to provide another year of seasoning for "The Kid," as Johnny Orlando dubbed Williams, and Williams admitted as much.

Williams played right field for the Millers and manager Donie Bush. A veteran of 16 years in the majors (1908–1923, with the Tigers and Nationals), and a big-league manager for seven seasons, Bush was nothing if not experienced. Reflecting 30 years later, Bush called him "a lovable little tiger," but at the time Bush wasn't so pleased with The Kid's demeanor, reportedly telling Millers owner Mike Kelley at one point, "It's Williams or me, one has to go." Kelley allowed as how Williams wasn't going, saying something along the lines of "Gee, we'd miss you, Donie"—so the choice was up to Bush.[2] The manager and his player eventually learned to work with each other. Williams was particularly pleased to have Rogers Hornsby working with the Millers as a batting instructor. They hit it off, as hitters. "Every day I'd stay out after practice with Hornsby and maybe one or two others who wanted extra hitting. Hornsby was like any of the really great players I have known—he just couldn't get enough of it. He was pushing fifty, then, I guess, but we'd have hitting contests and he'd be right in there, hitting one line drive after another...."[3]

Williams was impressed by one thing. Hornsby—with Cobb, one of just two men since 1901 to hit .400 more than once—never criticized Ted, a powerful pull hitter, for hitting to his strength. He never pushed Ted to hit to left field. And it was Hornsby in 1938 who taught Ted the words that became his mantra: "Get a good ball to hit."[4] Williams took the message to heart. He learned the strike zone cold, he refused to bite at pitches outside it, and he waited for his pitch. It is said that big-league umpires don't give rookies the benefit

COURTESY MINNESOTA HISTORICAL SOCIETY

Ted Williams at Nicollet Park.

BARNSTORMING WITH TED

We chummed around together. We'd go out and eat after the ballgame, that's all. We went on a barnstorming trip after the season was over. We had a guy named Cohen. Second baseman, an oldtimer and he [Andy Cohen] organized a trip after the season was over, driving from one town to another. Ted was on that team. I used to ride with him in his car.

They used to give us an appreciation day, Radio Appreciation Day. You'd get a sponsor and the sponsor would ask you what do you want? You could get a sports coat, a pair of pants, a shirt, whatever it was, you know. And when it came to Ted, he said, "I want a case of shotgun shells." He was going to go hunting. He used to like to go hunting. Minnesota up there. We played in upper Minnesota up there, and southern North Dakota.

He had heard that there was a lot of big jackrabbits out there, so he got that case of shotgun shells and he put them between his legs. He had Walter Tauscher driving his car and he was sitting in the front seat with a shotgun.

We'd go from one town to the next, barnstorming. We'd be playing ball at night—twilight, because nobody had lights. We'd play from like five 'til eight. Then they always threw a big spread for us, you know, a big cookout. We'd have a few drinks and we'd go to bed late, and the next day we'd get in the car again and go to the next town, maybe a hundred miles away. A hundred miles was nothing up there. Christ, he was shooting at everything! We'd be going about fifty miles an hour. Stan Spence and I'd be sitting in the back seat, you know, falling asleep from the night before, and all of a sudden we'd hear BANG! We thought we had a flat tire or something. He thought he saw a jackrabbit. Well, in about fifteen days, he emptied that whole case. By the end of the trip I think he was shooting at cats and dogs. He probably killed a couple of cows, I don't know. It's a wonder we never got pinched.

— Lefty Lefebvre, interview with author, June 19, 1997

of the doubt, yet when Williams reached the big leagues in 1939, he drew 107 bases on balls—setting an American League rookie record that still stands. Ted Williams led the league in walks eight times, and still today holds the record (minimum 1,000 games) for the highest walks percentage (20.64%) of any player who ever played the game.

Williams had a great year with the Millers, and it was one he enjoyed immensely from the start. Predictions as to how he might do differed. In March, he himself had declared to the *Providence Bulletin*'s Joe McGlone, "I'll rattle those fences in the American Association."[5] But the *Boston Post*'s Bill Cunningham wrote that same month, "I don't believe this kid will ever hit half a Singer midget's weight in a bathing suit."[6] Rogers Hornsby, better situated than either sportswriter, said, "He'll be the sensation of the major leagues in three years."[7] The Millers opened the season with 12 road games. Williams played right field but was hitless in the first three. In the fourth game, he walked five times and was 1-for-1 at the plate. On April 21, he hit two inside-the-park home runs in Louisville.[8]

The team played its first home game at Nicollet Park on April 29. Williams had a 3-for-4 day with two singles and a long home run that exited the park and, according to *Minneapolis Tribune* writer George A. Barton, "landed on the roof of a building on the far side of Nicollet Avenue."[9]

Dick Cullum wrote in the *Minneapolis Journal*:

> There was not a fan in the park who did not form an immediate attachment to gangling Ted. He is as loose as red flannels on a clothes line but as beautifully coordinated as a fine watch when he tenses for action. He is six feet and several inches of athlete and the same number of feet and inches in likeable boyishness…You see a lot of players you THINK will make the big league grade. You accord them a good chance; but once in a long while you have one quick glance of a natural and you KNOW he will make it, and not as just an average big leaguer, but as a star. That would be Ted Williams. He's a dead mortal cinch.[10]

The young Williams was a challenge, though. He'd often be spotted out in right field, taking cuts with an imaginary bat rather than focusing on defensive positioning. As early as May 5, Frank Haven wrote in the *San Diego Sun* that Ted had already been nominated "the screwball king of the American Association."[11] Williams, meanwhile, was bragging about what a good

Ted Williams and manager Donie Bush, 1938.

pitcher he'd been in high school, and maybe betraying a little homesickness as well.

Donie Bush's influence could only go so far, it seemed. There were routine fly balls Williams failed to catch, his mind seemingly elsewhere, and others he should have run out but did not—including a couple during spring training that he thought were foul. By the time he saw they were fair, the opposing outfielder earned an assist throwing him out at first base.[12]

Get him in the batter's box, though, and it was a different matter. On April 21, at Louisville, he hit two home runs off Jack Tising—and they were said to have been the two longest home runs in American Association history, the first one 425 feet and the second reportedly traveling 512 feet.[13] He enjoyed a 21-game hitting streak that ran from May 30 (when he put a ball onto the roof of the St. Paul Coliseum) through June 19. By that time, he'd already hit 21 homers, almost twice as many as the league's number two slugger. And a Chicago sportswriter noted that before the season was two months old, Williams had already hit at least one homer in every park in the league.[14]

Ted Williams was drawing fans to Nicollet, and he was beginning to draw raves with his fielding as well. For instance, Frank Haven wrote in late June, "He has polished his seemingly awkward, gangling fielding style to the point of near perfection, coming with 'impossible' stops and catches, as well as bullet-like throws from the outfield."[15]

Minneapolis Millers, 1938. Williams is top row, third from left.

MINNEAPOLIS BASEBALL CLUB—1938

FRONT ROW LEFT TO RIGHT:—WILFRED LEFEBVRE, ANDY COHEN, ROY PFLEGER, COAKER TRIPLETT, BUD PARMELEE.
MIDDLE ROW LEFT TO RIGHT:—KEN RICHARDSON, STAN SPENCE, JOHN MIHALIC, CHARLIE WAGNER, DONIE BUSH, FABIAN GAFFKE, ALTA COHEN, EARL GRACE.
LAST ROW LEFT TO RIGHT:—HARRY TAYLOR, JIM HENRY, TED WILLIAMS, WALT TAUSCHER, OTTO DENNING, BELVE BEAN, JOHN CHAMBERS.
LEFT:—EDDIE GALLAHER, MOBILGAS-WHEATIES SPORTS ANNOUNCER, WCCO.

RADIO APPRECIATION DAY—NICOLLET PARK—MINNEAPOLIS, 1938

At midseason, Ted Williams and Indianapolis pitcher Vance Page were the only two unanimous choices for the American Association All-Star team.

On August 3, after driving in four runs off Bill Zuber, Ted was beaned and taken out of the game. The RBIs brought him to 102 on the season. He missed one game, and it rained the next day, but he was back on August 6 at Kansas City with a double and home run number 33, and four more runs batted in. An unidentified clipping from the *Kansas City Journal-Post* said he'd been called "Peter Pan" in spring training. Now he'd established himself. Against visiting Toledo in late August, he was walked intentionally five times in two games (after he'd driven in five runs in the first game of the set, his 41st home run "clearing the buildings on the far side of Nicollet Avenue.")[16]

By the time the year was over, Ted Williams had won the Triple Crown in the American Association, with a batting average of .366, 43 home runs, and 142 runs batted in. He'd also hit 30 doubles and 9 triples. He drew 114 bases on balls.

There seemed no question but that Williams had earned promotion to the big leagues, and the Red Sox didn't hesitate to clear the decks for him, trading away right-fielder Ben Chapman in December. Ted truly enjoyed his time with the Millers, though, and had even declared late in the season, "I want to stay right here in Minneapolis with the Millers, for another year at least. I'm not ready for the major leagues. Another year under Donie Bush will do me a lot of good. I'm young yet. I figure that if a fellow gets to the majors when he's 21 or 22, that's time enough. He's got a better chance of sticking if he takes his time getting there. I don't want to be rushed. I've got plenty to learn and I've learned plenty under Donie this year. Maybe one more year and I'll be ready."[17]

Was Williams ready? All he did when he got to Boston was set two rookie records that have still never been matched. He showed plate discipline, walking 107 times, and driving in 145 runs. The 145 RBIs led the American League in 1939, 19 more than second-place Joe DiMaggio and 17 more than National League leader Frank McCormick. His 344 total bases also led the league.

And after the 1939 season, Ted chose to spend the winter in Minnesota. As Jim Smith wrote, "Ted took a $5 room at the King Cole Hotel in downtown Minneapolis, traveled west to hunt mallards, north to fish for walleyes at Lake Mille Lacs, out to the city park rinks to learn ice skating, and enjoyed the heated hotel pool as well…He also began courting the daughter of a hunting guide from Princeton, Minnesota, Doris Soule, who a few years later (during World War II duty), would become his wife."[18] ■

Notes

1. Ted Williams, *My Turn At Bat* (New York: Simon & Schuster, 1969), 47. Ted's autobiography was first published in 1969. Were it published today, it's a fair guess that we would learn the word "frigging" was sanitized.
2. James D. Smith, in *The Kid: Ted Williams in San Diego*, edited by Bill Nowlin (Cambridge MA: Rounder Books, 2005), 162.
3. Ted Williams, 53.
4. Ted Williams, *The Science of Hitting* (New York: Simon & Schuster, 1970), 20.
5. *Providence Bulletin*, date uncertain, March 1938.
6. Undated San Diego newspaper clipping.
7. Frank Haven, *San Diego Sun*, May 5, 1938.
8. Thanks to Stew Thornley for compiling the day-by-day records of Ted Williams during the 1938 season. The records have been reproduced in *The Kid: Ted Williams in San Diego*, pp. 165–169.
9. George A. Barton, *Minneapolis Tribune* game account "Williams, Galvin, Parmelee Shine in the Nicollet Opener."
10. Dick Cullum, *Minneapolis Journal*, April 30, 1938.
11. Frank Haven, op. cit.
12. According to an unidentified clipping from the *Kansas City Journal-Post*.
13. George Barton, *Minneapolis Tribune*, April 22, 1938.
14. Francis J. Powers, *Chicago Daily News*, June 20, 1938.
15. *San Diego Sun*, June 23, 1938.
16. George A. Barton, "Kels Thump Hens, 15–11, in Bat Spree, *Minneapolis Tribune*.
17. Unidentified news clipping.
18. James D. Smith, 164.

Two African American Pioneers Cross Paths

Roy Campanella and Carl Rowan

Joel Rippel

In May of 1948, two pioneers arrived at Lexington Park in St. Paul. One was Roy Campanella, who became the first African American to play in the American Association (which began play in 1902), when he was assigned to the St. Paul Saints by the Brooklyn Dodgers. Chronicling Campanella's pivotal role was another African American pioneer reporter, Carl Rowan, who was just beginning his newspaper career after receiving a Master's Degree from the University of Minnesota.

But the career paths of Campanella and Rowan almost didn't meet. Brooklyn Dodgers general manager Branch Rickey had considered sending Campanella to St. Paul earlier. In 1946, he placed Campanella in Nashua (New Hampshire) of the Class B New England League instead of St. Paul because he thought the American Association might not be ready to be integrated. In 1947, Campanella was sent to Montreal of the International League because Rickey, after considering the verbal abuse directed at Montreal's Jackie Robinson by Louisville fans during the 1946 Junior World Series, still didn't think the American Association was ready.

Campanella began the 1948 season with the Brooklyn Dodgers before being farmed to St. Paul, where he was reunited with manager Walt Alston, who had managed Nashua in 1946.

One St. Paul newspaper reporter had anticipated Campanella joining the Saints. In the May 18 edition of the *St. Paul Pioneer Press*, Joe Hennessy wrote:

> Never before has a Negro played in the American Association. Branch Rickey gave at least a hint that this move had been planned for some time when he watched the Saints in spring training at Fort Worth.
>
> He shattered a precedent or two there by playing a Negro with the Dodgers against both Fort Worth and Dallas—the first time it had been tried in the state of Texas.
>
> Afterwards he explained that any baseball man who would not make use of a good player, regardless of color, was just not showing good business judgment.

Campanella joined the Saints on May 22 in Columbus, Ohio.

The *Minneapolis Spokesman*, an African American newspaper, said in its May 28 edition, that Campanella would "be well received in the Twin Cities. Comment of Twin City fans and sports writers alike, indicates that the peppery backstop will be accepted as just another ballplayer." Campanella's play ensured that. He made his Minnesota debut in a Memorial Day twin-bill between the Saints and the Minneapolis Millers (with a game in each team's home park).

In the next edition of the *Minneapolis Spokesman*, Rowan, now on staff at the paper, wrote that Campanella was "a big hit with fans in St. Paul and Minneapolis."

Rowan summed up Campanella's initial appearance in Minnesota, writing: "Nobody seemed bothered that the first Negro was playing triple A baseball on

Roy Campanella with the Saints.

their fields. Few, indeed, seemed to wonder why it had taken so long."

Over the next month Campanella continued to impress the fans.

In late June, Rowan mentioned some of Campanella's highlights in the *Minneapolis Spokesman*: a home run in six consecutive games, 20 RBIs in one week and raising his batting average to .346. All of which made Campanella, "a tremendous favorite of St. Paul fans."

Rowan added that Saints fans had become "fearful Brooklyn might recall him."

Rowan continued, "It would be a terrific blow to the fans if the spunky, quiet-mannered catcher were recalled. He has completely soothed any hard feelings the fans had over not getting Duke Snider [who had been with the Saints in 1947 but was assigned to Montreal in 1948]."

According to Rowan, Campanella was enjoying his stay in St. Paul. Campanella and his family were renting an apartment from a St. Paul couple. On the road, Campanella stayed in the team's hotel except in Kansas City and Louisville, where he stayed with families.

Campanella told Rowan that there hadn't been any incidents in any city and that he "expected none."

On June 30, the Dodgers recalled Campanella. Rowan wrote in the July 9 edition of the *Minneapolis Spokesman*, "... and the Saintly City's baseball fans weren't the least bit happy about it. Although the fans admitted they disliked the move, many paused to say that they wished Campy a lot of luck in the big show."

In 35 games with the Saints, Campanella batted .325 with 13 home runs and 39 RBIs.

Campanella would go on to be the Dodgers' starting catcher for ten seasons—earning eight All-Star selections and being named the National League MVP three times.

Rowan joined the *Minneapolis Tribune* later in 1948. Over the next decade he would become one of just a few African American journalists covering civil rights issues in the South. He wrote five novels on racial issues and in 1960 wrote Jackie Robinson's biography, *Wait Till Next Year: The Life Story of Jackie Robinson*.

Carl Rowan, 1952.

In the late 1950s, Rowan was a mentor to the first group of African American scholarship athletes at the University of Minnesota—a group which included future Pro Football Hall of Famer Bobby Bell.

In the early 1960s, Rowan joined the U.S. State Department. He later served as the U.S. Ambassador to Finland and as the head of the United States Information Agency. Rowan eventually returned to newspapers and became a nationally syndicated columnist. ■

Sources

Lanctot, Neil. *Campy: The Two Lives of Roy Campanella*. New York: Simon & Schuster, 2011.

Lowenfish, Lee. *Branch Rickey: Baseball's Ferocious Gentleman*. Lincoln, NB: Bison Books, 2009.

Rippel, Joel A. *75 Memorable Moments in Minnesota Sports*. St. Paul, MN: Minnesota Historical Society Press, 2003.

Rowan, Carl. *Wait Till Next Year: The Life Story of Jackie Robinson*. New York: Random House, 1960.

Newspapers

Minneapolis Spokesman, *St. Paul Dispatch*, and *St. Paul Pioneer Press*.

SABR Collector Finds Mays Jersey

Stew Thornley

Longtime SABR member Bob Evans has been a collector most of his life. Born in 1935 and raised in West Orange, New Jersey, Evans started acquiring military memorabilia from relatives who fought in World War II and discovered baseball, as a fan and then as a collector, around the same time. His focus in military and baseball collecting were uniforms and equipment.

Evans played baseball at Lehigh University in Bethlehem, Pennsylvania (batting against Dallas Green of the Delaware Blue Hens) and amateur ball in West Orange (batting against Hank Borowy of nearby Bloomfield) and, following college, worked for Economics Laboratory, a company that transferred him to Minnesota in 1967. He acquired more uniforms and

spent time at military and baseball collector shows. In 1980 he was at a baseball show at a hotel across Killebrew Drive from Metropolitan Stadium in Bloomington, Minnesota. An elderly man, accompanied by his daughter, had brought a Minneapolis Millers uniform to show to dealers although he had nothing in mind in terms of what to do with it. The man, a former Minneapolis cop, had gotten the uniform when he played in a benefit game between the Minneapolis and St. Paul police in the mid-1950s.

Evans spotted the man with the uniform slung over his shoulder and asked if he was looking to sell. The man said yes in a reluctant fashion and added that he didn't know what it was worth. Evans said, "It's worth $50 to me." The man turned away and said, "It can't

The photo Bob Evans used to confirm his Mays uniform find.

The front and back of the Willie Mays 1950 uniform.

be worth that much." The man's daughter, however, convinced him to accept the offer, and Evans came away with the uniform, which included a jersey with 28 on the back.

Evans later determined that the uniform was from 1950 and also that Willie Mays had worn 28 for the Millers, although it was in 1951 when he played 35 games for Minneapolis. Evans found photos of Mays with the Millers and did magnification studies of details—the lettering, the shape of the piping around the yoke of the collar—and could make out anomalies that are unique to individual uniforms. He started to suspect that his jersey had been worn by Mays, meaning that he would have received a holdover uniform from 1950.

One detail in particular could confirm the connection. On the right sleeve of the jersey was a team repair of an L-shaped tear. However, in all the photos Evans had seen of Mays, none had clearly shown the right sleeve. Finally, in 2003, the Halsey Hall Chapter of SABR held its spring meeting at the Minnesota Historical So-

ciety, which had an exhibit on Minnesota baseball. In that exhibit, Evans saw the photo he was looking for. He acquired a copy of the photo, which clearly showed the tear on the right sleeve.

In 2004, the *Antiques Roadshow* came to St. Paul. Evans attended and brought the photo and the jersey to Simeon Lipman for appraisal. "It's obviously a remarkable piece," Lipman told Evans. "It's a remarkable story. It's in immaculate condition. That helps it. You spent $50 on it. I would estimate it conservatively in the $60,000 to $80,000 range today."

Evans decided to market it through a national auction company and consulted with his tax adviser. He learned that collectables are subject to a higher capital-gains tax, and he ultimately set up a charitable trust, to which he donated the jersey. The jersey sold through the auction house for an undisclosed amount. ∎

Sources

Interview with Bob Evans, December 18, 2010; *Antiques Roadshow* website: www.pbs.org/wgbh/roadshow/archive/200401A24.html

The Minnesota Twins Story

John Bonnes

The Minnesota Twins first home baseball game was played on April 21, 1961, but that 5–3 loss was the tip of a large and rocky iceberg. Minneapolis and St. Paul civic leaders, yearning for their metro area to be considered "big league," had been chasing a major league team for almost a decade. It did not go smoothly.

The St. Louis Browns, Philadelphia Athletics, New York Giants, and Cleveland Indians had been wooed unsuccessfully. In their pursuit, the Twin Cities sibling rivalry flared up so that each built a major league stadium—but neither had a major league team. Civic leaders went so far as to back a new major league, the Continental League, which was to begin play in 1961 along with New York, Denver, Houston, Toronto, and other frustrated metro areas. To short-circuit the new league, Major League Baseball responded by expanding by four teams, but even then it looked like Minnesota would miss the cut.

When the expansion meetings ended, however, Minnesota had their team. They weren't awarded one of the expansion teams, but the Washington Senators, owned by Calvin Griffith, were relocating to Metropolitan Stadium in Bloomington. To ease the political backlash of that move—the American League owners rightfully feared the nation's lawmakers retaliating with additional antitrust hearings or potentially punitive legislation—the D.C. area was awarded one of the two American League expansion teams. Griffith and the Twin Cities leaders had been talking about moving his franchise to the region for several years. In the face of pressure from minority owners and politicians, Griffith had never committed. However, with guarantees in place for attendance, moving expenses, and bank credit, the quest had finally been completed.

The franchise which Minnesota adopted was a team on the rise, though not by a terribly high standard. The Senators had not finished higher than fifth in the American League since 1946. Their inaugural season as the Twins didn't change that trend; the team finished 70–90 and in seventh place in 1961. It also led to manager Cookie Lavagetto being replaced by Sam Mele, who would manage into the 1967 season.

But Mele inherited a solid core of players. Catcher Earl Battey's work in the 1960 season had earned him Most Valuable Player (MVP) votes, and he would garner multiple Gold Gloves and All-Star Game appearances.

COURTESY MINNESOTA TWINS

The Washington Senators management is welcomed as they land in Minnesota to become the Twins, 1961.

Outfielder Bob Allison had been named Rookie of the Year just two years earlier, and would rank in the top ten in home runs eight times. Starting pitcher Camilo Pascual would win 20 or more games in 1962 and 1963 and be recognized as an All-Star five times. And 22-year-old Jim Kaat was beginning a career that would end with 283 wins and 16 Gold Gloves. Each was capable of doing significant harm to an opposing team, but they were joined by an absolute Killer.

Harmon "Killer" Killebrew was hardly a giant, just 5-foot-11 with a stocky build. That physique didn't hide his power potential. He was valuable enough to be signed for a bonus above $4,000, qualifying Killebrew as a "bonus baby." As a way of discouraging high bonuses, this classification required the young slugger to spend two years in the majors before being sent to the minors to begin his minor league training. His two-year stint riding the major league bench delayed Killebrew from playing full time in the majors until 1959, when he was 22 years old. When he returned to the majors, he burst on the scene with a league-leading 42 home runs. He would lead the league another five times before his career was over, and finish in the top five an astounding 12 times. He won the American League MVP in 1969 and received votes for the first 11 years of the Twins existence, with the exception of 1968, when he was hurt.

Killebrew had a quiet demeanor. He was known as a listener, not a screamer, someone who wasn't comfortable setting himself apart from the other guys. But his performance couldn't help but do so, and he was inducted into the National Baseball Hall of Fame in 1984.

With that kind of talent, it wouldn't be long before the Twins escaped the American League's second division. The team won 91 games in both 1962 and 1963, climbing to second in 1962 and then finishing third in 1963. When the club slipped back to 79–83 in 1964, despite Tony Oliva's Rookie of the Year award, the players, fans, and team management were all dissatisfied. That disappointment may have provided the fuel the team needed to finally reach the World Series.

In 1965, Mele and pitching coach John Sain were joined on the coaching staff by Billy Martin, and he is credited with helping shortstop Zoilo Versalles win the American League MVP. But the pennant the team won was certainly a group effort; so many players were injured that the success required contributions from all available hands. The best remembered hit was provided by Killebrew, who hit a two-out, two-run blast in the bottom of the ninth to beat the Yankees the day before the All-Star break. The Twins would not relinquish first place for the rest of the year. For 26 years that hit would be the considered the most dramatic home run in the organization's history.

The World Series pitted the Twins against the favored Dodgers. The Twins won the first two games handily in Minnesota, but scored just two runs in three games as they were swept in Los Angeles. Mudcat Grant, who led the club with 21 wins, pitched a one-run complete game to tie up the series, three games apiece. But the Dodgers prevailed in Game Seven when Sandy Koufax outdueled Kaat, throwing a shutout on two days of rest.

The next couple of years would feature lots of success, but no return to the World Series. Nineteen-sixty-six was a year of silver medals. Jim Kaat won 25 games—but lost to Koufax in the Cy Young voting, since there was only one award given between the two leagues. Meanwhile, Killebrew finished second in the American League in home runs and runs batted in, behind Frank Robinson who won the Triple Crown. The Twins also finished second, though they were never closer than nine games back after mid-June.

Finishing second was a lot tougher to swallow in 1967. As of September 6, four teams—the Twins, White Sox, Red Sox, and Tigers—were in a virtual tie for the division lead. For the last month, those teams would battle in a ten-team league for the pennant. As the final weekend approached, the Twins held a one-game

Slugging outfielder Bob Allison hitting a home run.

lead over Boston and Detroit with two games to play against Boston. But in the third inning, while holding a one-run lead, Kaat tore a tendon in his pitching elbow, and the Red Sox rallied to win 6–4, helped by a three–run home run from Carl Yastrzemski. The next day the Sox won the final game of the season 5–3, featuring more highlights from "Yaz." The Twins finished second best again.

After a disappointing 1968 that included a hamstring injury to Killebrew in the All-Star game and a seventh-place finish, changes were made for 1969. Billy Martin, who had managed the AAA team in Denver the year before, was installed as manager. Martin's aggressive style would make headlines on and off the field.

On the field, the Twins, a team known for its power, displayed a renewed interest in running wild on the bases. In the second game in which Martin managed, he had Rod Carew steal home. Carew would do so another six times that season, which at the time apparently tied a major league record. The Twins four triple steals that year did tie the major league record. In one game on May 18, both Carew and Cesar Tovar stole home in the same at-bat. More astounding? Killebrew was the batter.

Martin's well-known aggression off the field boiled over in early August, when it was revealed that he had become involved in a bar fight in Detroit—against his own player. And not just any player, but Dave Boswell, who would go on to win 20 games that season. Both Boswell and Martin required stitches from the incident. But there is no question that the team responded to Martin. They finished with 97 wins, capturing the newly formed West Division by nine games.

The postseason was not as kind. In the first American League Championship Series, the Orioles swept the Twins, who lost two extra inning affairs in Baltimore. When they came back to the Met, Martin started journeyman Bob Miller over Jim Kaat. The Twins lost that game 11–2, and Martin was fired at the end of the exhilarating season amid media and fan outrage.

Replacing Martin was Bill Rigney, a former player and manager for the Minneapolis Millers. He could rely on several outstanding performances in his first year as manager. Oliva (.325 batting average) and Killebrew (41 home runs) finished secnd and third in 1970's AL MVP voting and Jim Perry won the Twins first AL Cy Young award with a 24–12 record, throwing 278.2 innings with a 3.04 ERA.

First Minnesota Twins night game, 1961.

Together, they would lead the Twins to another division in 1970, despite several significant injuries. Most detrimental were the torn ligaments in Rod Carew's knee, limiting him to just 51 games. A different injury led to the debut of a future Hall of Fame inductee. Bert Blyleven, only nineteen years old, was called up to replace the injured Luis Tiant in the rotation. Blyleven would win that first game (despite giving up a home run to the first batter he faced) and nine more that year while throwing 164 innings. It was the last time he would not throw 200 innings for the rest of the decade, and he exceeded 270 innings each year he was with the Twins until he was traded in 1976. He would retire 22 years later with 287 wins, a career ERA of 3.31, and the third most strikeouts in baseball history.

The Twins won the division comfortably by nine games, but again couldn't take the pennant, which they lost in three games to the Orioles for the second year in a row. It wasn't obvious at the time, but the team would not make another postseason appearance for 17 years.

The Twins would remain marginally competitive over the next decade or so, but injuries and age would chip away enough to lower them from elite to mediocre. Killebrew turned 35 in 1971 and would never again hit even 30 home runs in a season. Oliva hurt his knee on a shoestring catch in June 1971 and would never again garner MVP votes, which he had done for eight straight years. Killebrew departed the Twins after the 1974 season and retired a year later. A year after that, Oliva played his last major league game. Rod Carew, however, bounced back from his 1970 injury and resumed his Hall of Fame career. He won batting titles every season from 1972 through 1978, except for 1976, when he missed it by two hits. He was an All-Star every year from his rookie year in 1967 through 1984.

The clubhouse was handed to manager Frank Quilici who guided the team to nearly a .500 record from 1972 through 1975, but they never finished higher than third in the division, and never fewer than eight games back. The results took their toll on attendance. The Twins did not break the 1,000,000 attendance mark for the first time in 1971, but it wouldn't be the last. The Twins wouldn't reach that mark again until 1977, thanks to Carew's stellar season, a new manager, and a "Lumber Company." The manager was Gene Mauch, a veteran manager from the National League who also happened to be a former member of the St. Paul Saints and Minneapolis Millers. He took over the Twins in 1976, and, despite the midseason trade of Bert Blyleven, the Twins posted a winning record.

The next year was even more exciting, and over 1,100,000 Twins fans watched it live. The Twins offense, known as the "Lumber Company," scored 867 runs and featured career years from Larry Hisle (119 RBI) and Lyman Bostock (.336 batting average). That level of run support helped make a 20-game winner out of Dave Goltz, who posted a 3.36 ERA. On August 23, the Twins were 18 games above .500 and a game back of the Royals. A late season fade to fourth place and 84 wins didn't tarnish the return of interest to the franchise.

COURTESY MINNESOTA TWINS

Kirby Puckett celebrates his game winning home run in Game Six of the 1991 World Series.

That interest was further fueled by Carew's remarkable 1977 season. He entered June hitting .365 but proceeded to gather hits in every June game save two of them. On July 1 he was hitting .411 and would keep his average above the .400 level through July 10, about the same time he was on the cover of *Time* magazine. He would not reach .400 again, but finished the year with a .388 average, eight hits shy of the magical mark. It would be the zenith of Carew's career with the Twins. Things turned sharply downhill that offseason.

The roots of that decline could be traced back to late 1975, when an arbitrator's ruling essentially struck down MLB's reserve clause and granted players free agency at the expiration of their contracts. Griffith had a miserly reputation—the Twins built an advertising campaign around that very topic in 1976—and baseball's new economic reality hit the Twins hard. Before the 1978 season, both Bostock and Hisle signed with other teams and the offense suffered to the tune of 200 fewer runs. The team finished 16 games under .500 and attendance fell with it, down to just 787,000, which perpetuated the problem of retaining premier players.

But even if the Twins had continued to draw fans, circumstances had deteriorated to the point where keeping a superstar like Carew with the club might have been impossible. For starters, Carew wanted more quality ballplayers around him to give the team a better chance at winning. Moreover, the relationship between Carew and the Twins became irreparable after Griffith made several off-color remarks—some of a racial nature—at a Lions Club function in Waseca, Minnesota. Carew, due to become a free agent following the 1979 season, was traded for four players to the California Angels, where he would finish his career.

Without their superstar, the Twins competed in two of the next three years. They finished above .500 in 1979 and had a surprise run at a division title in the second half of the strike-impacted 1981 season. But the focus was shifting from the present to the future, which would include overwhelming changes for the franchise.

The first of those changes was a brand new indoor ballpark. The Metrodome was the result of a 1977 Minnesota Legislature stadium bill, but could only be built if the Vikings and Twins both signed 30-year leases. Griffith, skeptical of the facility but intrigued by an increase in outstate attendance due to no rainouts, negotiated an out-clause: if the team failed to average 1.4 million in attendance over three consecutive years (a level the Twins had not averaged over a three-year period in their history), he could break the lease.

When the new stadium opened in 1982, the honeymoon lasted exactly one night. In its inaugural home

COURTESY MINNESOTA TWINS

Eric Milton celebrates his no-hitter against the Angels on September 11, 1999.

opener, the Metrodome drew 52,279 fans amid much pageantry. The next night the club drew 5,213. By the end of the season, attendance would fail to reach the 1,000,000 mark. And by the end of the first week, Griffith started dismantling the team for a youth movement, trading quality shortstop Roy Smalley to the Yankees. Two more trades would complete the fire sale by the middle of May. The 1982 team, in their brand new home, would finish with 102 losses.

But 1982 wouldn't just be remembered for a record-setting number of losses for the Twins. It would also become known as the beginning of a new generation of Twins that would finally reach the mountaintop. Nineteen-eighty-two was the rookie season for Kent Hrbek (22 years old), Tom Brunansky (21) and Gary Gaetti (23), all of whom slugged at least 20 home runs. Starting pitcher Frank Viola (22) would also debut that season, pitching to battery-mate and rookie Tim Laudner (24). Griffith had put together the cornerstones of the next contending Twins team. But it wouldn't be his Twins team.

It was becoming clear that the 1.4 million attendance threshold included in the Metrodome lease was not going to be met, giving Griffith the option of breaking the lease and perhaps moving to another market. Local business leaders responded by mounting a ticket-buying campaign of the cheapest unused tickets available to artificially inflate the attendance. For instance, on May 16, 1984, the paid attendance was 51,863, but the number of fans present was closer to 8,700. Flirtations with other markets, particularly Tampa Bay, were made, but instead local banker and

business executive Carl Pohlad purchased the team in the summer of 1984.

On the field, the team was growing—and experiencing growing pains. The promise of brighter days was apparent in 1984 when the Twins suddenly competed for the division, even though they had finished just 70-92 the year before. They led the AL West for all of August except two days and found themselves tied for first place as late as September 23. But six straight losses, including blowing a 10-run lead versus Cleveland in the last series of the year, left them in second place.

Those brighter days were also personified by a rookie call-up. Center fielder Kirby Puckett made his debut just 32 games into the season, hit .296 and finished third in the Rookie of the Year balloting. The next year he would collect his first MVP vote. These were previews.

The feature presentation started in 1986 when Puckett hit .328 and added power to his resume, slugging 31 home runs. Over the next 10 years, he would finish in the top 10 of American League MVP voting seven times, make 10 straight All-Star teams, and win six Gold Gloves. His success endeared him to the fans, but not as much as his zeal for the game. The Twins would retire his number in 1997 and he was voted into the Baseball Hall of Fame in 2001, his first year of eligibility.

While Puckett signified an apparently brighter future, the Twins struggled in 1985 and 1986, in part due to an explosive bullpen. Closer Ron Davis became the symbol for the team's failings, both supported and reviled by Twins fans. In 1985, after several blown games, a sympathetic newspaper story led to "I believe in R.D." T-shirts becoming fashionable in the Metrodome. But equally as popular was the trade that sent him and his 9.08 ERA to the Cubs in August of 1986.

There were big changes off the field, too. The Pohlads hired 32-year-old Andy MacPhail in August of 1985 to be the vice-president of player personnel, eventually promoting him to general manager. Two years later, MacPhail pushed for 37-year-old Tom Kelly, who had been the interim manager in 1986, to take over fulltime for 1987.

During the offseason, the team added a new closer, Jeff Reardon, and outfielder Dan Gladden. MacPhail also brought in utility infielder Al Newman and reliever Juan Berenguer, both of whom would prove useful additions. Blyleven and Smalley had also returned to the team in 1985.

As they battled for their first postseason appearance in 17 years, the Twins were seemingly assisted by some magic in the Metrodome. During the regular season, the team finished 56–25 at home and just 29–52 on the road. They went on a 16–7 tear starting

Gold Glove center fielder Torii Hunter making one of his typical stellar catches.

August 29 to move from a first-place tie to leading the AL West by six games. During that critical stretch, Puckett carried the team, hitting .407 with 10 home runs, 21 RBIs, and 18 runs.

In the American League Championship Series the Twins faced the AL East's 98-win Detroit Tigers, one of four AL East teams with more wins than the Twins' 85. But the Twins were a more formidable playoff team than regular season team due to the one-two pitching punch of Frank "Sweet Music" Viola (2.90 ERA in 251.2 innings pitched) and Bert Blyleven (4.01 ERA in 267 IP). The Twins won their two at home and two more in Detroit, returning home to an impromptu gathering at a packed Metrodome, an emotional homecoming that many players still point to as the pinnacle of their Minnesota career.

In the World Series, the Metrodome and its "Homer Hankies" held serve once again, as the Twins won all four games played there, winning their first world championship. Throughout the playoff run, the noise that championship-starved Minnesotans generated under the Teflon-coated roof was a major story. That noise overflowed outside for a raucous celebration and into a parade a few days later.

The sounds coming out of the Metrodome the next couple of years were not as harmonious. At the beginning of the 1988 season, fan favorite Tom Brunansky was traded away for second baseman Tommy Herr. Herr arrived and moped, mirroring the clubhouse's somber reaction to losing "Bruno." The Twins won six more games than the previous year, but never seriously threatened the 104-win Athletics for the division lead after the All-Star Break. They were led by 24-game winner Frank Viola, who also won the Cy Young Award. But that would lead to another discordant clash.

In 1989, Viola was in a free-agent year, and his contract negotiations with the team became public and sour. At the trade deadline, the Twins sent Viola to the New York Mets, where he received his multi-million dollar deal. A little over a year later, another core player would leave when Gary Gaetti signed with the Angels. While dealing with the departures, the Twins were also dealing with two losing seasons, including a last-place finish in 1990.

All those departures meant MacPhail was busy securing new talent. Viola's trade added pitchers Kevin Tapani and Rick Aguilera to the staff, and "Aggie" was converted to the team's closer in 1990. To replace Gaetti's glove at third base, the Twins signed Mike Pagliarulo, and to replace his bat they added designated hitter Chili Davis. In 1990, the Twins called up

Scott Erickson to the rotation and he impressed, posting a 2.87 ERA in 17 starts. The Twins farm system produced another key contributor in 1991, second baseman Chuck Knoblauch, who would go on to win the Rookie of the Year award. And in February 1991, just a few weeks before spring training, the Twins added a veteran ace by signing St. Paul's Jack Morris.

The rebuilt Twins rotation, centered around Morris, Erickson, and Tapani, would sparkle in 1991. Each won at least 16 games, and Erickson won 20; in fact over his first 116.1 innings pitched through June 24, Erickson was 12-2 with a 1.39 ERA. For the season, the highest ERA was Morris's 3.43. All three pitched over 200 innings. And all three finished in the top seven in the AL Cy Young voting.

Nevertheless, on June 1, the club was two games below .500 and in fifth place in the AL West. But June started with a 15-game winning streak that lifted the team to first. They never again relinquished at least a share of that lead, finishing with 95 wins, and beating the Blue Jays in the ALCS.

The Twins AL pennant set the stage for the "worst to first" World Series versus the Atlanta Braves, who has also finished last in their division in 1990. It has been labeled as the greatest World Series ever by *Sports Illustrated* and ESPN, and anything shorter than a novel is probably not doing it justice. Five of the games were won by a single run. Four of the final five games were won on the last at-bat.

The Twins again won the first two home games, just like in 1987, but again lost the next three games on the road. However, for Game Six the series returned to the Metrodome. In a 3-3 game, Puckett led off the bottom of the 11th inning with a solo home run, extending the series to a seventh game so announcer Jack Buck could see us all again "tomorrow night."

The climactic seventh game did not disappoint. Morris and John Smoltz and the Braves bullpen pitched goose eggs through nine innings, although both teams had chances to score, especially in the eighth inning. Finally, in the bottom of the 10th inning, Dan Gladden broke his bat on a short fly ball to left field that he hustled into a leadoff double. He was sacrificed to third base, and Puckett and Hrbek were intentionally walked to load the bases. Pinch-hitter Gene Larkin lifted a high fly to left that fell behind the drawn-in outfield, and the Twins had their second world championship.

The next season started with similar promise. Near the end of July the team was 60-38 and leading the AL West by three games over the second place Athletics. But the Athletics came to a packed Metrodome and swept the Twins, gaining a share of the division lead with a 5-4 win in which Eric Fox hit a three-run, ninth inning home run off of closer Rick Aguilera. The Twins limped to a 30-31 record the rest of the season and finished in second place.

Those doldrums extended into the rest of the decade. Gradually the core members from those championship teams departed. Morris had left after the 1991 season, shortstop Greg Gagne left after 1992, and Hrbek retired in 1994 after a couple of injury-plagued seasons. General manager Andy MacPhail accepted the president/CEO position with the Cubs in 1994 and was replaced by player personnel director Terry Ryan. Puckett's 1995 season ended early when his jaw was broken by a fastball from Dennis Martinez. In spring training the next year, he awoke on March 28 without vision in his right eye. After three surgeries failed to restore his vision, he officially retired in July.

From 1993 through 2000, the Twins never finished fewer than six games under .500. The teams were characterized by a low payroll, suspect pitching, and the signing of several native Minnesota veterans. During that decade St. Paul natives Dave Winfield and Paul Molitor both got their 3000th hits with the Twins, and Terry Steinbach from New Ulm also returned to play for his home state. As another bright spot, Knoblauch and starting pitcher Brad Radke turned in several excellent seasons and both of them would end up contributing to the Twins next postseason appearances. Knoblauch's contribution, however, came in what the team received in a trade. After the 1997 season in which the Twins only won 68 games, Knoblauch demanded a trade and was sent to the Yankees for a package of players that included shortstop Cristian Guzman and pitcher Eric Milton.

The two former Yankees prospects joined a nucleus of young Twins led by third baseman Corey Koskie, catcher A. J. Pierzynski, first-baseman Doug Mientkiewicz and outfielders Jacque Jones and Torii Hunter. Terry Ryan's rebuilt squad broke through in 2001. At the All-Star break, the Twins were 55-32 and leading the AL Central by five games. That lead faded fast in the second half of the season as the Twins posted a 30-45 record amidst a questionable trade that sent talented right fielder Matt Lawton to the New York Mets for pitcher Rick Reed, who posted a 5.19 ERA. Despite the fade, optimism reigned for the coming decade. It didn't last long.

First, Tom Kelly, the manager with the most wins in Minnesota Twins history, retired within a week of season's end. But a bigger shock came in November, when Commissioner Bud Selig announced that that the owners had approved a plan to reduce the number of major league teams by two. Reports indicated that one of those two teams would be the Twins.

Thus, the 2002 season was in question until Hennepin County District Judge Harry Crump ruled that the Twins were required to honor their Metrodome lease through at least 2002. Plans for contraction were shelved for one year (and eventually dropped altogether), and the Twins brought in new manager Ron Gardenhire to lead their young roster.

It would mark a turning point for the franchise. The Twins were in contention from the very beginning and grabbed first place for good by the end of May. They won their American League Division Series versus the "Moneyball" Oakland Athletics before losing the American League Championship Series to the Angels in five games. Maybe most importantly, attendance increased again, nearing the 2,000,000 mark.

Attendance would hover around that mark for the next three years as the Twins continued their success. In 2003 the team overcame a slow start and won the division with a late-season charge fueled by a trade for outfielder and leadoff hitter Shannon Stewart. In 2004 they were led to their third straight division title by Johan Santana's dominant year (2.61 ERA with 265 strikeouts), which earned him a unanimous American League Cy Young Award. However, in both years the team lost to the Yankees in four games in the first round of the playoffs.

The Twins were back at the top of the division again two years later, led again by Santana, who won his second Cy Young Award. He was joined by Justin Morneau, who was voted the American League MVP, and Joe Mauer, who led the league in batting average. Together, they propelled the team to a 71–33 record over

their last 104 games, winning the AL Central on the last day of the season. But again they were thwarted in the divisional series, being swept by the A's.

However, there was also a bigger victory for the organization than the division, Cy Young, MVP, and batting title combined. In May, after more than a decade of efforts, the Twins secured their funding from Hennepin County for a new ballpark to replace the Metrodome. Groundbreaking took place a year later.

Hunter and Santana left for greener pastures following the 2007 season (Hunter as a free agent and Santana by a trade), and general manager Terry Ryan stepped down, being replaced by assistant GM Bill Smith. Over the next two years the Twins finished the 162-game schedule tied for the AL Central title. In 2008, they fell to the White Sox 1–0 in tie-breaking Game 163, narrowly missing out on their fifth divisional title of the decade. They would get it the next year, when an extra-inning hit by Alexi Casilla lifted them over the Tigers in another Game 163, the last regular-season game at the dome. As they were swept by the Yankees in the divisional series, it was also the last win by the Twins in the dome.

The Twins' new ballpark, Target Field, opened in 2010, earning rave reviews locally and nationally. The new venue drew over 3,000,000 fans and fueled a 94-win season and sixth Central Division crown. But once again, the team would fall in the playoffs to the Yankees without recording a win. The second year of the ballpark was significantly more somber, as injuries devastated the team, with only two Opening Day regulars finishing with even 100 games. The Twins fell to last in the division, narrowly missing only their second 100-loss season. ■

Calvin Griffith

The Ups and Downs of the last Family-Owned Baseball Team

Kevin Hennessy

When Calvin Griffith sold the Minnesota Twins in 1984, he bowed out of baseball as the last of the family owners whose franchise represented their principal business and source of wealth. Griffith spent practically his entire life in baseball, spending his young adulthood working in one capacity or another for the Washington Nationals organization that his uncle Clark owned. Upon the death of his uncle, Griffith took over the franchise and ran it from 1955 to 1984. He ran the operation as a family company, with relatives holding nearly all of the key positions. In 1961 he moved the Senators from Washington to Minnesota, and for the next ten years he oversaw one of baseball's most profitable and successful franchises. Griffith struggled during his last decade in Minnesota, however, after a couple of key family members died and baseball's changing economics undercut his operational philosophies.

Calvin Griffith was born Calvin Robertson on December 1, 1911, in Montreal, Quebec. Calvin was the second child of seven children born to Jane Davies and James Robertson, who married in 1908. His family included an older sister, Mildred (who later would marry Joe Cronin, Washington shortstop and future American League President), a younger sister, Thelma (who would marry Washington pitcher Joe Haynes), and younger brothers Bruce, Sherrod, Jimmy, and Billy. Jimmy and Billy were twins born in 1921. By that time the situation with his family had become a struggle due to Calvin's father's alcoholism, which eventually would cut James' life short in 1923 at the age of 42. The family had little money and it was necessary for Calvin to work to help support the family.

In the summer of 1922 the family was visited by James' sister Addie Griffith, wife of Clark Griffith, at that time the owner of the Washington Nationals. It was decided that Calvin (age 11) and his younger sister, Thelma (age 9), would return to Washington, D.C., and stay with the Griffiths. From this point on Calvin and his sister were raised as members of the Griffith family. Upon the death of Calvin's father, the rest of the Robertson family also moved to Washington. Although Calvin and Thelma were never formally adopted by the Griffiths, they did have their names legally changed—in Calvin's case from Calvin Griffith Robertson to Calvin Robertson Griffith.

Calvin began his involvement with baseball as the Washington batboy in 1922. This continued on through the world championship season of 1924 and the American League championship season of 1925. In 1928 he entered the Staunton Military Academy, graduating in 1933. After Staunton, Griffith entered George Washington University, which he attended the next two years. During his time at Staunton and George Washington, he played baseball as a pitcher and catcher.

In the spring of 1935, Griffith left George Washington and went to work for the Washington organization at its Chattanooga farm club as secretary-treasurer, and in 1937 he took over as head man. With the team struggling in mid-season, Clark fired the manager and enlarged Calvin's duties to include field manager. In 1938 the elder Griffith promoted Calvin to the same all-inclusive post with their affiliate in Charlotte. In 1941 Clark called Calvin back to Washington to take over a newly opened position with the big league club as assistant secretary, head of concessions.

Gradually Calvin began taking over the responsibilities of his uncle. Specifically he began attending league meetings in place of Clark, along with taking charge of making player trades and negotiating contracts with the media.

Clark Griffith died on October 27, 1955, and on November 1, at age 43, Calvin was elected president of the Washington Nationals. In the reorganization, Joe Haynes was named roving minor league pitching instructor; Sherry Robertson became assistant farm director; Billy Robertson assumed the position of supervisor of Griffith Stadium personnel and maintenance; Jimmy Robertson remained as director of concessions. Calvin had inherited, along with his sister Thelma, 52% of the Nationals' essentially debt-free franchise. The ballclub and the stadium were valued at approximately $4 million.

THE MOVE TO MINNESOTA

By 1955 the Washington franchise had suffered through years of poor performance and attendance. Rumors of offers from Louisville, Los Angeles, and Minnesota's Twin Cities were confirmed by Calvin in the authorized biography written by Jon Kerr in 1990. But political difficulties in moving a franchise out of the nation's capitol and a one-franchise city likely led to the delay in any transfer of the Senators. An article in the *Washington Post* January 15, 1958, bylined by Calvin, stated:

> I have lived in Washington, D.C., for about 35 years. I attended school here and established many roots here. The city has been good to my family and me. This is my home. I intend that it shall remain my home for the rest of my life. As long as I have any say in the matter, and I expect that I shall for a long, long time, the Washington Senators will stay here, too. Next year. The year after that. Forever.[1]

Shirley Povich's article in *Baseball Digest* later that year detailed Griffith's testimony before the U. S. Senate's Anti-Trust Committee. There Calvin tried to backpedal, explaining that what he had said above did not mean that he would not stay should the club no longer be able to financially function in Washington.

With many large cities clamoring for major league baseball and the major leagues dragging their heels on expansion, in 1959 52-year-old New York lawyer William Shea championed the creation on of a new eight-team major league—in Shea's case largely to replace the Brooklyn Dodgers and New York Giants who had departed for the West Coast in 1957. The threat of Shea's Continental League sparked further talks by the American and National Leagues regarding expansion. Part of this discussion included consideration of Minneapolis-St. Paul as an expansion site, or alternatively, as a site for relocation of Griffith's Washington franchise. Griffith had been promised a guaranteed annual attendance of 750,000 and an estimated $430,000 media contract by the Twin Cities delegation. Part of a possible expansion plan included the addition of a new team in the nation's capitol, as Griffith's possible relocation of the Senators was being challenged in the courts at the time by minority owner H. Gabriel Murphy.

The next year expansion finally became a reality. The National League voted at a meeting on October 17, 1960, to expand to New York and Houston, with those teams beginning operation for the 1962 season. In a meeting on October 26, the American League voted to expand to 10 teams for the following season (1961). Calvin Griffith would be allowed to move his franchise to Minnesota, with a new American League franchise replacing his in Washington.

SUCCESS IN THE 1960s

The Senators were greeted warmly in Minnesota. Ticket orders rolled in well in advance of tickets going on sale for the opening of the 1961 season. Minneapolis sportswriter Sid Hartman probably put it best:

> The Senators became the Minnesota Twins, moved into Met Stadium, took over the concessions business, and there were relatives all over the place: Joe Haynes, Thelma Haynes, Sherry Robertson, Billy Robertson, Jimmy Robertson. You didn't know who was in charge of what. Your reaction was, "What is this? We didn't get a ballclub. We got a family." It was like being around the Beverly Hillbillies.

> And then there was this guy Howard Fox. He wasn't a relative, but he was the guy hanging out at Woodhill and Wayzata Country Clubs with Calvin. We wondered, "How does Fox fit in?"...

> It was an odd organization, but who cared? It was terrific to have major league baseball. The Upper Midwest went crazy, sending buses throughout the summer from every little town in Minnesota, the Dakotas, Iowa, Nebraska, and even Montana.[2]

The Twins were very successful at the gate from the beginning. From 1961 though the 1970 season Minnesota topped one million in attendance each year, including totals of over 1.4 million in four of those years: 1962, 1963, 1965, and 1967. The team also showed dramatic improvement on the field. With last-place finishes in four of the last six seasons in Washington, the Twins started with a seventh-place finish in 1961 (in the expanded ten-team American League), jumping to second in 1962 and third in 1963. After a sub-par 1964 season, the Twins won the American League pennant in 1965 and came close in 1967.

Much of the improvement was due to quality players that were signed and developed in the Senators/Twins farm system, most notably Hall of Famer Harmon Killebrew, outfielders Bob Allison, Jimmie Hall, and three-time batting champion Tony Oliva, first baseman Don Mincher, 1965 Most Valuable Player and shortstop Zoilo Versalles, and pitchers Camilo Pascual

Twins President Calvin Griffith presents Harmon Killebrew with a boat in recognition of Killebrew's 500th home run.

and Jim Kaat—all important members of the 1965 pennant-winning ballclub. By the end of the decade the system had also produced future Hall of Famers Rod Carew and Bert Blyleven.

Calvin was not above interjecting his opinions or directives when it came to his managers. A commonly cited example was when he insisted that Sam Mele stick with rookie Rod Carew during the 1967 season, when Carew was making the jump from playing class A ball in 1966.

In the mid-1960s, Calvin's son, Clark II, joined the organization. Joe Haynes passed away in 1967 due to a heart attack at age 49; Sherry Robertson died due to injuries suffered in an automobile crash in Houghton, South Dakota in 1970 at the age of 51. George Brophy took over as farm director for Sherry Robertson, and Howard Fox became even closer to Calvin as a confidant/advisor.

THE HIRING/FIRING OF BILLY MARTIN AS MANAGER

Since the move to Minnesota, Calvin had been through three managers. Cookie Lavagetto, the holdover manager from Washington, was dismissed during the 1961 season and replaced by coach Sam Mele. Griffith let Mele go early in the 1967 season and replaced him with coach Cal Ermer, who lasted through 1968.

To lead his club on the field, Griffith appointed Billy Martin as manager on October 11, 1968. Billy had played for the Twins in 1961, his final season as a player. In 1965 the Twins brought Martin back to the major league club as a coach—a position he held through the 1967 season. In 1968 Billy was sent to the Twins' triple-A affiliate in Denver to manage the team.

Billy's tenure as a coach with the Twins had been controversial—most notably his physical altercation with Traveling Secretary Howard Fox in 1966, which had carried over from a charter flight into the hotel. The two publicly made peace, but Fox would continue to dislike Martin. Another notable altercation occurred during the 1969 season when Martin fought with his own pitcher, Dave Boswell, outside a bar on August 7. This event was not popular with Calvin, who said he had warned Martin against going to the same establishments as his players before he was hired as manager. Calvin did, however, support Martin's fine of Boswell for the incident.

The Twins won the West Division of the American League that season, the first year of divisional play, and they entered the best-of-five playoff series against the East Division champion Baltimore Orioles. The Orioles won the first two games in Baltimore by one run each and then beat the Twins at home 11–2. In the third game, Billy had chosen to start Bob Miller over Jim Kaat, a decision which Calvin let be known he did not approve.

According to Tom Mee, the Twin's public-relations director at the time, the decision to fire Martin came at a meeting during the World Series in New York City on October 13. Everyone in the assembled group of six was asked to express his opinion about whether or not Martin, working 1969 under a one-year contract, should be rehired. Everyone spoke against Martin until it got to Mee. According to Mee, the "pro-Billy" people were not there—Sherry Robertson, in particular—and only Mee ended up speaking up in favor of Martin. After everyone had spoken, Howard Fox called the question, saying, "Well, what are you going to do?" to Calvin, who responded, "I'm gonna fire his ass."[3]

The firing was very unpopular with fans and the media. Don Riley wrote in the *St. Paul Pioneer Press* the day before the firing:

Just remember what I told you. Griffith may not be popular with the masses but I don't believe he's stupid. If he didn't rehire Martin, he leaves himself open to the biggest fan revolt since Gopher [University of Minnesota] fans learned there are football fields where you can see the game for five bucks . . .[4]

And in his column the day after:

Griffith couldn't have done a more dastardly work of unpopularity if he turned down a reprieve for Joan of Arc—or got caught drilling holes in Washington's rowboat.[5]

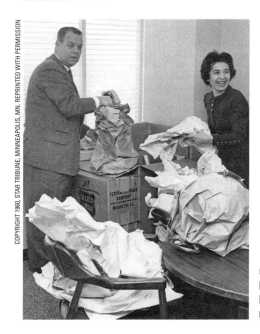

Calvin Griffith, with the help of assistant Vivian Hallow, moving into his new office in Minnesota.

Arno Goethel, the Twins' beat writer for the *St. Paul Pioneer Press*, added an analysis of the situation a couple days later. All the sources of conflict were mentioned: Martin's temperament, the Howard Fox conflict, Calvin's second-guessing of Billy's managerial style, the fact that Billy did not have complete control over the make-up of his coaching staff, and that Martin couldn't tolerate the nature of the Twins charter flights, which frequently included relatives and associates of Twins front office personnel. According to Tom Mee, the organization never did fully recover from the firing of Billy Martin as it moved into the 1970s.[6]

FAILURES IN THE 1970s

As Griffith searched for a replacement for Martin, he uttered one of his more memorable quotes: "I can't tell you what I intend to do, but I can tell you one thing; it won't be anything rational."[7] Griffith eventually hired Bill Rigney, and in 1970 the Twins' again won the West Division. And again they lost the American League Championship Series in three straight games to the Orioles. This was to be the Twins' last division championship under Calvin's ownership. Rigney survived as manager until 1972, when he was replaced mid-season by Frank Quilici.

Aging stars combined with lack of replacements led to the Twins failures of the early 1970s. As the decade wore on, the change in baseball's reserve system led to further problems for Calvin. He had been brought through the Nationals organization, learning from his uncle that a baseball team was operated with a bottom line, and was concerned with making a profit, not spending money that team didn't have. Avoiding debt

and interest payments were always foremost in his management style.

After 1970 the team drew over a million in attendance only twice (1977, 1979) at Metropolitan Stadium. These lower attendance figures meant less revenue for salaries, which Calvin already considered too high for mere ballplayers. Calvin reacted to the new baseball economics by futilely trying to resist changes such as salary arbitration, player agents, free agency, and the increasing importance of television revenue, which gave an advantage to teams in larger markets. As time moved on, Griffith was considered a "dinosaur" or a "vestige of yesterday" relative to the new baseball owners of the late 1970s.

On the personal side, 1974 was the year Calvin separated from his wife and moved out of his Lake Minnetonka home. Calvin had married Natalie Morris of Charlotte, North Carolina, in 1940; the couple had three children: Clark, Corinne, and Claire. The two never did reconcile or divorce.

1978—THE LIONS CLUB TALK IN WASECA

On Thursday, September 28, 1978, Calvin accepted an invitation to travel south to the rural town of Waseca, Minnesota, to spend the afternoon playing golf with his friend, sportswriter Tony Sybilrud, and speak to the Waseca Lions Club that evening.

Coincidentally, *Minneapolis Tribune* staff writer Nick Coleman was also in attendance that night. Coleman was not there to cover the event (Coleman lived in Rochester, Minnesota, and covered southern Minnesota for the paper) but rather a guest of his father-in-law. It was later said that during the introduction of the audience Coleman identified himself by name only and not by vocation.

The meeting proceeded in a question and answer format. Griffith began to make comments about specific players and about race in general. Coleman is quoted as saying "I was wincing the whole time thinking, you don't want to say that."[8] He was not there with a tape recorder or anything with which to write, so when he returned from the meeting he wrote everything down from memory. The next day he called his editors to ask if they wanted him to write a story based on what he had heard. They called back and said yes, and that it would run in the Sunday paper.

In the most damaging part of the article, Coleman detailed:

At that point, Griffith interrupted himself, lowered his voice and asked if there were any blacks around. After he looked around the room and assured himself that his audience was white, Griffith resumed his answer.

"I'll tell you why we came to Minnesota," he said. "It was when I found out you only had 15,000 blacks here. Black people don't go to ball games, but they'll fill up a rassling ring and put up such a chant it'll scare you to death. It's unbelievable. We came here because you've got good, hardworking, white people here."[9]

A few of the comments were specifically about Griffith's star first baseman, Rod Carew. Calvin's comments are believed to have underlined his dislike for agents and multi-year player contracts but clearly also impugned Carew's intelligence:

> Carew was a damn fool to sign that contract. He only gets $170,000 and we all know damn well that he's worth a lot more than that, but that's what his agent asked for, that's what he gets. Last year, I thought I was generous and gave him an extra 100 grand, but this year I'm not making any money so he gets 170—that's it.[10]

This, and comments that Calvin made in general about "blacks," led to Carew's public response in the papers a couple of days later on the final day of the 1978 baseball season, which also happened to be his thirty-third birthday:

> I will not ever sign another contract with this organization. I don't care how much money or how many options Calvin Griffith offers me. I definitely will not be back next year.

> I will not come back and play for a bigot. I'm not going to be another n— on his plantation.

> How does he expect these players to respect the thing that's across their chest—Twins—when it's coming right from the top that he doesn't care about the players?

> He respects nobody and expects nobody to respect him. Spit on Calvin Griffith.[11]

Carew never again played for the Twins. Going into the 1979 season, at the end of which Carew would be a free agent, Griffith traded him to the California Angels for four players. Time however, softened Carew's feelings for Calvin. In Bob Showers's book, *The Twins at the Met*, Carew is included as one of the narrators. He praised Calvin for sticking with him early in his career. Recalling his Hall of Fame election, Carew also said:

> When I first got the news that I was going into the Hall of Fame, he was the first person I called. It was 3 o'clock in the morning for him in Helena, Montana, and I woke him up. I called him before my mom because I owed him that much respect.[12]

From Calvin's perspective the comments from the meeting were blown out of proportion and misunderstood. Also from his perspective, comments made in a Lions Club meeting were meant to stay within the walls of the Lions Club meeting. It also had been reported that Calvin had had "a few" drinks over the course of the afternoon and evening.

The Waseca talk haunted Calvin the rest of his life. Personally, I have been working in Waseca the past three years, and it appears that even the most marginal baseball fan is aware of the story of that day. Few obituaries for Calvin in 1999 were run without mention of the Waseca talk being the low point in Calvin's career, and his life.

CALVIN AND HIS FAMILY BUSINESS

As already alluded to, the Senators/Twins franchise under Calvin (and to some extent under his uncle) was a family business. Calvin's son, Clark II, joined the organization in 1966. Thelma's son, Bruce Haynes, joined the team in 1974 as farm director.

In the latter years of the Griffith-owned franchise much was made of the rift that existed between Calvin and his son. Disagreements that may have germinated when Clark did not consent to an apprenticeship in the minor leagues as his father had done, led to the elder Griffith gradually losing trust in his son's judgments. These disagreements manifested themselves in the organization's response to the changing nature of the business: free agency, advertising, and negotiations between the players' union and the representatives of management, in which Clark II played a significant role. Calvin described his relationship with Clark in a curious comment: "This is a very close-knit family. I imagine you talked to Clark yesterday, and I imagine he may have told you that we don't talk."[13] The addition of Bruce Haynes to the executive mix further complicated the question of who would eventually inherit ultimate decision-making power after Calvin stepped down as president.

MOVE TO THE METRODOME, MORE RELOCATION TALK, AND SALE

Beginning in the early 1970s and fueled by the Minnesota Vikings' desire to have a stadium with more capacity and one that could shelter the team from brutal Minnesota winter weather, talks began regarding a new domed facility for Minnesota sports teams. By 1975, the year that the Twins' and Vikings' leases were set to expire at Metropolitan Stadium, negotiations began in earnest.

Eventually funding for the domed stadium in downtown Minneapolis's Industry Square location on the east side of downtown made its way through the Minnesota legislature. In July of 1979 the lease agreement was worked out with the Vikings. The Twins, on the other hand, had been sending Calvin's son, Clark Griffith II, nephew Bruce Haynes (both Clark and Bruce were executive vice presidents), and lawyer Peter Dorsey to the lease meetings with no results. Eventually Calvin entered into the lease negotiations, landing some favorable clauses for the club:

The Twins would get 30 percent of the stadium's gross concession receipts up to an attendance of 1.4 million. After that they would receive 20 percent. In contrast, the Viking's lease was for 10 percent.

The lease contained an escape clause which allowed the team to be released from the contract if attendance fell below an average of 1.4 million for three successive years or if the team experienced net operating losses in three successive years.

If the team could produce evidence of lack of attendance due to summer heat (the architects felt that the Metrodome, being mostly underground, would make air conditioning unnecessary), then the Twins were not bound to play in the Metrodome if the commission did not install air conditioning.

The Twins would pay no more than $700,000 of the $1.7 million needed to build the team new offices in the Metrodome.

In 1982 the Twins moved into the Metrodome after experiencing a dismal strike-shortened 1981, both at the gate and on the field. In response Griffith unloaded five high salaried veterans—a couple of whom had just been signed to large multi-year contracts by Clark—and instead relied on group of young, untested rookies to fill out the roster. The season rivaled 1981 for results: the Twins went 60-102 and drew less than a million fans–this in their first season in a new stadium. The next season the Twins' record improved to 70–92 but attendance slipped further to 858,939. The Twins were poised to test the three-year escape clause Calvin had negotiated.

Perhaps the most serious threat of relocation was to Tampa Bay. In 1983, Earle Halstead Jr., retired publisher of *The Baseball Blue Book*, took a potential ownership group from Tampa Bay to visit Calvin in Winter Park, Florida, where Calvin stayed during spring training. The group purchased the 41 percent of the Twins owned by H. Gabriel Murphy. Their plan was then to go after Calvin or Thelma's ownership in the Twins and offer Calvin an opportunity to continue to run the team. The move to Tampa Bay was to take place for the 1986 season. Calvin denied that any deal had been struck and further added that if anyone was going to move the team to Florida, it would be him.[14]

As the 1984 season proceeded, it appeared obvious that the Twins would not draw the 2.4 million fans required to bind the team to the Metrodome lease (the number needed to average the three-year total needed to meet the lease requirement), and the community began to worry. Local businessman Harvey Mackay

Calvin Griffith celebrating the team's surprising 1984 season.

organized a ticket buyout that would eliminate the escape clause and force Calvin to sell to a local buyer. Calvin claimed that this attempt, in the end, was in vain, as he could still have claimed net operating losses over the three seasons at the Metrodome.

Griffith contended he felt a loyalty toward Minnesota and in the end wanted to sell to a Minnesota buyer and keep the team in the Twin Cities. He ended up selling the club to local businessman Carl Pohlad for a price of $32 million in payments and salaries over a period of 20 years. Calvin thought Pohlad was also buying his management team, but in the end few were held over from the Griffith ownership. After the sale he had an office in the Metrodome but was never involved in any decisions. In the end, Calvin had not only brought major league baseball to Minnesota but also allowed it to stay there.

Three years later, when the Twins won their first World Series, it was with a core of players from the 1982 team. Both 1982 and 1987 rosters included Kent Hrbek, Gary Gaetti, Tom Brunansky, Tim Laudner, Frank Viola, and Randy Bush. Twins farmhands Kirby Puckett, Greg Gagne, Gene Larkin, and Mark Davidson also played key roles on the 1987 World Champions. The new management had also reacquired former Griffith-era stars Bert Blyleven and Roy Smalley.

Griffith died October 20, 1999, at the age of 87 due to a kidney infection, 15 years after he had sold his interest in the ballclub that was his life. He is buried outside Washington, D.C. ■

Notes

1. "Griffith Not Happy with Armory Stadium Site." *Washington Post*, January 17, 1958.
2. Sid Hartman, with Patrick Reusse. *Sid!* (Stillwater, MN: Voyager Press, Inc. 1997) 95–96.
3. Tom Mee. Interview September 7, 2011.
4. Don Riley. "Sports Eye Opener." *St. Paul Pioneer Press*, October 13, 1969.
5. Don Riley. "Sports Eye Opener." *St. Paul Pioneer Press*, October 14, 1969.
6. Mee, op. cit.
7. Jon Kerr. Calvin, *Baseball's Last Dinosaur: An Authorized Biography*. (Dubuque, IA: William C. Brown Publishers, 1990).
8. Jordan Osterman. "Griffith's Gaffe." *Waseca County News*, July 5, 2011.
9. Nick Coleman. "Griffith Spares Few Targets in Waseca Remarks." *Minneapolis Tribune*, October 1, 1978.
10. Ibid.
11. Gary Libman. "Angry Twins beat Carew vows he will not play for Griffith's Twins again." *Minneapolis Tribune*, October 2, 1978.
12. Bob Showers. *The Twins at the Met*. (Minneapolis: Beaver's Pond Press, 2009) 64.
13. Michael Lenehan. "The Last Pure Men of Baseball." *Atlantic Monthly*, August, 1981.
14. Bob Andelman. *Stadium for Rent: Tampa Bay's Quest for Major League Baseball*. (Jefferson, NC: McFarland and Company, Inc., Publishers, 1993) 34.

Sources

Andelman, Bob. *Stadium for Rent: Tampa Bay's Quest for Major League Baseball*. Jefferson, North Carolina: McFarland and Company, Inc., Publishers, 1993.

Anderson, David (editor). *Quotations from Chairman Calvin*. Stillwater, Minnesota: Brick Alley Books Press. 1984.

Baseball Guide and Record Book. St. Louis, Missouri: Charles Spink & Son, 1960.

Brackin, Dennis and Patrick Reusse. *Minnesota Twins: The Complete Illustrated History*. Minneapolis, Minnesota: MVP Books, 2010.

Coleman, Nick. "Griffith Spares Few Targets in Waseca Remarks." *Minneapolis Tribune*, October 1, 1978.

Goethel, Arno. "Martin Showed Foresight When Named Twins' Pilot." *St. Paul Pioneer Press*, October 14, 1969.

Goethel, Arno. "Why Did Cal Bounce Billy?" *St. Paul Pioneer Press*, October 15, 1969.

Griffith, Calvin R. "Griffith Not Happy with Armory Stadium Site." *The Washington Post*, January 17, 1958.

Griffith, Clark II. Interview September 6, 2011.

Grow, Doug. *We're Gonna Win Twins!* Minneapolis, Minnesota: University of Minnesota Press, 2010.

Hartman, Sid with Patrick Reusse. *Sid!* Stillwater, Minnesota: Voyager Press, Inc. 1997.

Johnson, Charles. "The Story of How Minnesota Got Major League Baseball." *Greater Minneapolis*, December, 1960, pgs. 11–13.

Kahan, Oscar. "Boss of Twins Bombarded by Advance Ticket Orders." *The Sporting News*, January 11, 1961, 9.

Kerr, Jon. Calvin, *Baseball's Last Dinosaur: An Authorized Biography*. William C. Brown Publishers, 1990.

Klobuchar, Amy. *Uncovering the Dome*. Minneapolis, Minnesota: Bolger Publications, Inc., 1982.

Leavengood, Ted. *Clark Griffith: The Old Fox of Washington Baseball*. Jefferson, North Carolina: McFarland and Company, Inc., 2011.

Lenehan, Michael. "The Last Pure Men of Baseball." *Atlantic Monthly*, August, 1981.

Libman, Gary. "Angry Twins beat K.C. in 11." *Minneapolis Tribune*, October 2, 1978.

Libman, Gary. "Angry Carew vows he will not play for Griffith's Twins again." *Minneapolis Tribune*, October 2, 1978.

McCarthy, Kevin. *Baseball in Florida*. Pineapple Press, Inc., 1996.

McKenna, Brian. *Clark Griffith: Baseball Statesman*. 2010.

Mee, Tom. Interview September 7, 2011.

Minnesota Twins Media Guides, 1961–1988.

Osterman, Jordan. "Griffith's Gaffe." *Waseca County News*, July 5, 2011.

Povich, Shirley. "Cal Griffith Tries to Explain." *Baseball Digest*, September, 1958, pgs. 51–52.

Riley, Don. "Sports Eye Opener." *St. Paul Pioneer Press*, October 13, 1969.

Riley, Don. "Sports Eye Opener." *St. Paul Pioneer Press*, October 14, 1969.

Ringolsby, Tracy. "Sport Interview: Calvin Griffith." *Sport*. April, 1984.

Sarasota Herald-Tribune. "Griffith Nixes Report He'll Sell Twins to Tampa Bay Group." July 2, 1983.

Showers, Bob. *The Twins at the Met*. Beaver's Pond Press, 2009.

Sinker, Howard. "Griffith: Talk Misunderstood." *Minneapolis Tribune*, October 2, 1978.

Smith, Gary. "A Lingering Vestige of Yesterday." *Sports Illustrated*, April 4, 1983.

Sport. "Minneapolis: Big-League Town in Waiting." December, 1959.

Thornley, Stew. *Baseball in Minnesota: The Definitive History*. Saint Paul, Minnesota: Minnesota Historical Society Press. 2006.

Washington Post. "Clark Griffith Brings Home 5 More Children to Adopt." November 24, 1925.

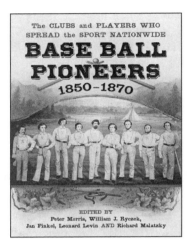

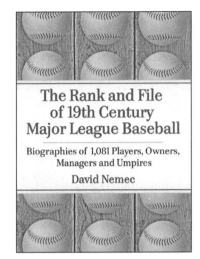
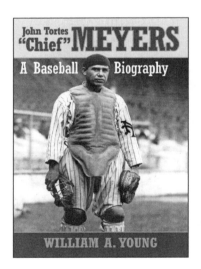

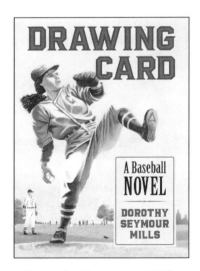

A Surprising Disappointment

The Minnesota Twins of the Late 1960s

Daniel R. Levitt

On October 14, 1965, the Minnesota Twins lost a heartbreaking World Series Game Seven to Sandy Koufax and the Los Angeles Dodgers, 2–0. While the disappointment was palpable, there was every reason to believe the Twins would soon be back in the Series. The team had won the pennant convincingly with a record of 102-60, seven games ahead of the second place White Sox. Owner Calvin Griffith, acting as his own general manager, had built a deep and talented club. And the once mighty New York Yankees dynasty that had dominated the American League over the previous four decades appeared to have run its course.

In Harmon Killebrew and Tony Oliva, the Twins had two of the top hitters in the league. Shortstop Zoilo Versalles led the league in total bases and runs scored, won a Gold Glove, and was named the league's Most Valuable Player. Along with Versalles, among the team's position players *The Sporting News* named Oliva, center fielder Jimmie Hall, and catcher Earl Battey to their year-end all-star team representing the American League's top players. Left fielder Bob Allison was only one season removed from finishing second in the league in OBP and fourth in slugging.

Led by these and other stars, the team dominated the league's scoring with 774 runs; Detroit finished a distant second with 680. In 1963 and 1964 the team had hit 225 and 221 home runs respectively, the second and third highest single-season totals of all time up to that point. In 1965 manager Sam Mele chose to emphasize the team's speed and the club stole 92 bases—fourth in the league—while being caught only 33 times. The Twins featured a terrific blend of power and speed.

The team also sported an excellent and deep pitching staff. Minnesota finished third in the league in ERA despite pitching in one of the league's better hitters' parks. Six pitchers started at least nine games, and every one could boast an ERA below the league average. Between 1963 and 1970 each of the six would win twenty games in a season at least once.

With 283 lifetime wins, then-rotation anchor Jim Kaat is currently on the Hall of Fame ballot and would not be a poor choice if elected. One of the league's best left-handers, in 1965 Kaat went 18–11 with a 2.83 ERA while leading the league in games started. Teammate Jim "Mudcat" Grant led the league with 21 wins and a .750 winning percentage. At that time only one Cy Young Award winner was named for the major leagues, which in 1965 went to the National League's Sandy Koufax. *The Sporting News*, however, named a Pitcher of the Year for each league and awarded the American League honor to Grant.

Curveball pitcher Camilo Pascual was the third Twins pitcher with over 20 starts in 1965. He led the league in strikeouts from 1961 to 1963, finished second in 1964, and won at least twenty games in both 1962 and 1963. Unfortunately, after a great start to the 1965 season that included winning his first eight decisions, he tore a muscle in his back near his shoulder. Pascual made it back by early September and started Game Three of the World Series. Although he pitched with less than stellar success after his return, Pascual was only 31, and the Twins had every reason to believe he would bounce back in 1966.

The other three hurlers who started at least nine games consisted of two youngsters, 20-year-old Dave Boswell and 21-year-old Jim Merritt along with swingman Jim Perry. Boswell and Merritt both turned in an ERA below the league average and struck out more than seven batters per game. Fourth starter Perry finished ninth in the league in ERA. Al Worthington, with 21 saves and a 2.13 ERA, anchored a good bullpen.

The Twins were not only talented but young. No player with over 150 at bats was yet on the wrong side of 30; of the pitchers, only Pascual was older than 30. With good reason, the Twins and their fans looked forward to a promising future.

*   *   *

But it was not to be. The Twins would not again win the pennant for more than 20 years, behind a completely different generation of players. The club came agonizingly close in 1967 when no dominant team emerged, and after some retooling, won division titles in 1969 and 1970. Nevertheless, with a boatload of young talent that had already proved it could win at the highest level, Minnesota averaged only 86 wins from 1966 though 1968. This was not going to win a pennant in the ten-team American League.

So what happened? Why did the Twins, who showed so much promise in 1965, fail to capture another flag? Like many complex questions, one can identify several causes for the failure to repeat. Most significant was the unexpected and dramatic falloff in production from the top position players. Table 1 highlights the players' performance before and after their pennant winning season. Every single player batted worse over the remainder of his career than through 1965. And not just a little bit worse, several simply collapsed below the level of a major-league-caliber baseball player.

Jimmie Hall played for several years after 1965, but never again as a more than a stop-gap. Some of his decline may be attributed to a beaning, but in any case, his dramatic fall-off left the Twins with a gaping hole in center field. Catcher Earl Battey suffered from chronically sore knees, exacerbated by goiter and weight gain that likely led to a premature end to his career. But the suddenness from which he fell from one of the league's top catchers to out of the league in just two years would surprise almost any organization. Third baseman Rich Rollins had regressed since breaking in as a regular in 1962, when he actually led all American League players in votes for the All-Star game. The next year he hit .307 to finish third in the batting race, and in 1964 he led the league in triples. Nevertheless, despite his still young age, after 1965 Rollins would never again be a quality major league regular. In 1966 Bob Allison suffered a broken bone in his hand and turned in only two more quality seasons. Tony Oliva's recurring problems with his right knee and a shoulder separation in 1968 left him a star but well below the level he had established during his first two years as a regular.

Zoilo Versalles, though, may have been the saddest case of all. Uncovered by legendary scout Joe Cambria, in the summer of 1957 Versalles arrived in Key West as a 17-year-old: hopeful, scared, unable to communicate in English, and thrown into a segregated society he didn't understand. Versalles covered much of his anxiety with a cocky swagger and a reputation as a hot dog. The talented youngster quickly worked his way through the Twins system and by 1961 was the team's regular shortstop as 21-year-old.

After his 1965 MVP season, however, Versalles completely lost his ability to play baseball. By 1967 Versalles was one of the worst starting regulars in the league; both his on-base and slugging percentages fell below .285. Sportswriter Doug Grow once asked Griffith what happened. Griffith told him, "drugs." Versalles had been prescribed pain killers for a chronically bad back. Unfamiliar with the culture and the language, Versalles often ignored the correct dosage, taking well over the prescribed amount.[1]

How exactly leadership of a baseball team affects performance on the field has long been debated. The Oakland A's of the 1970s fought each other and owner Charles Finley to three World Series victories. In many other instances, however, turmoil and dissension have often been used to explain the failure of otherwise talented clubs. The Twins of the late 1960s were fractured into several distinct cliques, and unlike the A's with a strong, skilled manager in Dick Williams, they had no one with a firm hand on the reins.

Twins owner Calvin Griffith grew up in baseball and by the early 1960s directed a truly family operation. Brothers Sherry, Jimmy, and Billy Robertson along with brother-in-law Joe Haynes all held down key executive positions within the organization. By the time Griffith moved the franchise to Minnesota, he had become an astute judge of baseball talent and was ably assisted by his family and scouts. Moreover, prior to the death of Haynes in 1967 and Sherry in 1970 and the changing

Table 1. Change in Twins Player Batting Statistics After 1965

Player	Age in 1965	Through 1965 AVG/OBP/SLG	OPS	After 1965 AVG/OBP/SLG	OPS	dOPS
Zoilo Versalles	25	259/303/408	711	217/270/304	573	-138
Tony Oliva	26	324/371/526	897	299/349/464	813	-84
Jimmie Hall	27	276/342/488	830	229/296/371	667	-163
Bob Allison	30	259/364/482	846	243/340/443	784	-63
Rich Rollins	27	283/347/405	752	239/289/353	642	-110
H Killebrew	29	261/368/534	902	252/382/486	868	-34
Earl Battey	30	276/353/425	778	235/318/300	619	-160
Don Mincher	27	242/340/501	842	252/352/429	781	-61

Star outfielder Tony Oliva is carried off the field on August 31, 1968 after separating his shoulder while diving for a fly ball. A great player for his first several years in the majors, injuries robbed him of a Hall of Fame career.

baseball economics that Griffith never really understood, the Twins organization should be regarded as one of the league's more successful, both on the field and in the stands. Over their first decade after moving from Washington to Minnesota in 1961, the Twins actually led the American League in attendance.

Despite his success, Griffith represented the last of the family owners; by the late 1960s baseball teams were owned by men who had made their fortunes in other lines of work and bought into baseball. Because Griffith operated as his own general manager and was not particularly skilled at leadership, he often micromanaged and rankled those who worked for him, somewhat akin to the problems George Steinbrenner experienced in the 1980s when not buffered by a solid general manager. His desire for hands-on involvement also occasionally hindered his hiring judgment.

After a disappointing 1964 season in which the Twins won only 79 games, Griffith cut manager Sam Mele's salary by $3,000 and publicly criticized his manager for being "too nice a guy" and managing a team that played sloppy baseball. Mele's managing philosophy of offering criticism and encouragement in private and highlighting what he wanted each player to practice, but not providing a lot of specific instruction, played into Griffith's concerns.[2]

To remedy the situation, Griffith foisted two brilliant but strong-willed coaches on Mele: pitching coach Johnny Sain and third-base coach Billy Martin. Much of the hullabaloo surrounding Sain derived from his tendency to separate the pitchers from the position players. Many pitchers he coached were his ardent students and in particular on the Twins, Jim Kaat. Martin was a ferocious competitor and helped enormously in relating to the Latino players. He was also a short-tempered, paranoid bully.

By 1966 Martin and Sain hated each other, and Mele was at odds with his pitching coach as well. The antagonism flared midseason in Kansas City when Sain confronted Martin after the third-base coach had cussed out a pitcher over a squeeze play. Martin and Sain were both angry and neither felt that Mele sufficiently took control of the situation. Moreover, in the aftermath of the altercation, players began to take sides, always a dangerous situation. After the season in which the Twins finished 89–73, nine games behind the Orioles, Griffith jettisoned Sain. In response, star pitcher Jim Kaat, who finished 25–13 and surely would have won the American League Cy Young Award had the award been bestowed in both leagues, sent a widely-circulated open letter defending Sain and criticizing the decision to fire him.

Finally, after a 25–25 start to the 1967 season, Griffith fired Mele and promoted Cal Ermer from the Twins triple-A farm team in Denver. Ermer found himself in an almost impossible situation: a man with little major league experience as either a player or coach thrust into a team fractured into cliques, both racial and otherwise, made up of stars who had tasted a pennant, and with a hands-on owner breathing over his shoulder.

To Calvin Griffith's credit, he had assembled one of baseball's more racially mixed teams. Many of the team's stars were African-Americans and Cubans who would have been banned for being too dark-skinned before 1947. But race relations in America in the 1960s were in flux, and baseball was not exempt. Just twelve days into his tenure, Ermer was faced with a difficult situation on the team bus in Detroit, a city teeming with racial tension.

White pitcher Dave Boswell was playing with a gun, when Grant, who is black, told him to put it away. When Boswell ignored him, Oliva also told Boswell to

Calvin Griffith (right) and beleaguered manager Sam Mele, 1962.

knock it off. "You Cubans play with guns down there," Boswell reportedly replied. "We got a right to play with guns up here."[3] Sandy Valdespino and Ted Uhlaender nearly came to blows, before cooler heads held them back. Ermer went to the back of the bus to calm things down and later held a meeting at the hotel to simmer down the tensions. Many of the black players remained unconvinced, but there can be no doubt that the team responded on the field. "Cal Ermer was a great guy," Kaat remembered. "I don't know if he ever had control over big league players, but he was a different presence than Sam and it worked for the rest of that season."[4] At least for the next 112 games: the Twins went 66–44 (with 2 ties), taking a slim lead in the pennant race.

But the Twins could not seem to shake their controversies. Holding onto a one game lead, the team once again faced off against itself on September 29. In a contentious players-only meeting to divvy up the World Series money (a small portion was also allotted to high finishing teams that did not win the pennant), many of the players argued against giving Mele a share. Once this had been pushed through, five members the pro-Mele faction symbolically voted not to give Ermer a share either. More substantively, eleven players agreed to pool their own shares to give Mele a portion. Even the commissioner's office felt the need to weigh in and castigate the players but otherwise took no action. In the aftermath of this dramatic meeting, the Twins lost the final two games of the season, and the pennant, in Boston.

The team's success under Ermer over the last half of 1967 did not translate into 1968. In addition to the players' drop-off noted earlier, Killebrew suffered a brutal hamstring injury that contributed to a 79–83 record. "It has been quite apparent to me that Ermer has lost control over the club," Griffith complained

late in the season.[5] Moreover, this was not a lone sentiment. "Cal Ermer was a weak man," wrote catcher John Roseboro. "He was quiet like [Los Angeles Dodgers manager Walter] Alston, but he didn't have Walt's firmness and he didn't have the respect Walter had."[6] Griffith, a lifelong baseball man with strong opinions of his own, too often exacerbated the situation by criticizing Ermer, making it hard for him to exercise the necessary managerial authority.

With the firing of Ermer, for 1969 Griffith finally relented and hired fan-favorite and domineering personality, Billy Martin. In this first year of two divisions, Martin brought the Twins home first in the West. With young star Rod Carew and several other quality newcomers having joined the aging nucleus of 1965, the Twins could still perform at a fairly high level. But it was too little, too late. The Orioles had built a superior ballclub in Baltimore, ranked by some as one of the greatest of all time. The Twins window of opportunity had closed.

In one of the odder mistakes, the Twins had a potentially great pitcher that they simply didn't use. Early in 1963 season the Twins traded for Cleveland's Jim Perry, a good pitcher who had been struggling recently. During Perry's first two years in the majors, 1959 and 1960, he had won thirty games, while leading the league in wins, starts, and shutouts in 1960. He fell off over the next couple of years, but with the help of Twins pitching coach Johnny Sain and a new curveball, he rejuvenated his career in Minnesota. For some reason, however, the Twins relegated Perry to the periphery of the rotation, essentially keeping him as a swing man from 1965 to 1968. Only once during those four years did Perry start more than 20 games despite having an ERA better than any rotation regular in three of them. When Martin finally put Perry into the rotation in 1969 he went 20–6. The next year he won the Cy Young Award with a 24–12 record. Perry currently holds the Twins career record for lowest ERA (minimum 750 IP) at 3.15 and finished with a career total of 215 wins.

By 1965 Calvin Griffith had built a terrific young team in Minnesota. The team won the American League pennant by a comfortable margin and came within a Sandy Koufax three-hitter of winning Game Seven of the World Series. Griffith, a life-long baseball man, had built a solid organization manned primarily by baseball savvy family members and close friends. The team drew well at the gate, and Griffith paid his players well by the standards of the time. But this group of Twins players could not repeat. Too many of the stars suffered unexpected rapid and severe declines, and in fairness to Griffith, it is almost impossible to know when a star

Above: 1965 AL MVP Zoilo Versalles, shown here in the 1965 World Series, was no longer a major league caliber baseball player just two years later.

Right: Center fielder Jimmie Hall's rapid and dramatic fall-off left the Twins with a gaping hole in their lineup.

is truly declining and when it is simply a one-year aberration, especially at the young age of many of his players. Furthermore, Griffith did continue to add talent over the next couple of years, most notably second baseman Rod Carew.

Griffith also seemed to lose control over the team. The team bickered and fought with itself in nearly every possible permutation: coach versus coach, coach versus management, and player versus player. Until hiring Martin in 1969, Griffith was unwilling to vest in his managers the sort of authority necessary to truly manage a diverse group of stars with strong personalities. In the years after 1965 a combination of bad luck and ill-defined manager control thwarted the Twins from reprising their success. ∎

Notes

1. Doug Grow, Phone Interview, February 21, 2011.
2. Max Nichols, "Sam Mele: A Study in Pressure." *Sport*, April 1966. 81.
3. Bill Furlong. "The Feuding Twins: Inside a Team in Turmoil." *Sport*, April 1968. Rod Carew with Ira Berkow, *Carew*. (New York: Simon and Schuster, 1979) 82.
4. *Minneapolis Star Tribune*, July 21, 2007, C8.
5. Jon Kerr. Calvin, *Baseball's Last Dinosaur: An Authorized Biography*. (Dubuque, IA: William C. Brown Publishers, 1990) 78.
6. John Roseboro with Bill Libby. *Glory Days with the Dodgers and Other Days with Others*. (New York: Atheneum, 1978) 230.

Sources

Anderson, Dr. Wayne J. *Harmon Killebrew: Baseball's Superstar*. Salt Lake City: Deseret Book, 1971.

Armour, Mark L. and Daniel R. Levitt. *Paths to Glory: How Great Baseball Teams Got That Way*. Washington D.C.: Brassey's, 2003.

Carew, Rod with Ira Berkow. *Carew*. New York: Simon and Schuster, 1979.

Furlong, Bill. "The Feuding Twins: Inside a Team in Turmoil." *Sport*, April, 1968.

Golenback, Peter. *Wild, High and Tight: The Life and Death of Billy Martin*. New York: St. Martin's Press, 1994.

Jordan, Pat. "In a World of Windmills." *Sports Illustrated*, May 8, 1972.

Kerr, Jon. *Calvin: Baseball's Last Dinosaur*. Dubuque, IA: Wm. C. Brown, 1990.

Leggett, William. "A Wild Finale—and It's Boston." *Sports Illustrated*, October 9, 1967.

Nichols, Max. "The Kaat Organization." *Sport*, December, 1966.

———. "Sam Mele: A Study in Pressure." *Sport*, April, 1966.

Roseboro, John with Bill Libby. *Glory Days with the Dodgers and Other Days with Others*. New York: Atheneum, 1978.

Smith, Gary. "A Lingering Vestige Of Yesterday." *Sports Illustrated*, April 4, 1983.

Sporting News Baseball Guides. 1965 through 1970.

Sports Illustrated. "Minnesota Twins." April 18, 1966.

Urdahl, Dean. *Touching Base with Our Memories*. St. Cloud, MN: North Star Press of St. Cloud, 2001.

Williams, Jim. "Which Is the Real Jim Kaat." *All Star Sports*, August, 1968.

Zanger, Jack. *Major League Baseball*. 1965–1970. New York: Pocketbooks.

Felled By the Impossible

The 1967 Minnesota Twins

Mark Armour

On September 30, 1967, a Saturday afternoon, the Minnesota Twins played the first of a two-game season-ending series against the Red Sox at Boston's Fenway Park. The Twins led the Red Sox and the Tigers (who had to play two doubleheaders) by a single game. A Twins victory would eliminate the Red Sox, while the Tigers had to win either three or (if the Twins beat the Red Sox in both games) all four of their games against the Angels.

On the pitching mound for the Twins would be Jim Kaat, who had already posted a 7–0 record with a 1.57 ERA in 63 September innings. If he could win on the 30th, he would become just the second pitcher since 1946 (joining Whitey Ford) to win eight starts in a single month. The Red Sox would counter with Jose Santiago, making just his 11th start of the season. The Twins had 20-game-winner Dean Chance available on Sunday, but they had to like their chances to finish off Boston on Saturday. Of course, the season had been nothing if not unpredictable.

Heading in to the 1967 season many observers had conceded the pennant to the powerful Baltimore Orioles. After romping through the AL in 1966, the O's had summarily swept the Los Angeles Dodgers in the World Series. The club had a few middle-aged stars—Frank Robinson (30), Brooks Robinson (29) and Luis Aparicio (32)—who had shown no signs of slowing down. The rest of the starting lineup was in their early 20s, and Steve Barber, at 28, was the old man of a deep and talented pitching staff.

The toughest challenge, it was reasoned, would come from the Twins, who had won the pennant in 1965, finished second to the Orioles in 1966, and had as much front-line talent as any team in the league. The Twins were led by two star hitters—third baseman Harmon Killebrew, who had already won four home run titles, and right-fielder Tony Oliva, who had two batting crowns—along with a deep and flexible pitching staff.

The Twins regression in 1966—from 102 wins to 89—was completely due to a drop-off from their hitters. The team's offense dropped by 111 runs, while their pitchers allowed 19 fewer runs, more than the league wide average drop of 11 runs per team. While Killebrew (39 home runs, 110 RBI) and Oliva (.307, 25 home runs) were among the best hitters in the league, no other regular was any better than league average for his position. Among many setbacks, shortstop Zoilo Versalles, the league's MVP in 1965, dropped from 76 extra base hits to just 33 and provided very little offense from his leadoff spot. Meanwhile Jim Kaat won 25 games with a 2.75 ERA, and Mudcat Grant, Jim Perry, Dave Boswell, and Jim Merritt also provided solid starting pitching.

Right after the 1966 season, Twins manager Sam Mele parted ways with pitching coach Johnny Sain, an innovative thinker who got results from his pitchers but generally did not get along with his bosses. Sain demanded complete control over the pitching staff, a power his managers were usually reluctant to surrender. Jim Kaat in particular loved Sain, and in response to his mentor's dismissal wrote a critical open letter to the *Minneapolis Tribune*. The letter ran on page one, and said, among other things, "If I were ever in a position of general manager, I'd give Sain a 'name-your-own-figure' contract to handle my pitchers. (And, oh yes, I'd hire a manager that could take advantage of his talents.)" Not surprisingly, these comments did not sit well with Mele. Twins owner Calvin Griffith, who acted as his own general manager, spoke with Kaat and mostly seemed bewildered that Mele could not get along with his coaches.[1] Clearly the pressure was on Mele, and new pitching coach Early Wynn, to succeed in 1967.

Though the Twins had more pitching than hitting, this fact was largely misunderstood at the time due to the friendly hitting environment of Metropolitan Stadium. As an illustration, at the 1966 winter meetings the Twins traded Don Mincher and Jimmie Hall (likely their third and fourth best hitters), along with relief pitcher Pete Cimino, to the Angels for pitcher Dean Chance. After a brilliant 1964 season, Chance remained a good pitcher (12–17, 3.08 ERA in 1966), though not noticeably better than the five good starters the Twins already had.

Star left-hander Jim Kaat, shown here throwing his curveball, had a remarkable September, nearly carrying the Twins to the pennant.

To replace Mincher, Mele moved Killebrew to first base full-time (he had been playing there against left-handed pitchers), and returned Rich Rollins to full-time duty at third. To replace Hall, the Twins were counting on the return of Bob Allison from a broken hand, and were planning on playing the versatile Cesar Tovar in center field. With Earl Battey at catcher, the Twins hoped they could hit enough to make up for what they lost in the Angels trade.

On the mound, the Twins were set with Kaat, Chance, Grant, Boswell, and Merritt as starters, Jim Perry as the swingman, and Ron Kline and Al Worthington as the capable short relievers. It was a fine pitching staff, one of the best in the league.

When the season opened, the Twins played poorly for the first month. On May 15 Minnesota stood tied for eighth with an 11–15 record, 7½ games behind the first-place White Sox. They could take solace in being tied with the defending champion Orioles, but the White Sox and Tigers (just one and a half games out) were good teams who were threatening to leave other clubs behind. Although there were many culprits, the biggest disappointments were Battey, Oliva (.183 through May 20), Jim Kaat (1–6, with a 6.66 ERA through May), and Grant (who lost his first three starts and was battling a sore knee).

The one Twins player who started the season hitting well was Versalles, hitting over .350 in early May and briefly among the RBI leaders. Unfortunately, this success proved fleeting, and his average steadily plummeted for the next five months until it fell to .200 at the close of the season. Versalles stayed in the lineup all year and provided a steady drain on the offense with a dreadful 52 OPS+. American League MVP just two years earlier, the 27-year-old Versalles was finished as an effective major league player.

On the other side of the keystone, Griffith had been an early proponent for the promotion of Rod Carew. "Carew can do it all," said Griffith in March. "He can run, throw, and hit. He could be the American League All-Star second baseman if he sets his mind to it."[2] Pretty bold words about a 21-year-old fresh from the Carolina League. But Carew would fully justify Griffith's confidence, and would do so immediately. Carew's five hits on May 8 brought his average up over .300 for the first time, and he spent most of the summer among the league leaders. On June 15 his average reached .335, and he trailed only Al Kaline and Frank Robinson in the American League. It was therefore no surprise when Carew fulfilled Griffith's prediction and started that summer's All-Star game as a rookie.

The person most affected by the emergence of Carew was Cesar Tovar, who many observers felt would otherwise be the best all-around second baseman in the league. Tovar had won the job from Bernie Allen during the 1966 season, but with Carew on board Tovar was moved to center field to start the season. In the event, Tovar's versatility and the struggles or injuries of many of his teammates caused the club to move him around the diamond repeatedly throughout the next few seasons. By mid-May of 1967 he'd already seen action at six positions. This likely did not help Tovar's development, but he was a fine player, generally hitting at the top of the order and scoring 98 runs in 1967 (the third highest total in the league).

Adjusting to the team's slow start, Mele benched Battey in favor of Jerry Zimmerman, but the production from the catcher position remained inadequate. With Tovar moving to the infield to deal with slumps and injuries, Mele eventually played Ted Uhlaender full-time in center. He moved Jim Merritt into the rotation, turning away from Mudcat Grant. As for Kaat and Oliva, Mele kept playing them in hopes they would turn things around.

Meanwhile, the Twins managed to slog their way to .500 in mid-May and stay near that level for a few weeks. After a tough loss on June 8, when the Indians scored four runs in the ninth to win, 7–5, and drop the Twins to 25–25, Griffith fired Mele and replaced him with Cal Ermer, who had been managing their

Triple-A club in Denver. The winner of four pennants as a minor-league manager, the 43-year-old Ermer's major-league resume included a single game, in 1947, and a year as a coach with the Orioles in 1962. Griffith had expected the team to be contending for the pennant, not floundering in sixth place. After splitting their first 16 games under Ermer, the team got hot in late June and was back in contention by the All-Star break.

Table 1. AL Standings, July 10, 1967

Chicago	47–33	—
Detroit	45–35	2.0
Minnesota	45–36	2.5
California	45–40	4.5
Boston	41–39	6.0

With the Orioles nine games back, it looked to have turned into a three-team race, as no one expected either the Angels or Red Sox to be able to hang with the front runners.

One Minnesota player who revived at about the time of the Mele firing was Jim Kaat, who had publicly called out his manager the previous winter. Coincidence or not, Kaat had been 1–7 with a 6.00 ERA at the time of the switch, but won his first three

Jim "Mudcat" Grant was a staff ace on Minnesota's pennant winner in 1965, but he struggled in 1967.

starts and pitched as well as ever under Ermer. His victory on June 10 was the 100th of his career but came after nine winless starts. "There never has been any bad feeling of any kind between Sam and myself this year," Kaat said. Either way, with Chance, Boswell, Merritt and Perry, the Twins had an excellent starting staff the rest of the season.

The biggest change for Harmon Killebrew in 1967 was that the club stopped moving him around the diamond to accommodate other players. With Mincher traded, Killebrew was a full-time first baseman for the first time in his career, and he responded with an excellent season, even by his lofty standards. It took him a few weeks to find his power stroke, but he hit 12 home runs in June on his way to 44, his sixth season over 40, and he coaxed a league leading 131 walks. Also important was the comeback of Bob Allison, after his lost season in 1966. Allison hit 24 home runs and provided valuable production hitting fifth behind Killebrew and Oliva. "This club definitely has the feeling we had in 1965," said Killebrew.[3]

As quick as the Twins had gotten hot, they lost six in a row in mid-July, just as the Red Sox were winning 10 straight and getting into the thick of the race. At the end of July, the Twins were five games back and looking up at Chicago, Boston, and Detroit.

Tony Oliva was a remarkably consistent ballplayer over his first eight major-league seasons, but he never started slower than he did in 1967. Although Oliva's hitting had steadily improved after his poor start, his average was still just .256 at the end of July. Fortunately, no one did more during the pennant race than Oliva, as he hit .333 the last two months with 6 home runs and 18 doubles.

Although Mele made changes to his lineup and rotation, Griffith did not make any moves to fix the holes on his club. The Red Sox picked up Jerry Adair, Gary Bell, and Elston Howard, all quality veterans who played a large role in the team's pennant drive, and then signed Ken Harrelson as a reaction to Tony Conigliaro's August eye injury. The White Sox acquired Don McMahon, Ken Boyer, and Rocky Colavito, and all were given important roles. The Tigers obtained veteran Eddie Mathews, and he played a key role down the stretch at both third and first base. With the closeness of the race and at least two poor hitters in the lineup every day (at shortstop and catcher), the Twins could have used another bat.

In early August, the White Sox went through their first rough patch of the season, and relinquished first place after two months at the top, the longest any team would hold the lead that season. All of the contenders went through a bad stretch at one point during the season, and as August ended it was difficult to separate the first four teams.

Table 2. AL Standings, August 31, 1967

Boston	76–59	—
Minnesota	74–58	0.5
Detroit	74–59	1.0
Chicago	73–59	1.5

The standings for every day the rest of the season were a slight variation of the above, with the teams dropping from first to third or rising from fourth to second regularly. No first place team would lead by more than a single game on any day hereafter. On September 6, there was a virtual four-way tie at the top.

The Twins held at least a share of the lead from September 2 through September 14, and looked to be the favorite when they went to Chicago to play three games. They lost all three, including a crushing defeat on the 16th when Dean Chance entered the ninth with a six-hitter but allowed three hits and his own error and ultimately lost the game 5–4. Just like that, the Twins were tied for third place. Never fear: a four-game sweep in Kansas City and they were back on top with eight games to go.

The Twins' outstanding pitching continued in September, with their third straight month with an ERA under 3.00. For the season, the team finished at 3.14, second best in the league despite playing in a hitter's park. The reason the Twins did not run away with the pennant was their imbalanced offense, a problem which only grew worse in the final month. In September, Killebrew, Oliva, and Allison hit .317 with 17 home runs. The rest of the team hit .216 with four round trippers. Still, a pennant was within reach.

It is interesting to note how Ermer used his pitchers in September. Beginning on September 9, the day after their final doubleheader, he used Kaat-Boswell-Chance-Merritt in rotation four straight times. After Kaat's seventh consecutive September victory on the 26th gave the Twins a one-game lead with three to play, Ermer switched up and went with Chance on two days rest on Wednesday the 27th. Dave Boswell, who was passed over, had not pitched well in his previous start but had three complete game victories in September. Chance, who had won his 20th game on Sunday, could not get through the fourth on Wednesday, and the Twins dropped the game, 5–1. This was huge, but then again, weren't they all?

In the latter stages of this great pennant race, the Red Sox had become the dominant story. Everyone loves an underdog, and while the other contenders had been good teams for several years the Red Sox had finished ninth in 1966 and had not really been in a pennant race since 1950. It was the Red Sox, and their star Carl Yastrzemski, who were featured on the cover of *Life* and *Newsweek* that September. Their loss of local favorite Tony Conigliaro to a brutal eye injury in August only heightened the drama of their story.

The Red Sox and Twins would have two days off to prepare for their two-game series, while the Tigers and Angels were rained out on both Thursday and Friday, necessitating consecutive doubleheaders over the weekend. The White Sox, who had led the race for more days than any other team, finally dropped out with their loss on Friday night. The remaining three teams all had a shot at winning the league outright.

Table 3. AL Standings, September, 29, 1967

Minnesota	91–69	—
Detroit	89–69	1.0
Boston	90–70	1.0

Though the final games would be played in Boston, the two days off allowed Ermer to pitch Kaat (with seven September wins) and Chance (20–13, 2.62 ERA,

Despite being 38-years-old, relief ace Al Worthington led the 1967 Twins in games pitched and saves.

18 complete games) on their regular three days of rest. Though just 28-years-old, Kaat had been a dependable workhorse for many years, averaging 17 wins since 1962, including 25 in 1966. For good measure, he had already won five Gold Gloves, and was one of the game's top hitting pitchers (nine home runs in the past six seasons). He was the man the Twins wanted on the mound.

As it happened, Kaat got through the first two innings, and led 1–0 heading into the bottom of the third. While striking out opposing pitcher Jose Santiago to lead off the inning, Kaat felt a "pop" in his elbow and had to leave the game a few pitchers later, a game-changing break for the Red Sox. After throwing a heroic 66 innings over 30 September days, with a 1.51 ERA for the month, Kaat was done. A succession of normally excellent Twins pitchers—Perry, Ron Kline, and Merritt—failed to shut down the home team, and Killebrew's 44th home run in the ninth was not enough as the Twins fell, 6–4.

Heading into Sunday, the Twins and Red Sox were tied, while the Tigers were a half game back with a doubleheader to play. If the Tigers swept, they would tie the winner of the game in Boston, necessitating a three-game playoff series beginning the next day. The Fenway match up featured two 20-game winners—Dean Chance and Boston's Jim Lonborg, both of whom had pitched Wednesday on two days rest and lost. The Twins seemed to have the pitching advantage—Chance had been 4–1 with a 1.58 ERA against

the Red Sox, including a five-inning perfect game, while Lonborg had gone 0–3, 6.75 against the Twins.

The Twins scratched out unearned runs in the first and third innings, and led 2–0 after five. Chance had scattered four hits and looked to be cruising. Leading off the sixth, Lonborg dropped a perfect bunt down the third base line to reach first. Singles by Jerry Adair, Dalton Jones, and Yastrzemski tied the score, and the go-ahead run scored on a ground ball to Versalles that the shortstop elected to throw home rather than to second base to try for the double play.

Al Worthington came in and threw two wild pitches, Killebrew contributed an error, and suddenly it was 5–2, Boston. The Twins managed a run in the eighth, but lost the game and the pennant shortly thereafter. In Detroit, the Tigers dropped the second game of their twin bill, giving the Red Sox their miracle pennant.

Forty-five years later, this remains one of baseball greatest and most historic pennant races. Many books have been written about the season, most focused on the winning Red Sox. Looking back, it is obvious that none of the contenders was a great club. The Red Sox winning percentage was the lowest ever for an American League champion prior to divisional play. Each of the teams had notable flaws, and the three teams that fell short could point to a game or two that should have been won and could have made a difference. For the Twins, Kaat's injury on September 30 is the most common lament.

On October 1 the Twins boarded an airplane which took them back to Minneapolis and 1,200 waiting fans. Cal Ermer promised the gathered faithful a pennant in 1968. "We've got to give Boston credit," said Kaat, "but I think the best team and the best fans will be watching the Series on television."[4] ■

Notes

1. Max Nichols, "Sain's Exit Puts Mele on Win-or-Else' Spot," *The Sporting News*, October 22, 1966, 15.
2. Max Nichols, "Rookie Rod Carew Stakes Out Claim To Twin Keystone," *The Sporting News*, March 25, 1967, 27.
3. Max Nichols, "Allison Regains Hot Touch With Stick— Harvest for Twins," *The Sporting News*, August 5, 1967, 9.
4. "1,200 Greet Twins, Hear Ermer Promise 1968 Flag," *The Sporting News*, October 14, 1967, 27.

Bob Allison loses an argument to umpire Emmett Ashford after being called out trying to steal second base.

Top 50 Players In Minnesota Twins History

Aaron Gleeman

When the Senators moved from Washington to Minnesota in 1961 the roster that became the Twins included an incredible combination of young, established stars and MLB-ready prospects. Harmon Killebrew was already one of baseball's elite sluggers at age 24, catcher Earl Battey and right fielder Bob Allison were among their respective positions' top players at age 26, and the rotation had a 27-year-old ace in Camilo Pascual.

That alone would have been an impressive collection of 27-and-under talent, but those four building-block players were also joined by 21-year-old rookie shortstop Zoilo Versalles and 22-year-old southpaw Jim Kaat. Of the 13 players to log at least 200 plate appearances or 75 innings for that first Twins team in 1961 six of them—Killebrew, Pascual, Battey, Allison, Kaat, and Versalles—went on to become among the 25 best players in Twins history.

One inner-circle Hall of Famer and five top-25 players in team history is one heck of a foundation for a franchise making a new start, but remarkably the Twins have continued to consistently stock the roster with star players ever since. Tony Oliva joined the mix in the Twins' second season, followed by Jim Perry in 1963, Cesar Tovar in 1965, and Rod Carew in 1967. And it didn't stop when the 1960s did.

In fact, at no point since coming to Minnesota in 1961 have the Twins gone more than five seasons without integrating at least one of the top 25 players in team history. Bert Blyleven, Dave Goltz, and Roy Smalley arrived in the 1970s, followed by Kent Hrbek, Gary Gaetti, Frank Viola, Kirby Puckett, and Rick Aguilera in the 1980s, Chuck Knoblauch, Brad Radke, Torii Hunter, and Corey Koskie in the 1990s, and Johan Santana, Michael Cuddyer, Justin Morneau, Joe Nathan, and Joe Mauer in the early 2000s.

Not only is the steady stream of top-level talent unique, the Twins' overall level of talent is well beyond the norm for a team with a relatively brief history. In their five decades of existence the Twins have had five Most Valuable Player (MVP) winners and three Cy Young Award winners (including Johan Santana, who

won twice), and sabermetrically speaking their star talent is immense.

Wins Above Replacement (WAR) measures a player's all-around contributions to determine how many runs—and in turn, wins—he was worth compared to a replacement-level player at the same position. For instance, during his MVP-winning 2009 season Mauer led the league among non-pitchers with 7.5 WAR, meaning he provided the Twins with nearly eight more wins than a replacement-level catcher—say one of the Buteras, either Sal or Drew—would have produced.

And to get a sense for what exactly a hypothetical "replacement-level player" looks like, consider that Denny Hocking, Danny Thompson, Luis Rivas, Pedro Munoz, and Al Newman have the most plate appearances in Twins history among players with a negative WAR.

Since moving to Minnesota the Twins have had seven different players accumulate at least 40 Wins Above Replacement while with the team. Of the nine other American League teams that were around in 1961, only the Yankees have more 40-WAR players during that time.

Players with 40+ WAR from 1961–2011

Yankees	11
Twins	7
Red Sox	7
Tigers	6
Orioles	5
White Sox	3
Indians	3
Angels	3
Royals	3
Rangers	2

Source: Baseball-Reference.com

When only the Yankees have produced more superstars during a 50-year period, that's a pretty amazing distinction. Those seven 40-plus WAR players are Carew, Killebrew, Puckett, Oliva, Mauer, Blyleven, and

Radke. And all seven of them were originally signed or drafted by the Twins (or, as in Killebrew's case, the Senators).

Here's the same list, but with 20+ WAR players

Yankees	27
Red Sox	24
Twins	20
Orioles	20
Royals	18
Tigers	17
Angels	17
Indians	17
Rangers	14
White Sox	13

Source: Baseball-Reference.com

Whether you focus on superstars or above-average regulars, the Twins come out looking very good, with only the Yankees and Red Sox holding an advantage in churning out sustained talent.

WAR isn't perfect, of course, but it provides a great framework for analysis that can be supplemented further with other measures both objective and subjective, such as Value Over Replacement Player (VORP), Win Shares, postseason performance, peak value, perceived impact, and tenure with the team.

How do you compare, say, Randy Bush's fairly modest contributions during 12 years with the Twins to Jack Morris's massive contribution during his one season in Minnesota? I've spent the past several years doing just that at my blog, *AaronGleeman.com*, and what follows is my sabermetric ranking of the top 50 players in Twins history.

50. Randy Bush
49. Rich Rollins
48. Francisco Liriano
47. John Castino
46. Denard Span

Bush was never flashy and more often than not filled a part-time role for manager Tom Kelly, but he spent a dozen seasons in Minnesota—only eight guys have played more games in a Twins uniform—and he was one of seven players on both the 1987 and 1991 championship teams. He earns a spot on this list, along with other longtime contributors, rather than stars like Morris or Chili Davis who made one- and two-year impacts.

Ranking active players like Liriano and Span alongside long-retired players like Castino and Rollins can be

Third baseman John Castino tied for the AL Rookie of the Year Award in 1979, but his career was cut short by chronic back problems.

difficult because their cumulative value is always changing and it's tough to put their impact into proper context without being able to look back. I've been somewhat conservative with active players throughout this list.

45. Jason Kubel
44. Scott Erickson
43. Eric Milton
42. Jimmie Hall
41. Steve Braun

Erickson's career got off to one of the fastest starts in Twins history, but he went from 23-year-old ace on a championship team and Cy Young runner-up to winning a total of just 61 games in Minnesota. His overall Twins numbers (979 innings, 61 wins, 104 adjusted ERA+) are nearly identical to Milton's (987 innings, 57 wins, 101 adjusted ERA+) and they also both threw no-hitters, but Erickson went 20-36 with a 5.40 ERA in his final three Twins seasons. [Note that the "+" after a statistic normalizes that statistic for the ballpark and offensive context of the season. A value of 100 is league average; higher is better, so in the context of ERA a value above 100 reflects an ERA below league average.]

Hall flamed out quickly, but his impact on the Twins was significant. He packed 98 homers into just four seasons in Minnesota despite playing at a time when big offensive numbers were rare, and played a passable center field while doing so. Braun is similarly underrepresented in team lore, but ranks sixth in

Twins history with a .376 on-base percentage and his raw numbers are underrated by the low-scoring 1970s.

40. Dave Boswell
39. Matt Lawton
38. Greg Gagne
37. Al Worthington
36. Butch Wynegar

In many ways Lawton, along with Radke, was the bridge from the 1987 and 1991 teams to the current era, and because of that, his contributions are often lost in the Twins' ineptitude during that time, but his .379 OBP is the fifth-best in team history and he also ranks eighth in steals.

Gagne's hitting numbers look puny compared to modern shortstops, but he had plus power for the position in the 1980s and was fantastic defensively. Similarly, Worthington was the Twins' first of many standout closers and because of the way relievers were used in the 1960s his save totals are underwhelming, but he actually led the league with 18 saves in 1968 and had the second-most saves in baseball 1964–1968.

Wynegar was Mauer before there was a Mauer, tearing through the minor leagues to debut at age 20. He made the All-Star team in each of his first two

COURTESY MINNESOTA TWINS

Outfielder Shane Mack was a mainstay of the Twins in the early 1990s and a key member of the 1991 World Series team.

seasons, but unfortunately peaked by 22, was traded to the Yankees at 26, and retired at 32.

35. Jacque Jones
34. Scott Baker
33. Kevin Tapani
32. Tom Brunansky
31. Larry Hisle

Brunansky broke in alongside fellow rookies Hrbek and Gaetti in 1982 and his walks-and-power approach would have been much more appreciated by modern analysis that doesn't focus on batting average. Dwight Evans, Eddie Murray, and Dave Winfield were the only AL hitters with more homers than Brunansky 1982–1987, and he smacked the ninth-most homers in Twins history before being traded to the Cardinals for Tommy Herr.

Hisle's career with the Twins was short and sweet, with 662 games spread over five seasons, yet he's all over the team leaderboard. Hisle ranks among the top 20 in batting average, slugging percentage, on-base percentage, homers, steals, and RBIs, with a top-10 mark in adjusted OPS+, and his 1977 is one of the top years by any outfielder in Twins history. And all that came in low-offense eras.

30. Eddie Guardado
29. Michael Cuddyer
28. Brian Harper
27. Shane Mack
26. Cesar Tovar

Guardado went from starter to left-handed specialist to closer, and then Everyday Eddie returned to the Twins for a second go-around as a middle reliever in 2008, finishing with the most appearances and third-most saves in team history.

Hitting was Harper's specialty, as he batted .306 for the Twins and was arguably the best offensive catcher in the league 1989–1993, and the negative perception of his defense behind the plate isn't fully supported by numbers. Teams ran on Harper a ton, but he threw out 31 percent of attempted basestealers for his career and often topped his backups (such as Tim Laudner) in throw-out rate.

A tremendous athlete who covered tons of ground wherever the Twins put him in the outfield, Mack hit for big batting averages with great speed and had overlooked power. Among all MLB outfielders to play at least 600 games 1990–1994, only Barry Bonds, Ken Griffey Jr., Rickey Henderson, and David Justice had a better OPS than Mack, and his .854 mark with the Twins ranks fourth in team history.

While most fans have come to think of a "utility man" as someone like Denny Hocking or Nick Punto who's a capable backup at multiple spots, Tovar was more like an everyday player who just didn't know where he was going to play on a given day. And on September 22, 1968, he played literally everywhere in the same game.

25. Zoilo Versalles
24. Gary Gaetti
23. Camilo Pascual
22. Dave Goltz
21. Rick Aguilera

In recent years it has become fashionable to suggest that sabermetric analysis wouldn't agree with Versalles winning the MVP in 1965, but one of the hallmarks of good sabermetrics is being able to adjust raw numbers for historical context, and once you do that, Zoilo

COURTESY MINNESOTA TWINS

Manitoba native Corey Koskie anchored third base during the Twins streak of division championships in the early 2000s. His career was prematurely cut short by post-concussion syndrome.

led the league in WAR and VORP. Versalles' career fizzled shortly after the MVP campaign, but his place in Twins history is only amplified by a deeper look at the numbers.

More than any other player, Pascual's standing on this list suffers because his pre-1961 work with the Senators isn't included. He debuted at age 20 and bounced back from some early rough patches to post ERAs of 3.15, 2.64, and 3.03 in his final three seasons in Washington, finishing with 14.4 WAR for the Senators and 16.1 WAR with the Twins. If combined, he'd likely rank in the top 10. Little Potato was a helluva pitcher and his .607 winning percentage ranked first in Twins history until Santana came around.

Aguilera lost his spot atop the Twins' all-time saves list in mid-2011, but it's worth noting that his saves were longer and more difficult than Joe Nathan's. Aguilera inherited four times as many runners as did Nathan and recorded 55 more outs in his 254 saves than Nathan did in his first 254.

20. Earl Battey
19. Corey Koskie
18. Joe Nathan
17. Roy Smalley
16. Justin Morneau

Battey ranked among the AL's top five catchers in VORP during each of his six full seasons with the Twins, but as good as his bat was, it couldn't compete with his amazing arm. Battey allowed just 226 steals in 6,700 innings for the Twins despite playing in the run-heavy 1960s, throwing out 40 percent of attempted basestealers. He also led the AL in pickoffs four times, including 15 in 1962. That season Battey allowed only 34 steals and picked off or threw out 42 runners.

Koskie turned himself into a quality fielder at third after initially being banished to the outfield by manager Tom Kelly, and his combination of power and patience at the plate added up to an adjusted OPS+ of 115 that ranks ninth in Twins history among hitters with at least 3,000 plate appearances. Gaetti generally gets the nod when picking the best third baseman in Twins history, but a deeper look at the numbers suggests Koskie is a deserving pick.

Smalley was acquired from the Rangers for Blyleven and then, like Bert, returned to the Twins for a second go-around late in his career. His spot on this list is largely due to the six-season run he had as their starting shortstop 1976–1981. During that time he logged 3,330 plate appearances with a 104 adjusted OPS that led all MLB shortstops, with only Garry Templeton

(104), Dave Concepcion (101), and Robin Yount (100) also above 100.

15. Jim Perry
14. Frank Viola
13. Torii Hunter
12. Jim Kaat
11. Chuck Knoblauch

Advanced defensive metrics aren't nearly as kind to Hunter as his nine Gold Glove awards, and by the time he left the Twins his range and instincts had certainly diminished, but at his peak no center fielder was more spectacular and fearless. And he could hit a little, too, ranking among the Twins' top 10 in homers, doubles, runs, RBIs, and hits. If you're convinced that Hunter's glove was truly spectacular rather than merely very good, he'd move up a couple spots.

Knoblauch left the Twins on horrible terms and remains hated by most fans, but during his seven seasons in Minnesota he ranked second among all MLB second basemen in WAR, between Craig Biggio and Roberto Alomar. His 1996 season—in which Knoblauch hit .341 with a .448 OBP and .517 slugging percentage while scoring 140 runs—is the second-highest WAR total in team history behind Carew hitting .388 and winning the MVP in 1977. Mauer (.403), Carew (.393), Knoblauch (.391), and Killebrew (.383) are the only Twins hitters with an OBP above .380 over their career with the Twins.

10. Bob Allison
9. Brad Radke
8. Kent Hrbek
7. Johan Santana
6. Joe Mauer

Radke was never perceived as a star, but better support from the lineup, defense, and bullpen on those awful 1990s teams would have upped his win totals enough to potentially change that. WAR cares about his performance rather than his win-loss record—or a raw ERA that was inflated by one of the highest offensive eras ever—and Radke joins Blyleven and Santana as the only pitchers in Twins history to top 5.0 WAR in at least three seasons.

Santana is the only pitcher in Twins history with multiple Cy Young awards, winning the honor in 2004 and 2006, and he deserved a third in 2005. That year Santana led the league in strikeouts, opponents' batting average, and adjusted ERA +, yet Bartolo Colon won the award despite throwing 9 fewer innings with an ERA that was 0.61 runs higher. Santana is the all-time Twins leader in winning percentage, adjusted ERA +, strikeouts per nine innings, and strikeout-to-walk ratio.

Believe it or not, that number six ranking is conservative for Mauer. Not only did he lead the AL in WAR among non-pitchers during his MVP season in 2009, he also had the league's top WAR in 2008 and finished second in 2006. Among position players

Left-hander Jim Kaat, seen here chatting with some young fans, anchored Minnesota's rotation throughout the 1960s, topped by a league-leading 25 wins and 304 2/3 innings pitched in 1966.

Minnesota native Kent Hrbek, here celebrating the 1987 World Series championship, played 14 years for the Twins, anchoring first base.

COURTESY MINNESOTA TWINS

Brad Radke spent his entire 12 year career with the Twins and was a rotation anchor of the Twins division winning teams of the early 2000s.

COURTESY MINNESOTA TWINS

Hall of Fame pitcher Bert Blyleven returned to the Twins in the late 1980s and helped lead the team to the 1987 World Series championship.

Mauer already has three of the top dozen single-season WAR totals in Twins history, along with three batting titles, three Gold Glove awards, and an MVP.

> 5. Bert Blyleven
> 4. Tony Oliva
> 3. Kirby Puckett
> 2. Rod Carew
> 1. Harmon Killebrew

Blyleven played nearly half of his Hall of Fame career elsewhere, but still rates as the best pitcher in Twins history. He threw 325 innings with a 2.52 ERA in 1973 for the team's best single-season WAR among pitchers and also holds the fourth, ninth, and 15th spots on that list. He's the only pitcher to crack 45 WAR for his Twins career and also leads in complete games, shutouts, and strikeouts.

When it comes to choosing the greatest player in Twins history it's tough to go wrong. Do you pick a Gold Glove center fielder with a .318 batting average and unforgettable postseason heroics? Or how about a .334-hitting second baseman with seven batting titles and an MVP award? Or maybe an MVP-winning, five-time home run leader who ranked among the AL's top 10 in OPS for 10 of his 12 seasons in Minnesota?

Puckett is the clear-cut number three choice based on WAR, VORP, Win Shares, and various other metrics, although certainly it would have been a different story had his career not been cut short coming off one of his best seasons at age 35. There's no shame in finishing behind two of the greatest hitters in baseball history, of course, and it's possible that advanced defensive metrics underrate Puckett's work in center field somewhat compared to his collection of Gold Gloves and sterling reputation.

Ultimately the choice between Carew and Killebrew is a toss-up. Their skills couldn't have been any more different, but they each contributed massive value on a consistent and sustained basis. Carew was a second baseman for most of his career in Minnesota before shifting to first and a line-drive machine with great speed and bat control who rarely struck out but with only limited power. Killebrew was one of the greatest sluggers of all time and drew walks in bunches to go along with his high strikeout totals as a corner infielder.

Carew had a .334 batting average for his Twins career, while Killebrew hit .260, yet in terms of overall production Killebrew had a .901 OPS compared to an .841 OPS for Carew. Carew's speed cancels out some of that OPS difference and he also had the edge defen-

Many consider Harmon Killebrew, seen here blasting one of his 573 home runs, the greatest player in Minnesota Twins history.

sively, although the size of that gap draws mixed opinions. Killebrew played 300 more games and logged 1,000 more plate appearances for the Twins, which was a big factor in my giving him the ever-so-slight nod.

Killebrew is the only player in Twins history to hit 40 homers in a season … and he did it seven times (plus one more when the team was in Washington). He also drew 100 walks seven times, while Allison is the only other Twins hitter to do it even once. He hit 475 homers in a Twins uniform, while no one else has 300. He drew 1,321 walks and no one else has 850. And he did all that mashing in the low-scoring 1960s and 1970s, producing an adjusted OPS+ of 148 that stands atop the Twins' leader board ahead of Carew (137), Mauer (133), Oliva (131), Allison (130), Hrbek (128), and Puckett (124). In their fifty year plus history the Twins have turned out more than their fair share of talent, in particular among position players. While only one Hall of Fame pitcher spent an important portion of his career with the team, in Puckett, Carew and Killebrew the Twins could boast three of the best players of their eras, each of whom spent all, or at least the bulk, of his career in Minnesota. ∎

The Legacy of Twins Legends

Killebrew, Carew, Puckett, and Mauer

Charlie Beattie

Since the Washington Senators moved to Minnesota in 1961, the team has boasted many stars, including several of the greatest players in the game. Minnesotans have embraced these players differently, highlighting the changing nature of our complicated relationship with our sports heroes.

The team that Calvin Griffith moved to Minnesota featured a player who was rapidly becoming the most feared hitter in the league, Harmon Killebrew. Killebrew's numbers, and their place in the history of the Twins/Senators franchise, are hardly a well-kept secret. He either leads or places second in nearly every statistical category. The quiet, unassuming Killebrew's best qualities were thrust back into the spotlight in May 2011 after his passing due to complications of esophageal cancer. Lauded throughout his career as a "team guy," he proved this label correct even in death, as his funeral serendipitously coincided with a rare Twins interleague trip to Arizona, allowing the front office staff and current players, many of whom were affected both personally and professionally, to attend. Current Twins star Joe Mauer called Killebrew "a family member," right fielder Michael Cuddyer called him "the most genuine person he ever met," and team president Dave St. Peter called him the most important player ever to don a Twins uniform.[1] Bert Blyleven, in his eulogy, spoke of Killebrew telling players to autograph baseballs with a legible signature, the better for young fans to read whose name they had.

Famously scooped up by the Nationals out of his Idaho home at the age of 17 in 1954, as a "Bonus Baby" signing, Killebrew was forced to stay on the Nationals' active roster for at least two seasons, and he rarely saw the field. After just 11 home runs in his first five seasons (with the final three spent more in the minors than the majors), Killebrew busted out in 1959, slugging 42 and leading the American League. It was just in time for *Sports Illustrated* to brand him the living embodiment of Joe Hardy (the Senators hero in *Damn Yankees*), but too late to save the Senators, who were destined to move west. So, while Washington fans saw just a glimpse of his potential, he arrived in Minnesota a finished product, on and off the field. A quiet, family-oriented man, Killebrew was the perfect ambassador for baseball in the Midwest. Killebrew's early life is straight out of "All-American Boy" cliché. He had reportedly gained his strength by lifting 95-pound milk cans while working on his father's farm. He lettered in three different sports and was a high school All-American quarterback. His first wife, Elaine (the two were married from 1955 to 1985) was his high-school sweetheart.

Assigned to cover a man whose controversial side seemingly didn't exist, the media embarked on a career-long quest to attach idiosyncrasies where there were none. When *Sports Illustrated* writer Barbara Heilman asked him if he had any "curious" habits during a 1963 interview, Killebrew replied, "Doing the dishes, I guess."[2] Nicknames were applied liberally, yet none seemed to capture the man. "Hammerin' Harmon," "Harmin' Harmon," and "Bombin' Harmon" were all attempted, as well as the mildly ridiculous (yet oddly fitting) "Charmin' Harmon." Early in his career, *St. Paul Pioneer Press* columnist Arno Goethel tried the long-winded "Bashful Basher from Power Alley,"[3] but the only nickname that stuck was perhaps the least flattering of all: "Killer."

After Killebrew's death, Bob Nightengale of *USA Today* called the nickname "the most unsuitable nickname in sports."[4] On a personal level this is true, but of course the moniker had more to do with his ability to destroy a baseball. For a franchise that had long made its mark as one of the least powerful teams in the league, the '60s Twins boasted a lineup of thumpers. As he led the Twins to success in the 1960s, the quiet unassuming Killebrew was embraced as one of their own by his new hometown.

Rod Carew may have been the greatest pure hitter to put on a Twins uniform. His career average of .334 as a Twin (.328 over his entire career) is 11 points higher than Joe Mauer's and 16 ahead of Kirby Puckett. Twice he flirted with .400 deep into the season. In 1977, Ted Williams threw his support behind Carew becoming the first man since the Splendid Splinter to eclipse the magical mark, if only so reporters would "stop asking [Williams] if it could be done again."[5] Nevertheless, despite his electric ability, as further evidenced by his 17 career steals of home, Carew's adoration from the public never reached the heights of Killebrew, Puckett, or Mauer.

By the 1970s, the relationship between the players and owners was changing. Players were lobbying for greater employment freedom, which they would gain by the middle of the decade, while baseball's owners were desperately clinging to the last vestiges of their absolute power over the game's finances. Though owner Calvin Griffith's cheapness angered the public, players like Carew did not escape the notion that while owners may be tyrannical, the players were becoming increasingly greedy.

The sad reality of Carew's Twins' career is that it was played out in nearly uninhabited stadiums. In 1974, the season in which Rod made his first (albeit short-lived) charge at the .400 mark, the Twins drew just 662,401 fans, an average of fewer than 9,000 per game. Few years after their division titles were significantly better. Only in 1977, when Carew had a big season, and in 1979, the year after Carew left and the team stayed in contention until late in the season, did the Twins top one million fans during the 1970s.

Though Carew was not intentionally an unpleasant person, his public persona did him no favors with the few fans that did come to see him play. In his autobiography, *Carew*, he describes himself as a player who was "moody, intense, lonely, insecure, quick to anger."[6] He further writes that his desire to "jump the club" and quit nearly overcame him several times throughout his playing days, often for what could be described as the mildest of slights. Though the knowledge of Carew's impoverished upbringing in Panama by an emotionally abusive, distant, and often absent father might go a long way towards explaining Carew's insecurities, his autobiography would not be published until 1979, after his acrimonious departure from Griffith's Twins, leaving fans without many of the vital details to understand their star.

The most notable of Carew and Griffith's many battles was their last, which destroyed their relationship (later rehabilitated) and fostered Carew's exit to California. After many seasons of contract disputes, in which Griffith admitted to Carew that he was underpaid yet refused to raise his salary, Griffith gave an (admittedly drunken) speech to a rural Minnesota Lions club in 1978 in which he called Carew a "damn fool"[7] for signing a contract that paid him less than he could make elsewhere. He also claimed that he was

Harmon Killebrew, one of the most popular players in Minnesota sports history, hitting his 500th home run versus the Baltimore Orioles at Metropolitan Stadium.

glad he moved to Minnesota because it had "only 15,000 black people,"[8] while claiming that black fans didn't come to ballgames. An incensed Carew responded by branding Griffith a "bigot" and refusing to be "another slave on his plantation."[9] He was traded to the California Angels in the ensuing offseason.

Carew's accomplishments did not entirely escape the consciousness of Twins fans. Though he was overshadowed by Killebrew in their overlapping playing days, forced to play the singles-hitting second fiddle to Harmon's power show, Carew had the attention of the baseball world thrust upon him during his most serious challenge to the .400 mark, in 1977. With *Time* magazine featuring his pursuit and Ted Williams offering his support, fans took notice, especially on June 26. Entering the game with a .396 average and, in front of a crowd of 46,463 clad in Twins T-shirts with his number 29 on the back (the stadium giveaway that day), Carew went 4-for-5 and paced the team to a 19–12 drubbing of the White Sox. With the scoreboard detailing his exact batting average after each hit (his last hit put his batting average at .403), the crowd showered him with four separate standing ovations, the last of which lasted until Carew finally doffed his cap in recognition from first base. Carew recognized the magnitude of the moment in his autobiography, stating, "I had goose bumps, and I kept thinking that the fans had finally accepted me, that they'd finally come over on my side."[10] Years later, Twins broadcaster Dick Bremer summed up the moment well: "It was the first public acknowledgement that this guy was the best hitter [the fans] were ever going to see."[11]

It was the next Twins superstar, however, that Bremer labeled "the most electrifying player in Twins history."[12] Few who watched center fielder Kirby Puckett regularly would disagree. Puckett was the first

The best player on the Twins during the 1970s, Carew led the league in batting average seven times. He electrified the Twin Cities in 1977 as he pursued a possible .400 season.

superstar in the team's Metrodome era and the catalyst for their only two world championship teams. Flashy, brash, and highly quotable, he was the perfect combination of talent and personality to lead the franchise into the era of 24-hour sports television, and his madcap style of hitting and defense was made for fans both in the ballpark and on the small screen.

Puckett started his professional career relatively late, as he was 22 when drafted out of Bradley University in 1982 and 24 when he debuted in the majors in 1984.Glaucoma robbed Puckett of his playing ability in 1996, but he was already 36 when forced into retirement, and he had reached the 200-hit mark just once after his 30th birthday. In between, he astounded fans with his exploits. Puckett had four hits in his major league debut and his .318 career batting average at the time of his retirement was one of the ten best among AL righties. Moreover, he was the rare great offensive player who may be better remembered for his defense. The elastic centerfield fence was his personal jungle gym for eleven years. In recognition of his stellar career, the Hall of Fame voters elected him into the Hall on the first ballot.

Puckett would be a Minnesota legend even if he had played just one game in a Twins uniform, provided that game was Game Six of the 1991 World Series. Postseason legends are measured lyrically, and Puckett's Game Six was one of the finest offensive and defensive solo acts in World Series history. Puckett was 3-for-18 entering the game, but finished it a double short of the cycle, and of course extended the series with his eleventh inning home run off Charlie Leibrandt. In true Puckett fashion, however, his fielding in the game may

be more famous. His third-inning robbery of Atlanta's Ron Gant is still a World Series highlight-reel must 20 years later. As Tim Kurkjian put it, "It was the kind of performance that elevates a player to legendary status."[13]

What amplifies Puckett's eternally shining star is not the performance itself, but the details that surround it. First of all, Puckett essentially predicted the outcome. Before the game, in what has now become an oft-retold story, Puckett sauntered into the clubhouse and told his teammates to "get on his back" so he could "carry them." Perhaps less remembered is Puckett's second prediction of the night. After Puckett's death in 2006, Terry Crowley (the Twins hitting coach in 1991) shared a story—possibly apocryphal—that Puckett, when Bobby Cox visited the mound before Puckett's fateful eleventh inning at-bat, turned to Crowley and said "If they leave this guy in the game, the game is over."[14]

Beyond the one box score, Puckett's impact on the Twins can be measured by the effort the player made to weave himself to the "Minnesota lifestyle." The man who grew up in the predominantly black South Side of Chicago moved his home to Minnesota and blended himself in with a predominantly white public with little difficulty. He developed a love of fishing, though not ice fishing, once telling a reporter "I ain't gonna die on no ice."[15] During the run of two World Series championships, Puckett may have been the most popular and best recognized celebrity in Minnesota. For a populace that has long accepted its place in American culture as a self-contained outpost, far removed from the mainstream, Minnesotans are quick to adopt outsiders who respect their outlook. As Bremer put it, "There's something very parochial about those of us who live here. We like people who like being here. You don't have to be from here, but it really matters to fans that you become part of the community."[16]

After his career was over, Puckett fell prey to several personal scandals, suffering through a highly public divorce from his wife, Tonya, amid allegations of violence inflicted upon not only his wife but multiple other women with whom he was involved. Years later, with time to heal the wounds suffered by fans who before his divorce had held Puckett up as an icon, reasonable people who neither condone his private actions nor support his personal choices can separate his failings from his accomplishments that brought them happiness.

Comparing Joe Mauer's place within the Minnesota's baseball zeitgeist to three franchise legends is an awkward proposition at this point in time. For starters, Mauer is still a young man (turning 28 early in the 2011 season) seemingly with years to add to or detract from his legacy. At the time of this writing, however, hometown-hero Mauer's previously golden image is being tarnished for the first time in his career. During the 2011 season he was labeled "soft" after a slow recovery from offseason leg injuries. Aggressive fans altered his Wikipedia entry to strategically add the word "lazy."[17] Writers and fans questioned the sanity of his $184 million contract that kicked in before the season. One ESPN writer questioned whether or not Mauer had, in one season, gone from one of the game's most productive and popular players to an albatross in his own clubhouse. In fact, in today's Internet age all superstars are subject to heightened scrutiny. Moreover, advanced metrics are used to measure a player's value in ways that previous generations of players did not have to deal with, adding another angle for possible criticism.

Mauer's miniature fall in 2011 testifies to the staggering nature of his popularity in the years preceding it. A brief flirtation with a scholarship offer to play football for Bobby Bowden's Florida State football powerhouse as well as the suggestion that the Twins take Mark Prior, not Mauer, with the top pick in the 2001 draft might have derailed Mauer's eventual appearance on the Twins, but in retrospect his selection by Minnesota was the culmination of an unstoppable three-year magnetic attraction between player and community.

Joining a team in 2004 that already featured Puckett's heir, Torii Hunter, in center field as well as star hurler Johan Santana and Justin Morneau, a future AL MVP who debuted a year earlier, Mauer's celebrity instantly trumped them all. Without the need to ingratiate himself to a public that already knew him intimately, and never indicating that any team apart from Minnesota would be a better option for his career, Twins fans became very protective of their home-grown star. Their support was evident on the backs of replica jerseys on a nightly basis at both home and away ballparks. "He is very much one of us," Bremer stated succinctly.[18]

As arguably the best player on Minnesota's only two World Series championship squads, Kirby Puckett became one of the most beloved athletes in Minnesota history. Puckett's extra-base robbing catch in the third of inning of Game Six of the 1991 World Series remains one of his most memorable.

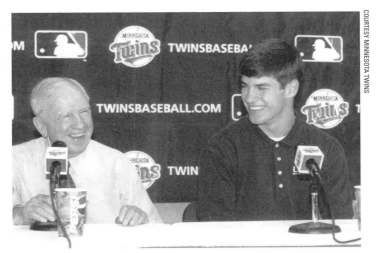

The Twins and their owner, Minneapolis businessman Carl Pohlad, made St. Paul schoolboy sensation Joe Mauer the number one overall pick in the 2001 amateur draft.

As Mauer's statistical totals rose, so did the interest in his personality. Not once but twice he was featured on the cover of *Sports Illustrated*, characterized as the all-American, hometown neighbor with the unique ability to hit .350 at the most demanding defensive position. When the story broke that Mauer struck out just once in all of his high school games, the local alternative newspaper *City Pages* sought to track down the pitcher who pulled the trick. They did, and Paul Feiner, unwilling to crow about his victory over Minnesota's golden child, immediately deflected the attention back to Mauer, pointing out that the catcher both homered and singled off of him in the same game.[19] His trademark sideburns even achieved a personality of its own, in the vein of Rollie Fingers' handlebar moustache in Oakland in the '70s. The team once gave away stick-on replica sideburns at the ballpark as a promotion.

With the notion that Mauer will always be more of a Carew than a Killebrew offensively, the debate over Mauer's positional future still rages. Those who maintain that longevity of the 6-foot-5 Mauer will be increased via a permanent move to another less-demanding position clash with those who cite that his new, heightened contract significantly decreases his perceived value elsewhere. From a purely statistical standpoint these arguments are valid, but measuring the value of a star player as merely a player and not an attraction to be connected to by millions of fans who flood the turnstiles is to tell only half of the story. Mauer is the spiritual heir to Killebrew for his humble nature, the statistical heir to Carew through his playing style, and the popular heir to Puckett. As Bremer sums up, "He's the Ted Williams of catchers. How lucky are [Twins fans] to be able to witness that from the beginning of his career to the end?"[20] ■

Notes

1. Nightengale, Bob. "Appreciation: Harmon Killebrew Recalled as Great Player, Person" *USA Today* (2011): www.usatoday.com.
2. Heilman, Barbara. "Out of the Park on a Half Swing." *Sports Illustrated* 18, no. 14 (1963): 85–92.
3. Brackin, Dennis and Patrick Reusse. *The Minnesota Twins, a Complete Illustrated History*. Minneapolis: MVP, 2010.
4. Nightengale, op. cit.
5. Williams, Ted, Underwood, John. "I Hope Rod Carew Hits .400." *Sports Illustrated* 47, no.3 (1977): 20–25.
6. Carew, Rod and Ira Berkow. *Carew*. Minneapolis: Simon and Schuster, 1979.
7. Lenehan. Michael. "The Last of the Pure Baseball Men." *The Atlantic* (1981). www.theatlantic.com.
8. Ibid.
9. Carew and Berkow, op. cit.
10. Ibid.
11. Dick Bremer of Fox Sports North Television was interviewed at Target Field on August 23, 2011.
12. Ibid.
13. Kurkjian, Tim. "For 11 Innings, Puckett's Greatness Took Center Stage." www.espn.com (2006).
14. Christensen, Joe. "Goodbye, Kirby." *Minneapolis Star Tribune* (2006): www.startribune.com.
15. Rushin, Steve. "End of the Fairy Tale." *Sports Illustrated* 104, no. 12 (2003): www.sportsillustrated.com.
16. Bremer, op. cit.
17. Howard, Johnette. "Is Joe Mauer Dragging Twins Down?" www.espn.com (2011).
18. Bremer, op. cit.
19. Walsh, Jim. "The Kid who Struck Out Joe Mauer." *City Pages* (2006): www.citypages.com.
20. Bremer, op. cit.

Sources

Anderson, Kelli. "The Perfect Catch." *Sports Illustrated* 105 no. 5 (2006): www.sportsillustrated.com.

Bingham, Walter. "The Killer Strikes in May." *Sports Illustrated* 10, no. 22 (1959): 55–58.

Carry, Peter. "A Head Fit for a Triple Crown." *Sports Illustrated* 33, no. 5 (1970): 14–15.

Deford, Frank. "The Rise and Fall of Kirby Puckett." *Sports Illustrated* 98, no.11 (2003): www.sportsillustrated.com.

Fimrite, Ron. "Hitters of Singular Skills." *Sports Illustrated* 41, no. 1 (1974): 14–17.

Murphy, Austin. "A Better Set of Twins." *Sports Illustrated* 67, no. 4 (1987): 36–38, 59.

O'Keefe, John. "Harmon Killebrew: Twins Slugger." *Sports Illustrated* 91, no. 18, (1999):16.

Rushin, Steve. "Does the Puck Stop Here?" *Sports Illustrated* 76, no. 24 (1992): 22–30.

Rushin, Steve. "A Series to Savor." *Sports Illustrated* 75, no. 20 (1991): 16–27.

Telander, Rick. "Minny's Mighty Mite." *Sports Illustrated* 66, no. 24 (1987): 46–49.

Verducci, Tom. "Joe Mauer Will Serenely, Politely, Crush You." *Sports Illustrated* 110, no. 26 (2009): www.sportsillustrated.com.

May 17, 2011

A Strong Man Dies

Francis Kinlaw

Harmon Killebrew died today,
Another on a list of boyhood heroes gone;
Passing years deprive us of the joys of our youth
And of icons who made it special.

Wasn't it only last month that a "Bonus Baby" was born…
This quiet son of Idaho, bringing excitement to staid Washington?
A diamond star from "The Gem State," lifting spirits and his struggling team,
Enlivening the City of Power in the era of Ike.

It was he who sparked the imagination of a Southern kid
Who in backyard games dreamed of playing for the Senators;
Not for the Yankees with all their stars,
But for the lowly Nats, with their emerging slugger.

Wasn't it only last week that this man with the solid physique
And a simple yet distinctive stance and swing,
Pounded a triple to the deep recesses of Yankee Stadium's outfield
That would become ingrained in the mind of a soldier on his way to Vietnam?

No, that blow occurred back on Easter Sunday in '68
When the future Hall of Famer was in his prime;
When he was hitting towering fly balls and home runs
With humility in the face of success which invited arrogance.

Wasn't it only yesterday that the statistics of this genuine star
Confirmed his exalted status among the sport's best?
If there were a Mount Rushmore for the sluggers of his time,
His face would be chiseled in stone more firm than his arms.

The Reaper claims even the strong and the great,
Legends are removed from the scenes of their glory;
Physical features are taken, no matter how imposing,
But spirits and impressions and respect are left behind!

"The Killer" lives now in memory with a number "3" on his back
Like the immortal Bambino—though with much less flair;
As time marches on, as notable moments float into the past,
These traits we remember:

Young phenom with modesty…Kind and gentle man…
Loyal and supportive teammate…Universally respected…
Role model in life…Role model in death.

PHOTOGRAPH BY HOWARD THORNLEY

COURTESY MINNESOTA HISTORICAL SOCIETY

Left: Shown here on May 25, 1963, Harmon Killebrew would go on to lead the league in slugging average and home runs that season, one of his six home run championships.

Right: This bumper sticker highlights Harmon Killebrew's popularity among Minnesotans.

KILLEBREW for GOVERNOR

Twin Cities Ballparks of the 20th Century and Beyond

Stew Thornley

Early baseball teams in Minneapolis and St. Paul played in a number of hastily built and short-lived ballparks before settling on a pair that each lasted 60 years, longer than any other park or field used for professional baseball in the Twin Cities.

NICOLLET AND LEXINGTON

Opened and closed a year apart, Nicollet Park in Minneapolis and Lexington Park in St. Paul hosted numerous championship teams and were the hot spots during the major holidays when the Millers and Saints played twin-bills—a morning game at one park and an afternoon game at the other—on Decoration Day, Fourth of July, and Labor Day.

The Minneapolis Millers played in a number of locations, but the ballpark most closely associated with the team was the one described by former *Minneapolis Tribune* writer Dave Mona as "soggy, foul, rotten, and thoroughly wonderful Nicollet Park."

In 1896, Nicollet Park replaced a tiny ballpark in downtown Minneapolis, Athletic Park, and represented a move outside the core area of the city. The location was picked, in part, because of its proximity to public transit, just off the corner of Nicollet Avenue and Lake Street in south Minneapolis.

Although spacious compared to the band box that it had replaced, Nicollet Park soon became known for its modest dimensions, particularly the short distance to the right-field fence, which ran along Nicollet Avenue and was an easy target for strong left-handed hitters. Mike Kelley, who owned the Millers from 1924 to 1946, built his 1930s powerhouse around that fence, pouncing on sinewy southpaw swingers who could bombard Nicollet Avenue beyond. Joe Hauser played for the Millers from 1932 to 1936 and hit 202 home runs during those five years. In 1933, Hauser set a professional baseball record with 69 homers; 50 of them were hit at Nicollet Park. Halsey Hall remembers the right-field fence being made a little higher over the years and awnings going down in front of the plate-glass windows on Nicollet Avenue businesses as insurance rates on window breakage rose.

In 1938 Ted Williams spent his last season in the minors with the Millers. As a 19-year-old in his second season of pro ball, Williams won the American Association Triple Crown, hitting .366 with 43 home runs and 142 RBIs while also leading the league in runs, total bases, and walks. In addition to Williams, some of baseball's greatest players performed for the Millers at Nicollet Park, including Hall of Famers Willie Mays, Rube Waddell, Ray Dandridge, Monte Irvin, and Hoyt Wilhelm.

Known as a hitters' park, Nicollet Park witnessed "hits" of different kind in the morning game of the Fourth of July two-game set in 1929. A brawl between the Millers and Saints drew the description of veteran baseball (and boxing) reporter George Barton as "the most vicious affair ever witnessed at Nicollet." The trouble began in the third inning when Hughie McMullen grounded to Saints first-baseman Oscar Roettger. Pitcher Huck Betts covered first and was spiked by McMullen as he crossed the bag. The St. Paul and Minneapolis newspapers differed the next day as to whether the spiking was intentional, but apparently there was no doubt in Betts's mind as he took the ball from his glove and fired it at McMullen's head in retaliation. The throw missed, but Sammy Bohne didn't. Bohne, a reserve infielder who was coaching first at the time, rushed Betts with a series of punches as the dugouts emptied. McMullen recalled, "Both clubs met in the pitcher's box and you hit anyone near you." The headline over Halsey Hall's story in the *Minneapolis Journal* the next day read, "Sammy Bohne Doesn't Play, But Gets More Hits Than Those Who Do." There were plenty of ejections in the game, but Hugh McMullen was not among the ejectees—ironic because in a letter written by McMullen 55 years later, Hughie admitted that he had indeed spiked Betts intentionally in retaliation for a beanball Betts had thrown a few pitches earlier.

As opposed to a delay for brawling, Sunday doubleheaders were often cut short by a law requiring games to be stopped promptly at 6:00 P.M. (The ordinance was repealed in 1941, but Mike Kelley continued to honor the policy.) In 1935 the Millers saw a 3–0 lead disappear as Toledo scored five runs in the top of the ninth. But the clock at Nicollet read 5:54 as the Millers came to bat. With shrewd stalling by Fabian Gaffke, Buzz Arlett, and Joe Hauser, the clock struck six o'clock before the final out was made; as a result, the score reverted back to the last full inning, wiping out the Mud Hen runs and giving the Millers a 3–0 win.

That same season Babe Ruth made a Nicollet Park appearance in a game between the Minneapolis and St. Paul police teams. Ruth played half a game with each team, and contributed a double in five trips to the plate. Pitching for the Minneapolis Police team, Pete Guzy, former East High and Minnesota Gopher pitching sensation and later the longtime football and baseball coach at Edison High, was able to count Babe as one of his 18 strikeout victims in the game.

In 1983 a historical marker was erected in front of the Norwest (now Wells Fargo) Bank on 31st and Nicollet, on the former site of Nicollet Park. The plaque was paid for in large part by donations from ex-players and fans. With their contributions came letters and notes to indicate that memories of Nicollet Park have not faded. Hughie McMullen, who played in the late 1920s, remembers even then Nicollet as a very old, run down park. "The fences were held up only by the paint on them," says McMullen. Eddie Popowski managed the Millers in their final year at Met Stadium. But as an infielder with Louisville in 1943, he played at Nicollet and recalls players having their gloves and shoes chewed up by rats when they left them overnight. "Nicollet Park holds the best memories in baseball for me," said Al Worthington. The star of the 1955 playoffs recalls that he had great success at Nicollet Park (his three-year won-loss record at Nicollet was 24–5). Al also remembers the lack of heat in the clubhouse. "It was so cold in April that taking a shower was almost like being outside when the sub-zero wind blew."

* * *

Seven miles to the east of Nicollet Park was its St. Paul counterpart, Lexington Park, which opened in 1897 as home to Charles Comiskey's Western League team. The team had been playing in a small ballpark on Dale Street, a block south of University Avenue, six days a week, but because of neighborhood opposition was forced to find other venues for Sunday games. One of those sites, a large lot on the southwest corner of Lexington Avenue and University Avenue, approximately one mile west of the Dale Street park and bounded by Dunlap Avenue on the west and Fuller Avenue on the south, became the location for Lexington Park.

Like Nicollet Park, Lexington Park was well removed from the center city when it opened, which became an issue for owner George Lennon when his Saints joined the new American Association in 1902. Because Lennon found Lexington Park too remote, he built a new park on the northern edge of downtown St. Paul. Sunday games were played at Lexington Park, but from 1903 to 1909, the downtown site served as the primary home of the Saints. Starting in 1910, the Saints moved full time at Lexington Park.

Lexington Park had a serious fire in October of 1908, and following the 1915 season an even greater fire destroyed the grandstand. When the park was rebuilt, it was reconfigured, with the diamond turned 90 degrees, moving home plate from the southwest toward the northwest corner of the lot. The ballpark set back 100 feet from University Avenue, which was on the north side of the ballpark, and 100 feet from Lexington Avenue to the east. The main entrance to the grounds was behind home plate, at the corner of University and Dunlap.

With the new configuration came familiar landmarks outside the stadium. The most prominent was the Coliseum Pavilion beyond the left-field fence, its roof being the landing site for many home runs. To the south, behind right field, was Keys Well Drilling, which erected a sign bearing the company name that, although outside the ballpark, was clearly visible to those inside.

The 1903 opener at Nicollet Park between the Minneapolis Millers and Milwaukee Brewers.

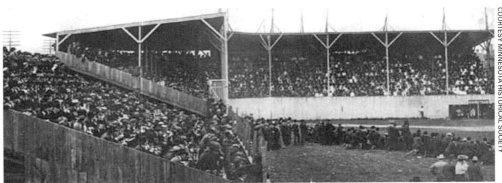

COURTESY MINNESOTA HISTORICAL SOCIETY

COURTESY MINNESOTA HISTORICAL SOCIETY

A panoramic look at Nicollet Park, 1954.

This sign wasn't hit by home runs with the frequency of the Coliseum roof (if the sign ever was hit). In fact, for most of the life of the rebuilt Lexington Park, few balls cleared the right-field fence. The distance down the foul line in right field was 365 feet. A 12-foot-high wooden fence sat atop an embankment that led up to the fence.

Home runs to right field at Lexington Park were so rare as to be memorable. When the New York Yankees came to St. Paul for an exhibition game in June of 1926, the *St. Paul Pioneer Press* reported that only nine home runs had been hit over the right-field fence since the park had been rebuilt. Bruno Haas was the only player to have done so twice. In 1950, in his only season with the Saints, Lou Limmer, a left-handed hitter, led the American Association in home runs, even though he hit only one at home.

Disaster struck the Twin Cities on Friday, July 20, 1951, as high winds and floods caused millions of dollars in damage. One of the casualties of the gale was the right-field fence at Lexington Park, torn apart by winds reported to have reached 100 miles per hour. The Saints were in Kansas City at the time, giving management a chance to rebuild the barrier before the team returned. By August, when the Saints were back from their road trip, Lexington Park had a new right-field fence, and this one was much closer to home plate. The distance down the line had been shortened to 330 feet. To make it a bit more challenging, a double-decked fence was erected that was 25 feet high, although the embankment that the previous fence had rested atop was gone. Limmer, though, wasn't around to enjoy new the fences; he had been promoted to the American League.

Lexington Park closed in 1956 and was replaced by a Red Owl grocery store. In 1958 Red Owl imbedded a plaque in the floor of the store to mark the spot of home plate (although it was not exact). Red Owl eventually moved out, but the property remained a supermarket. In the course of changing management, however, the home-plate plaque disappeared. In the summer of 1994, the Halsey Hall Chapter of the Society for American Baseball Research began raising money from former Saints players and fans to erect another marker. In April 1994 a new plaque was mounted on the outside of the structure. When the building was later abandoned the plaque was placed in storage and awaits an appropriate time to be re-mounted.

MIDWAY AND THE MET

By the middle of the 20th century, it was clear that the Twin Cities' minor league teams needed new ballparks. Around this same time, the itch for something more was emerging. The transfer of the Boston Braves to Milwaukee in 1953 gave local civic leaders and sports boosters hope that Minnesota could land a major league team, the pursuit of which would require a new ballpark. St. Paul and Minnesota both made plans for stadiums for their existing teams that they hoped would someday house a major league team.

St. Paul settled on a site in the midway area of the city, off Snelling Avenue just south of the State Fair grounds. Midway Stadium opened in 1957 and served the St. Paul Saints for four years. A single-decked stadium, the structure was designed to provide for additional decks if needed for a major league team. When major league baseball finally came, however, the team ended up in the new stadium built for the Minneapolis Millers. The arrival of the major leagues put the Saints and Millers out of business after the 1960 season, leaving Midway Stadium without either its primary tenant or the one it hoped to get.

For the next 20 years, Midway was used for a variety of activities: high-school and other amateur sports, exhibitions such as famed softball pitcher Eddie Feigner with the King and His Court, a practice facility for the Minnesota Vikings football team, and wrestling. Midway Stadium eventually became a drain on the city's coffers and was frequently referred to as a "white elephant." It was demolished in 1981, and the city successfully encouraged new office and industrial development on the site.

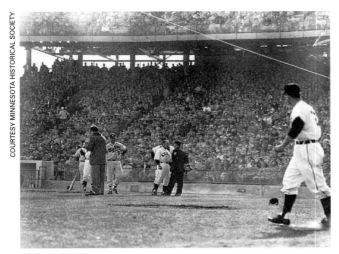

The Minneapolis Millers opened the new stadium in Bloomington (soon to be known as Metropolitan Stadium) against the Wichita Braves on April 24, 1956. Wichita won 5–3 in a game in which the Millers manager was ejected after drop-kicking his hat in the fifth inning when plate umpire Bob Phillips overturned his original decision three times on a steal of home by the Braves' Joe Koppe.

By the time Midway Stadium opened, the Minneapolis Millers already had a new stadium. Minneapolis business interests raised the money through bond sales for what became known as Metropolitan Stadium, located in Bloomington, a southern suburb. The new ballpark had three decks, which extended only to the end of each of the dugouts. What it didn't have were posts to support the upper decks; the cantilever construction, rare in sports structures at the time, allowed fans an unobstructed view of the field.

The Millers played at Met Stadium from 1956 through 1960. The announcement near the end of October 1960 that Washington Senators owner Calvin Griffith was moving his team to Minnesota culminated the state's quest for major league baseball. The incoming Twins would play at Met Stadium, which would be expanded. The first two decks were extended down the right-field line although the grandstand on the third-base line was never extended. Bleachers filled the gap down the left-field line, with wooden bleachers providing seating beyond the outfield fences. Eventually, a double-decked grandstand was built in left field for the Minnesota Vikings, the National Football League team that shared the stadium. In addition to the Twins and Vikings, the Met hosted the Minnesota Kicks soccer team as well as events ranging from wrestling matches to a Beatles concert.

The Met was primarily a baseball stadium, and it didn't work well for football. Even with the new grandstand, which provided more seats between the goal lines, spectators on both sides of the gridiron were far removed from the game. The Vikings were the first of the stadium's tenants to seek a new home, starting in the early 1970s.

Weather was an ongoing challenge, and games were sometimes postponed or delayed because of rain, snow, and at least once by a nearby tornado touchdown. One delay occurred for a completely different reason. In the fourth inning of a game versus the Boston Red Sox on August 25, 1970, first-base umpire Nestor Chylak ran in toward the infield, waving his arms to call time. The interruption was explained with an announcement that the Bloomington police had been told an explosion would take place at Met Stadium at 9:30. The week before, the Old Federal Building in downtown Minneapolis had been bombed, and officials were taking no chances, although they

Met Stadium was home to the Minneapolis Millers for five years and the Minnesota Twins for 21 years. It hosted the 1965 All-Star Game and four games of the World Series that year. The 1958 and 1959 Junior World Series were also played here.

allowed the game to start and be played until 9:15, approximately 45 minutes after the threat had been called in. The players congregated on the field, away from the stadium structure itself, and the fans were directed to the parking lots. Many of the fans, however, found their way onto the field where they mingled with the players and got autographs, while vendors worked the crowd, hawking concessions. Few people even noticed the time when the scoreboard clock showed 9:30, the time set for the explosion, which never occurred. Twenty minutes later, fans re-entered the stadium and cleared the field, and the game resumed shortly before 10:00. The only blast of the night was from Boston's Tony Conigliaro, who homered in the eighth inning to give the Red Sox a 1–0 victory.

Harmon Killebrew provided the most frequent blasts, hitting many of his 573 career home runs at the Met. Two of the longest came on the first weekend of June in 1967. On Saturday, June 3, Killebrew homered into the upper deck in left. The estimated distance of the drive was 430 feet. (Met Stadium had been one of the first stadiums to measure homers, the result of a table used to record the distance to each section and row of the outfield seats; the measurements given were to the point of impact, not the estimated distance of how far the ball would have traveled had there been no obstructions.) The next day the Twins announced that the estimated distance it would have traveled was 520 feet. This announcement had barely been made when Killebrew connected again, hitting a shot off the facing of the second deck, farther toward left-center field. The estimated distance it would have traveled was given as 550 feet although the point of impact was measured at 434 feet.

Metropolitan Stadium's biggest year was 1965, when it hosted both the All-Star Game and the World Series. The crowd at Metropolitan Stadium for the first game of the Series included a man from Illinois, Ralph Belcore. A veteran of 21 World Series, the 60-year-old Belcore had arrived at Met Stadium at 7:30 the morning of Sunday, September 26 to stake out the first spot in the ticket line for general admission seats, even though this left him with a wait of more than 245 hours before the first game. The Twins lost the World Series to the Los Angeles Dodgers, four games to three, with more than 50,000 fans present for the decisive seventh game, the only time the Twins topped 50,000 in a game at Met Stadium.

The Twins were successful during their first decade in Minnesota. Their attendance topped 1,000,000 (then considered a benchmark for success) in each of their first 10 years at the Met, and they twice led the

league in attendance. In total, over this decade the Twins led the American League in attendance. As the team dropped in the standings during the 1970s, however, so did attendance. The Twins joined the Vikings in seeking either a new stadium or significant improvements to the existing one and eventually were successful.

The Twins played their last baseball game at Met Stadium on September 30, 1981, losing to the Kansas City Royals. The final event at the Met was a Vikings game against the Kansas City Chiefs on Sunday, December 20, 1981. Following the game, fans in search of souvenirs ravaged the stadium, taking what wasn't bolted down as well as many things that were.

Met Stadium remained partially dismantled for several years before being totally demolished, and it remained a vacant site for several more years before a large shopping center, dubbed the Mall of America, was erected on the site. A plaque marking the spot of home plate was installed in an amusement-park area in the middle of the shopping center.

HUBERT H. HUMPHREY METRODOME

The Minnesota Legislature passed a non-site specific stadium bill in 1977 and empowered a newly created stadium commission to evaluate options. In late 1978 the commission voted to erect a multi-purpose covered facility on the eastern edge of downtown Minneapolis, and the Hubert H. Humphrey Metrodome opened in 1982 with 55,000 seats available for baseball. The capacity for football—both the Vikings and the Minnesota Gophers, who abandoned Memorial Stadium on the University campus to play in the new domed facility—was 8,000 more than for baseball.

The first event was an exhibition baseball game between the Twins and Philadelphia Phillies on Saturday night, April 3. The temperature outside was 19 degrees, made colder by northwesterly winds of 30 miles per hour with gusts up to 45. Pete Redfern threw the first pitch for the Twins and the second batter up for the Phillies, Pete Rose, got the first hit. Kent Hrbek of the Twins hit the first two home runs in the new stadium. Three nights later, the first regular-season game was played, with the Twins losing to the Seattle Mariners. With two out in the bottom of the first, Minnesota's Dave Engle put one over the left-field fence for the first official hit and home run in the Metrodome.

The Metrodome was functional but short on amenities. The sterile nature of the stadium was not conducive to the aesthetic atmosphere desired by many fans. Other problems included the roof, which caused players to lose sight of fly balls. The first inside-the-park home run at the Metrodome came on Friday night, May 28, 1982, when Tom Brunansky hit a high fly to left. Yankees left fielder Lou Piniella stood helplessly, his arms outstretched, as he couldn't see the ball, which dropped to the ground and stayed in play by bouncing off the fence as Brunansky circled the bases. One ball that got lost in the roof in a more literal sense was hit on May 4, 1984, by Dave Kingman of Oakland, a pop up that didn't come down. The ball went through a vent hole in the roof, and, by the ground rules of the Metrodome, Kingman was awarded a double.

The artificial turf initially installed in the Metrodome was extremely spongy, causing high bounces that played havoc with fielders. White Sox right fielder Harold Baines suffered a related problem on Sunday, June 24, 1984. The Twins were trailing 2–0 with two on and one out in the last of the ninth when Tim Teufel dropped a hit into right field. Baines charged in to field the ball, which hit a seam in the turf, bounced over his head, and rolled to the fence. Teufel ended up

COURTESY MINNESOTA TWINS

The Minnesota Twins played in the Hubert H. Humphrey Metrodome from 1982 through 2009. The Metrodome is still used for baseball by the Minnesota Gophers and many other college, high school, and amateur teams.

with a game-winning, three-run inside-the-park home run. Different types of artificial turf have been installed since then, generally correcting the problem.

Although the roof insulated the Twins from weather problems, one game was postponed after a storm, which began the evening of Wednesday, April 13, 1983, and dumped 13½ inches of wet, heavy snow on the Twin Cities. The California Angels, scheduled to play the Twins on Thursday night, had taken an overnight flight from California and arrived over the Twin Cities at about 5:30 on Thursday morning. The plane, however, was unable to land and diverted to Chicago, where the Angels spent the day. The absence of the Angels, combined with concerns for the safety of players and fans trying to get to the Metrodome that night, prompted the Twins to postpone the game. That night, a chunk of ice tore a 20-foot gap in the roof of the Metrodome, causing it to deflate. The roof collapse is often given as the reason for the postponement, but in fact, the game had already been postponed nearly 12 hours earlier. On a side note, a roof collapse on the Metrodome in 2010 did cause a Minnesota Vikings game to be moved. The game, scheduled against the New York Giants for noon on Sunday, December 12, was first postponed until Monday night after the Giants' flight on Saturday was diverted to Kansas City. When the roof collapsed and tore later in the day, it became uncertain when the stadium would be available again, and the National Football League moved the game to Detroit. The Metrodome was still out of service the following week, so the Vikings played their final home game of the season at TCF Bank Stadium at the University of Minnesota.

A roof breach that did affect a game occurred on Saturday night, April 26, 1986. In the eighth inning, a storm ripped a hole in the roof, soaking fans in the upper deck in right field as water poured through. High winds also caused the light bars to sway and the game was delayed as fans were evacuated from the seating area. The game was eventually resumed, but the Twins may have wished it wasn't as the California Angels scored six runs in the ninth inning, capped by a two-out, two-run home run by Wally Joyner off Ron Davis, to win 7–6. In the end, despite its many complaints and flaws, the Metrodome's tenure as the home of the Twins and Vikings exceeded that of Met Stadium.

As part of the authorizing stadium legislation, the Twins and Vikings had been required to sign 30-year leases. However, Twins owner Calvin Griffith insisted on an escape clause, which could be triggered if, among other things, the Twins did not average at lease 1.4 million fans per year over three consecutive years.

COURTESY MINNESOTA TWINS

Derek Jeter of the Yankees at bat against the Twins in the Metrodome.

It also required the installation of air conditioning if the lack of it affected attendance. Although the duct work was in place, the stadium opened without air conditioning, and the Metrodome climate was oppressive during the first summer. Air conditioning was installed and was first used in June of 1983.

Even with the cooler temperatures in the Metrodome, drawing fans was a problem, mainly because of the poor performance by the Twins. Despite a number of players who would later become stars, in 1982 the Twins lost more than 100 games and attendance was only 921,186. In 1983, the Twins were 70–92 and it was becoming clear that attendance would probably not achieve the average of 1.4 million per season through 1984, allowing Griffith to terminate the lease.

In response the local business community began buying unused tickets to the games. The plan was to buy the least expensive tickets, which meant focusing on the weekday games when ticket prices were discounted. The first occurrence of a buyout was on Tuesday night, May 15, 1984, when the Twins played the Toronto Blue Jays. Although fewer than 10,000 fans attended the game, the paid attendance was 26,761. The next day, with discounted prices in effect, the paid attendance was 51,863, although the number of fans present was closer to 8,700 (with more than 2,300 of those being school-patrol members who got in free, leaving the turnstile count for paid ticket holders at 6,346). The Twins began announcing two attendance figures for games based on tickets sold and on the turnstile count. A legal battle loomed as to whether this artificial padding of attendance would actually stop Griffith from exercising his escape clause; instead, in June of 1984, Griffith signed a letter of intent to sell the Twins to banker and Pepsi bottling magnate Carl Pohlad.

Despite the new ownership, concerns over the lack of stadium revenues prompted the Twins to seek a new stadium in the latter part of the 1990s. The drawn out negotiations revealed that additional escape clauses in varying forms remained, and the threat for the team to leave (either by relocation or by being entirely eliminated, an issue that surfaced after the 2001 season) resurfaced.

As construction was in its final stages for a new Twins' stadium at the other end of downtown Minneapolis, major league baseball at the Metrodome featured a set of reprieves in October 2009. The Twins' final scheduled game of the season was at home, against Kansas City, on Sunday, October 4. Only three weeks before that, Minnesota was 5½ games behind first-place Detroit. However, the Twins won 11 of their next 12 and were back in the race. On October 4 Minnesota beat Kansas City 13–4 to tie the Tigers for first place, meaning at least one more game in the Metrodome. Two days later, Minnesota hosted a tiebreaker game against Detroit, an exciting back-and-forth contest that ended with a 6–5 win for the Twins in 12 innings.

The Metrodome lived on but faced another possible final game on Sunday, October 11. The Twins had dropped the first two games of their best-of-five playoff series against the Yankees in New York. In Game Three at the Metrodome, Minnesota carried a 1–0 lead into the seventh, but home runs by Alex Rodriguez and Jorge Posada (the latter one the last ever hit in a major league game in the stadium) sent the Yankees on to a 4–1 win, eliminating the Twins and ending their 28-season tenure in the Metrodome.

TARGET FIELD

Although the Metrodome was expected to serve the Twins for at least 30 years, by the mid-1990s the Twins were pushing for a new home. In 1997 owner Carl Pohlad unsuccessfully sought public funding for a new park, one with a retractable roof on a site along the Mississippi River, a few blocks from the Metrodome. The proposal turned into a public-relations disaster when what appeared to be the offer of a significant contribution by the Twins turned out to be more along the lines of a loan; in addition, the threat of a move by the Twins to North Carolina hung over the issue and turned off some fans. The level of distrust intensified after a book, Stadium Games by Society for American Baseball Research member Jay Weiner, suggested that the proposed ownership group in North Carolina was put in place more for the purpose of giving the Twins and Minnesota stadium proponents additional leverage than it was to present a serious offer to purchase and move the team.

Pohlad's talk of moving the Twins, combined with the illusory nature of the "contribution" to a new ballpark, turned the man once seen as the savior of the franchise when he purchased it in 1984 into a villain. Pohlad's popularity plummeted further a few years later when it was reported that he had volunteered the Twins as one of the two teams to be contracted in exchange for a large sum of money—reported to be anywhere from $150 million to $250 million—from Major League Baseball.

Baseball Commissioner Bud Selig faced many obstacles in carrying out his team-trimming, and one of the first hurdles tripped him up. The Metropolitan Sports Facilities Commission filed suit to compel the Twins to honor their lease at the Metrodome. On November 16, 2001, only 10 days after the vote by the owners for contraction, Hennepin County District Judge Harry Crump granted an injunction that prohibited the Twins from taking any action that would prevent them from playing in the Metrodome in 2002. The Minnesota Court of Appeals upheld the injunction in January, and the state Supreme Court the following month refused to hear the case. It is unlikely that contraction would have occurred even if the injunction had not been granted, but the court actions signaled the end of any hope Selig had for getting rid of two teams in 2002. Meanwhile the city of St. Paul had gotten into the act, making an attempt to lure the Twins from Minneapolis, but this effort died when St. Paul voters rejected a referendum to raise their sales tax to fund a new stadium.

By the time most of the controversy from these actions dissipated, another push began. In 2005 the Twins and Hennepin County, which encompasses Minneapolis, reached agreement on a package to fund a new ballpark. However, approval from the Minnesota Legislature was needed to allow the county to raise its sales tax without a county-wide referendum, and the Legislature adjourned its 2005 session without final action on a ballpark bill.

Finally in 2006, the state legislation was approved and that summer the Hennepin County Board of Commissioners authorized a .15 percent sales tax to partially fund a new ballpark. The site was on the

Joe Mauer got a run-scoring single when his grounder bounced off second base in the fourth-inning of the first regular-season game, between the Twins and Red Sox, at Target Field on April 12, 2010. Fourteen black spruce trees in front of the batter's eye in center field were removed after the 2010 season because they were a distraction for some hitters.

northwestern edge of Minneapolis's downtown, just over one mile from the Metrodome and one block beyond Target Center, the arena that houses the NBA's Minnesota Timberwolves. (Eventually the naming rights for the Twins' stadium were sold to Target Corporation, which already held the rights to the name of the basketball arena, and the new ballpark is called "Target Field.")

The plan called for an open-air stadium with no provisions for a retractable roof. Money for a roof wasn't available, and constraints on the eight-acre site do not allow for a movable roof to be added in the future. The site for the ballpark was being used as a parking lot and is located between two elevated roads: Fifth Street North to the northeast (beyond what would be the left-field stands) and Seventh Street North to the southwest (behind first base). To the northeast, behind third base, is the Hennepin Energy Recovery Center, a waste-to-energy facility commonly known as the "garbage burner." Interstate 394, to the southeast beyond right field, separates the site from Target Center, although a parking ramp is over the freeway and eventually a plaza was built over I-394 to allow better access to the ballpark. In addition, a light-rail line was extended a few blocks to get to Target Field, where it connects with commuter rail that runs to the northern and northwest suburbs and beyond. With the new site, in a small way baseball in Minnesota returned to its past; only a block away from the center field entrance was the left-field corner of Athletic Park, home to the Minneapolis Millers from 1889 to 1896.

A ceremonial groundbreaking scheduled for early August 2007 was postponed for several weeks following the collapse of the I-35W bridge over the Mississippi River. Construction progressed over the next two-and-a-half years. Much of the erecting was done from the inside out with cranes on the site of the field hoisting exterior panels and other materials over the top of the emerging structure.

Target Field includes many features and amenities, including a range of dining options, that had not been present in the Twins' previous homes. In addition, the Twins decided to use the high-profile nature of their new ballpark to highlight issues of sustainability. The ballpark includes a membrane filtration system to capture and treat rainwater for use in irrigating the field and washing the grandstand. Besides reducing municipal water usage by more than 50 percent, saving more than 2 million gallons of water each year, the arrangement brings attention to the global issue of water, raising awareness of the value of sustainability and the wise use of water.

The first event in Target Field was a college baseball game between the Minnesota Gophers and Louisiana Tech Bulldogs on Saturday, March 27, 2010. Clint Ewing of the Bulldogs hit the first home run in the park as Louisiana Tech beat Minnesota 9–1. Approximately 35,000 people passed through on the first day with fans watching the game while also checking out the features of the new digs.

The following weekend the Twins hosted a pair of exhibition games, both in front of sellout crowds, against the St. Louis Cardinals. Denard Span of Minnesota hit the first major league home run in Target Field during a win by the Cardinals on Friday, April 2.

The Twins went on the road to open the regular season and returned for a homestand, starting against the Boston Red Sox, on Monday, April 12. Under partly-cloudy skies with a temperature of 65 degrees, Minnesota's Carl Pavano delivered the first pitch at 3:13 P.M., officially bringing outdoor major league baseball back to Minnesota. The Twins won the game 5–2 with Jason Kubel of Minnesota hitting the only home run, a drive to right leading off the last of the seventh. Two innings earlier, Boston's Mike Cameron hit a long fly to left that disappeared in a narrow gap between the foul pole and a limestone wall. Third-base umpire Kerwin Danley ruled the ball foul, but the umpires conferred and decided to use video replay to confirm the call. Danley's foul ruling was upheld, and Cameron struck out on the next pitch. Video replay became a relatively common occurrence at Target Field during its first year; it was used eight times (with two calls being overturned and six upheld) in 2010, setting a record for the most uses of replay in a season at one stadium.

In its first season, Target Field demonstrated itself to be a pitchers' park as it was below average in runs scored and last in home runs. Joe Mauer, after hitting 28 home runs in 2009 (16 in the Metrodome), hit only 9 in 2010, 1 at home. On the other hand, the Twins' Jim Thome hit 15 of his team-high 25 home runs at Target Field in 2010, including a Labor Day blast off the top of the flag pole in right that was measured at 480 feet.

In 2011 the Twins added a video board above the stands in right field so that fans in left field could see it as well as a 100-foot-high tower in right field for animation and graphics. The top of the tower displays the time.

The Twins also made some changes to help their hitters, some of whom had complained about the surface of the center-field batters' eye as well as the spruce trees in front of the batters' eye. The hitters said they had trouble "locking in" on pitches with the trees swaying in the wind, so the 14 trees were removed. Nevertheless, the park continued to play to the benefit of the pitchers, particularly by depressing home runs for left-handed batters. In 2010 Target Field had a run index of 96, meaning it depressed runs by 4 percent relative to a neutral park; in 2011 the run index actually declined slightly to 94. The home run index for left-handed batters was only 65 and 72 respectively for the two seasons.

The opening of Target Field began another chapter in Minnesota baseball. Metropolitan Stadium was a workable stadium for major league baseball. With its often described erector-set construction, the Met didn't have the character of ballparks from the classic era of stadium design. However, it has become the symbol of nostalgia and happy memories for many who grew up with it. The Metrodome was functional—it could be converted to handle baseball and football, not to mention a wide range of other sports and activities—but completely without charm. It ensured games would be played as scheduled and protected fans from rain, cold, and sometimes snow, but it also shielded them from the sun and pleasant days and nights that are a common, if not constant, part of Minnesota summers. Target Field was built amid the period of retro-ballparks, facilities built for baseball only along with distinctive features for an old-feel look and modern amenities. Many fans embraced the idea of a smaller stadium for a seemingly more intimate feel and have had to face the realities of having a harder time getting tickets. Limiting supply, owners have found, has a way

of creating and maintaining demand and, Target Field proved a popular destination for fans during its first season. Out of 85 games (including two exhibition and two playoff games), all but two were sold out, and the Twins had a regular-season attendance of 3,223,640. The fortunes of the Twins will no doubt influence the demand in the future, but the new ballpark clearly appears to have brought a new look and feel to the game and re-energized baseball fans in Minnesota. ∎

Sources

Baseball Info Solutions. *The Bill James Handbook 2011*. Chicago: Acta Sports, 2010.

Baseball Info Solutions. *The Bill James Handbook 2012*. Chicago: Acta Sports, 2011.

Berg, Steve. *Target Field: The New Home of the Minnesota Twins*. Minneapolis: MVP Books, an imprint of MBI Publishing Company and Quayside Publishing Group, 2010.

Hinman, Jim. Unpublished manuscript on the history of the St. Paul Saints.

Johnson, Charles. *History of the Metropolitan Stadium and the Sports Center*. Minneapolis: Midwest Federal, 1970.

Klobuchar, Amy. *Uncovering the Dome*. Minneapolis: Bolger Publications, 1982

Metropolitan Sports Area Commission. Metropolitan Sports Area Stadium: Stadium Souvenir, 1956.

Minneapolis Chapter of Commerce. *10: A Decade at the Met*, 1966.

Mona, Dave, compiler. *The Hubert H. Humphrey Metrodome Souvenir Book*. Minneapolis: MSP Publications, 1982.

Quirk, James. *Stadiums and Major League Sports: The Twin Cities*. A publication of the Brookings Institute, 1997.

Weiner, Jay. *Stadium Games*. Minneapolis: University of Minnesota Press, 2000.

Personal Correspondence: Correspondence with Joe Hauser, 1983–85, as well as telephone interview with Hauser, December 6, 1984, and interview with Hauser, July 8, 1988; Correspondence with Hugh McMullen, March 1984; Correspondence with Al Worthington, March 1984; Telephone interview with Oscar Roettger, September 11, 1984; Correspondence with Ted Williams, November 1987; Interview with Willie Mays, July 11, 2002; Telephone interview with Monte Irvin, June 30, 2005; Interview with Don Zimmer, July 2, 2005.

How (Not) to Build a Ballpark

The 1884 Minneapolis Grounds

Chris Kimball and Kristin Anderson

Every day, about a quarter of a million cars race east and west along a one-block-wide corridor sunk below grade a few blocks south of downtown Minneapolis. It is here that Interstates 94 and 35W meet and briefly merge, with twelve lanes of traffic and assorted ramps filling the space between Park and Portland Avenues on the east and west sides, and Seventeenth and Eighteenth Streets on the north and south. The noise and commotion at this block is significant and dramatic.

Just over 125 years ago, this same block was the site of different noise and commotion when it contained, for one short season, the 1884 Minneapolis Northwestern League ballpark. The cacophony here was exactly what one might expect near a nineteenth-century ballpark, with fans, vendors, traffic, and brass bands crowding into the space for the team's home games, but this place created more than just ballgame-related sounds. The usual and expected chaos attendant to professional baseball was accompanied by social tensions and legal difficulties, and the ballpark became the proxy for this conflict.

While perhaps more pronounced than similar difficulties at other ballparks, what sets this ballpark and its story apart is the remarkable amount of surviving documentation. These resources reveal not only the story of the ballpark's construction and brief use, but they also present a lively snapshot of professional baseball in the late nineteenth century.

In the fall of 1883, Minneapolis baseball devotees set out to organize a professional team for the following season. With high expectations, public organizational meetings were announced. Attendees at the first gatherings included a range of citizens: some were established businessmen and professionals from the city's well-to-do families, while others were young middle-manager types. This relatively diverse group reflected widespread interest in the sport, and by November 1883, they had organized themselves and incorporated the Minneapolis Base Ball Association. Early enthusiasm waned, however, and as the months passed, the most prominent citizens largely disappeared from view, leaving the organization in the hands of the less-well-heeled clerks, bookkeepers, and bartenders.[1]

The new association quickly embarked on the many tasks necessary to fielding a professional team. Chief among these was raising money to hire a manager and players and to build a playing space. Appealing to civic boosterism and the possibility of financial returns, the association solicited funds through public stock sales. Although a number of leading Minneapolitans bought shares of stock, the subscribers were not a small group of wealthy individuals with a clear business plan. Instead, funding came in small increments of voluntary support from a variety of individuals paying their stock assessments over time. Further, the stock offering was never fully subscribed; just under half of the shares were sold by the time the new ballpark opened in June 1884. This precarious financial model left the association and its team inadequately capitalized. They had insufficient support for their initial pre-season costs, and then insufficient revenues during the season to pay their operating expenses. Nevertheless, as the season began, organizers expected that high profile games with leading teams in the league—and especially with cross-river rival Saint Paul—would generate enough income to help them succeed.[2]

In addition to finding financial backers from among the city's baseball fans, it was essential to recruit talented professional players. This was a significant challenge in 1884. A dramatic national expansion of league baseball, including the formation of the putatively major league Union Association, meant that quality players were in demand. The Minneapolis Base Ball Association sought to affiliate itself with the relatively new Northwestern League (1883), which began its 1884 season with twelve teams from five western Great Lakes states: Michigan, Wisconsin, Indiana, Illinois, and Minnesota. The Northwestern League's territory was geographically large and included Lake Michigan, a significant travel obstacle. The U-shaped territory created a circuit range of about 2,000 miles, and the Twin Cities were far afield from Fort Wayne, Grand Rapids, and Saginaw. Traveling so far north and

Minneapolis Baseball Team, 1884.

west for a single series was not feasible for the other teams and so in order for any Minnesota city to have a team in this league, more than one city and team needed to join. As a result, three closely spaced Minnesota cities—Stillwater, Saint Paul, and Minneapolis—helped form the league.[3]

The tasks of league affiliation and player recruitment were entrusted to the team's manager, Benjamin Tuthill (1861–1936) from Saginaw. A youthful manager who turned twenty-three as the season began, Tuthill was likely put forward for the job by Northwestern League president John Rust, also a Saginaw resident. While Tuthill's baseball career was quite brief—a single season as Minneapolis skipper and a little bit of umpiring—his larger entertainment career was lengthy. After leaving baseball in 1884, he went immediately to the theater worlds of New York and Chicago. Tuthill spent the remainder of his long career as a theatrical agent and manager, marrying various actresses along the way and finding himself involved in the occasional lawsuit or controversy.[4]

Selection of the playing grounds was another essential task for the Minneapolis Base Ball Association. In December 1883, the Minneapolis team announced that they would play at a site about two and a half miles south of downtown, along Nicollet Avenue at Thirty-first Street. The place had been used for baseball before; in fact, as recently as July 1883, the non-league Minneapolis Brown Stockings had built a facility there. A dozen years later, in 1896, the site would be chosen to replace the downtown Athletic Park (1889–96) and would become the location of

Nicollet Park (1896–1955), home for more than half a century to the Minneapolis Millers.[5]

In 1884, these grounds were relatively remote and beyond an acceptable walking distance from the city center, but they were served by two independent transit systems. The steam trains of the Minneapolis, Lyndale & Minnetonka railroad, known as the Motor Line, ran from downtown Minneapolis to this block, and then turned west to the increasingly popular Minneapolis lakes and Lake Minnetonka. The area was also served by the Minneapolis Street Railway, a streetcar company that would soon electrify its lines and expand to encompass both Minneapolis and Saint Paul's transit systems, operating for decades as the Twin City Rapid Transit Company.

Securing the ballpark's location in the fall preceding the season was typical of this era, as was waiting until just weeks before the season began to actually build the facility. In this case, the common delay between fall site selection and spring construction allowed the association to change its mind about where to locate the grounds. The association criticized transit magnates Thomas Lowry of the Street Railway and William McCrory of the Motor Line for not buying baseball stock. Claiming that they should not be rewarded with ballpark-related transit business if they were not willing to invest in the project themselves, the baseball association reconsidered the grounds arrangement in late March and sought a location that was closer to the center of the city and less reliant on mass transit.[6]

They found an open area just south of the city's grid change, where the street layout shifted from an

W. V. Herancourt, *Minneapolis, Minnesota*. (Minneapolis: Isador Monasch, 1885). The ballpark block is to the right of the center line near the top of the view.

angled alignment determined by the Mississippi River's course to a more traditional compass-oriented plan. A full block of approximately six acres, the land sat between Park and Portland Avenues and Seventeenth and Eighteenth Streets, approximately one and a half miles from St. Anthony Falls and a fifteen-minute walk from the old downtown center.[7]

The empty block was vacant in a couple of senses of the word. First, there was nothing built on it, and second, it was not subdivided. Most of the surrounding blocks had been subdivided in preparation for the construction of individual residences, but this block was visually, physically, and legally "open" space. The residents near this block, all of whom were relatively new to the neighborhood, were evidently accustomed to this open land and their views of it. They objected when it was leased for the baseball park, and they continued to protest as more than 40 trees were cleared to make room for the ballpark's field and structures.[8]

In objecting to the site preparations, the neighbors blamed the local agent who worked for the absentee landlords, inaccurately identified as New Yorkers who had inherited the property. In fact, a group from Massachusetts owned the land, including Roger Sherman Moore, a Springfield banker, lawyer, and real estate speculator who seems never to have lived in Minneapolis. Moore and his associates were originally

from Southwick and other nearby communities in Hampden County, Massachusetts, and they owned land in this part of Minneapolis as well as at a number of sites in St. Paul. Heman Laflin, Joseph M. Forward, and Edward Bates Gillett—Hampden County people all—were in and out of Moore's ownership group over the years. That their investment property produced some rental income was an advantage for these absentee landlords. Unlike the block's neighbors, then, Moore and his co-owners would have been pleased with the work of their local agent.[9]

Having found a new location, the baseball association hired Minneapolis's busiest architect, Leroy S. Buffington, to design the ballpark. Buffington (1847–1931) had been at work on many high-visibility projects, including the showplace Pillsbury A-Mill in Minneapolis (1881) and the second Minnesota State Capitol in Saint Paul (1883), as well as various commercial blocks and residences. His fashionable West Hotel (1884) in downtown Minneapolis was under construction when the baseball grounds were built. This may have been the first time that a prominent architect was hired for a ballpark job in the Twin Cities, though it was certainly not the last.[10]

Preparation of the grounds began in late April and construction began in late May. Home plate and the surrounding grandstand sat at the southeast corner of the block, placing the fans in full sun during the afternoon games and necessitating a late modification of the architectural plans to include an awning. In fact, most ballpark elements emphasized fan comfort. The *St. Paul Pioneer Press* described such features as "dressing and retiring rooms for both gentlemen and ladies, and bath rooms for the players," as well as "one hundred posts for horses."[11]

While taking great care to create a park that would please the fans inside, relatively little was done to ease the concerns of the neighbors around the park. Just three weeks into the season, the neighbors filed for an injunction to stop play at the site, basing their complaints on property damage, disorderly behavior, appearances, and noise, among other things. Acknowledging that these elements were "the natural, probable, and necessary consequences" of baseball grounds, they did not seek to alter the operations. Instead, they wanted the facility closed and removed. This direct legal action is unusual in the history of local ballparks and reveals much about the varying perceptions of life in the growing city of Minneapolis.[12]

The neighborhood's evolution explains much of the animosity. Both Park and Portland Avenues were emerging as important residential thoroughfares running out from the central business district. In keeping with the image they hoped to create, the residents exchanged the avenues' assigned numbers—Sixth Avenue and Seventh Avenue—for the more elegant and evocative "Portland" and "Park" Avenues. Within six years, neighbors would organize the Park Avenue Improvement Association and mansions would fill the large lots facing these streets.[13]

The name of lumber company owner Charles S. Bardwell appeared at the top of every legal document and press report about neighborhood objections. Bardwell's home, one of the largest in the area, was constructed in 1882 and cost $8,000 to build, making it far more expensive than the vast majority of Minneapolis residences built that year. The house sat at the southwest corner of Park Avenue and Eighteenth Street, and Bardwell could congratulate himself on both the beautiful house and its wonderful location, situated as it was on a large lot along this developing high-class residential boulevard. Its north side and many of its windows faced the empty lot that initially provided a park-like setting—

but not a *ballpark-like* setting, which is what it became once the block was cleared, fenced, and required a ticket for admission.[14]

It should be noted that not all the neighbors disliked the ballpark. Some supported the baseball association, saying that they and their families enjoyed the games. What's more, the team asserted that some of the complainants sold viewing space on their roofs and in their windows, thereby profiting from the baseball games they claimed to dislike.[15]

Bardwell and many of his neighbors launched a legal assault on the ballpark, weaving together several arguments about the importance of open space in an urbanizing environment, the need to segregate commerce and residence in the new industrial urban order, and the threat posed by the daily arrival of the wrong sort of people. In their complaint, they defined their neighborhood as quiet and residential, "suitable and agreeable for the purposes of the best class of family homes," and argued that they had improved their property with trees, flowers, and shrubs. The baseball grounds were detrimental to the identity, character, and carefully tended visual surroundings they sought to create.[16]

They complained about the noise: "a large and noisy crowd of several hundred men and boys has been attracted to and has collected in the streets" and then "during a great part of said times Bands of Brass instruments are playing loud and noisy tunes," while crowds of fifteen hundred to three thousand people "continually shout, clap their hands, stamp with their

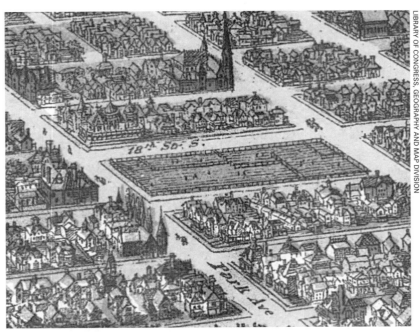

Detail of Frank Pezolt, *Bird's Eye View of Minneapolis, Minn.* (Minneapolis, A. M. Smith, c. 1891).

Charles S. Bardwell house, Minneapolis.

feet and make loud and deafening noises and demonstrations." The neighbors complained about the visual environment: in addition to the removal of the trees in May, they disliked the fences and stands being built on the block. They also claimed that the "defendant and other persons throw about, strew, and distribute large numbers of paper posters and advertisements of various descriptions in the streets and over plaintiffs [sic] premises." The temporary stands and booths erected on the sidewalks for selling lemonade, cigars, pop, and peanuts were also offensive.[17]

The traffic, both inside and outside of the grounds, was objectionable, including not only the vehicles parked on the field but also the "horses and wagons, carriages and buggies, which are not taken within the said enclosure but are hitched, tied or left standing" about the streets in front of the residences and blocking the streets for several hours—and "many of which are driven into the plaintiffs door yards and over and upon plaintiffs lawns and flowers, and are tied and fastened to plaintiffs trees, fences and posts." Not only were the animals and vehicles a problem, so too were the "large noisy and promiscuous crowds" of men and boys who "swarm over the lawns and flowers, and climb onto porches, roofs, sheds, barns and residences" and into the trees to see the games. Property damage and danger were among the concerns, including a broken window in the Bardwell house, which stood closest to the grandstand. "Balls used in said games are very hard and dangerous instruments and are frequently batted or

forced with great violence . . . endangering the lives and bodily safety of the plaintiffs families" and when the balls left the grounds, men and boys "rush upon the plaintiffs premises to recover said balls, trampling upon plaintiffs ornamental lawns, flower beds and shrubbery and brushing against, shaking and injuring the plaintiffs trees and otherwise injuring said premises."[18]

Any residential community might reasonably object to circumstances such as these. In the complaints, however, we can read of issues deeper than disliking big crowds and noisy brass bands. In general, the legal battle between neighborhood and ballpark revealed several community tensions. One dealt with understandings of open space. Minneapolis had just formed a park board in the previous year, something that had been a matter of significant public discussion. Talk of parks and their benefits was also an important part of recent national dialogue. Although not a public park, the ballpark's block had functioned like one, creating "open, ample breathing space" for Minneapolitans, "essential to the health, as well as the happiness, of thickly settled communities." Beauty and nature were commonly understood as an antidote to urban life, something increasingly essential as Minneapolis grew to face challenges already seen in the older and larger cities to the east, and the neighbors drew on the language of order, beauty, peace, and quiet in discussing the ball grounds' problems. They described their neighborhood as "fitted up," "improved," "beautiful," and "carefully kept," making it "quiet" and "agreeable," an exclusively residential area for a fine class of people. In contrast to the orderliness and beauty of their property, they emphasized the disorder, chaos, and damage created by the ballpark. They described the block's baseball use as an "appropriation" of the open space, rather than characterizing it as the result of a legal and orderly real estate transaction, and they failed to acknowledge the "improvement" of the grounds by the baseball association. Seeing the ballpark and its use as an assault on nature, the neighbors regularly spoke of—or on behalf of—the landscape features great and small, from the trees to the grass.[19]

A second area of tension arose from the proximity of residences and businesses. The area was described as being distant from the "crowded and noisy" portions of the city, which were associated with economic activity, not residential life. There were strong objections to the perceived intrusion of commercial activities into the neighborhood: ticket offices and gates for the collection of admittance fees, money-making "devices" like concession stands, and the extensive advertising, signs, and posters. Further, complaints about the appearance of the structures—with a "grand stand," "raised seats" and "high board fences"—were frequently associated with height, itself a characteristic of the buildings found in the central business district.[20]

In responding to this array of charges, the baseball association noted that it had made numerous concessions to the neighbors. For example, they had built lower fences than originally planned, and with higher quality lumber, in an attempt to make the facility less objectionable and more attractive. The purchase of surfaced lumber made the project more expensive, and an agreement not to post advertising on the fences cost the team expected income. Further, lower fences made it easier for people to see into the park without paying for tickets—another potential blow to the revenue. It was also noted that baseball would be played for only a few months out of the year, and then for only an hour or two a day. The brass bands played but for ten or fifteen minutes at the start of the game, and with an average attendance of only 800 respectable fans, the amount of disruption would be minimal. Streets would never be blocked and police would be present in the unlikely event that order needed to be restored. For most of the year and for most hours during the baseball season, the ballpark would be a quiet place fully compatible with its neighbors. The baseball association also deployed the discourse of nature as an antidote to urban and commercial disorder as they defended the ballpark. Most revealing was the association's response to the claim that baseballs represented a danger. Rather than describing them as propelled by the swing of a bat, the defendants noted that the baseballs were the size of apples, and argued that they "fell" into the street, much like fruit falling from a tree. In this, of course, the baseball club was turning the language of nature back against its opponents.[21]

Their arguments made, the association and the neighbors then awaited the district court's decision while the games continued. In the end, the residents around Park and Portland Avenues prevailed in their attempt to remove the baseball grounds from their neighborhood. In late August 1884, the court granted their request, and the baseball association was enjoined from playing at those grounds past October 15, 1884. They were also prohibited from scheduling additional events or games, and the structures on the property were to be removed within ten days of the October 15 deadline. These fall deadlines proved to be irrelevant, however, as the team folded in early September.[22]

The abrupt and early end to the Minneapolis season was not the end of the story, however, as problems with the 1884 ballpark's construction shifted into the courts. The project's contractor, Robert Fender, first put a lien on the property and later filed a lawsuit to receive full payment for his services. He had been paid about two-thirds of what was owed to him, probably in weekly wages to the construction workers, but had not received the remainder of his $600.63 payment within thirty days of the project's completion. His complaint, like those of the neighbors, provides some insight into the details of the project and the facility. The itemized bill hints at some of the details of the structure, including the installation of a bathtub (a $6.00 item) and the digging and making of two privy vaults (at $1.50 each). We learn that the facility included twelve gates, secured with Yale locks, and was fitted out with 21 dozen coat hooks.[23]

Even more extensive was the legal dispute with the lumber company, Farnham & Lovejoy. They had delivered approximately 107,000 board feet of lumber to the ball grounds in early June, running up a bill totaling $1,613.81. After unsuccessful attempts to collect payment, they followed the contractor's lead and put a lien on the property in October, shortly before the scheduled demolition. Unable to collect from the association, Farnham & Lovejoy filed suit against one of the group's directors, bartender Joseph H. Murch. Murch had been present when the lumber was ordered, and Farnham & Lovejoy claimed that he had agreed to be personally responsible for the billing. Murch denied this and refused to pay. The dispute resulted in two trials held in November and December 1885, more than a year after the facility was removed. In the first trial, the jury failed to agree, but in the December trial, the second jury decided against Murch. He asked for a new trial, but was rejected by the state Supreme Court in January 1887. Farnham & Lovejoy then sued for both the original claim and for interest and legal costs, but Murch prevailed in a January 1888 decision.[24]

The sad story of this short-lived ballpark, replete with conflict and difficulty, might indicate that nothing but high-end homes would ever be welcome in the Park Avenue neighborhood. Remarkably, after the professional baseball team and its facilities were gone, the block continued to be used for sports—for lacrosse matches, University of Minnesota football games, tennis clubs, and the like—but without the structures, crowds, and commercialism associated with the 1884 league team. It was not until the turn of the twentieth century that any permanent structures were built there. By that time, professional baseball teams in Minneapolis had built (and twice rebuilt) three new ballparks in other parts of the city, and in the last of these, Nicollet Park, the team finally found a long-term home. The Park/Portland neighborhood would remain quiet and largely residential until the interstate highway bisected the community. Compared to a multi-lane concrete trench filled with traffic, the sights and sounds of a small baseball park might not seem so unpleasant.[25] ■

Notes

1. Minneapolis Base Ball Association Articles of Incorporation, November 1883. *Minnesota State Archives: Secretary of State, Corporate Division, Incorporations Book I*, 528, Minnesota Historical Society; *Minneapolis Tribune*, "Base Ball: A New Northwestern League," September 22, 1883; *Minneapolis Tribune*, "A Base Ball Club," October 24, 1883; *Minneapolis Tribune*, "Gossip About Town: The Base Ball Association," November 8, 1883.

2. *Minneapolis Tribune*, "Gossip About Town," October 24, 1883; *Minneapolis Tribune*, "The National Game," October 30, 1883; *Minneapolis Tribune*, "Base Ball Stock: An Appeal to be Made to Business Men and Others," January 26, 1884; *Saturday Evening Spectator*, "Home-Hitters," June 28, 1884.

3. *Minneapolis Tribune*, "Base Ball: A New Northwestern League," September 22, 1883; *Minneapolis Tribune*, "The Base Ball Club: Manager Tuthill Returns and Reports Everything Lovely," January 3, 1884; *Minneapolis Journal*, "The National Game: The Expectations for Minneapolis Next Season," January 3, 1884; *Minneapolis Journal*, "The Base Ball League," January 8, 1884; *Minneapolis Journal*, "We are a League City," January 10, 1884; *St. Paul Daily Globe*, "Base Ball: Minneapolis and St. Paul Admitted to the Northwestern League, Composed of Twelve Teams," January 11, 1884; *Minneapolis Journal*, "Base Ball: The Question of Sunday Games," March 22, 1884. Later, Winona would take a spot in the league as other teams folded. *Saturday Evening Spectator*, August 16, 1884.

4. *Minneapolis Tribune*, "Base Ball in Minneapolis," October 19, 1883; *Minneapolis Journal*, "No Sunday Games," January 18, 1884; *St. Paul Daily Globe*, "Scraps of Sport," February 1, 1888; *St. Paul Daily Globe*, "All is Not Lovely in the Managerial Department of the 'Said Pasha' Company," January 12, 1890; *St. Paul Daily Globe*, "Romance to Reality," April 10, 1891; *New York Sun*, "Manager Tuthill Marries," September 19, 1892; *New York Clipper Annual*, 1893, 6; *New York Dramatic Mirror*, "A New Stock Company," January 5, 1898.

5. *Minneapolis Tribune*, "Gossip About Town," November 27, 1883, and December 12, 1883; *St. Paul Daily Globe*, "Twenty-Six to Three," June 29, 1883.

6. *Minneapolis Journal*, "Sporting Gossip: The Base Ball Grounds," March 31, 1884; *Saturday Evening Spectator*, "Home-Hitters," June 28, 1884.

7. *Minneapolis Tribune*, "The City," April 17, 1884; *Saturday Evening Spectator*, "Spectator About Town," April 19, 1884; *Minneapolis Tribune*, "The Base Ball Grounds," May 9, 1884.

8. C. M. Foote, *Atlas of the City of Minneapolis, Minnesota*, 1892 and 1898, plate 15. The baseball association had a three-year lease costing $1,000 a year; one resident claimed that he would have contributed one hundred dollars to help lease the land to prevent its alteration. *Saturday Evening Spectator*, "Spectator About Town," May 3, 1884.

9. *Minneapolis Tribune*, Legal notice, August 15, 1874; *Obituary Record of Graduates of Yale University Deceased from June, 1890, to June, 1900* (New Haven: Tuttle, Morehouse & Taylor, 1900), 209, accessed at

http://books.google.com/books?id=QFgdAQAAIAAJ&pg on June 25, 2011; William Richard Cutter and William Frederick Adams, *Genealogical and personal memoirs relating to the families of the state of Massachusetts*, vol. 3, 1815, accessed at http://books.google.com/books?id= Bc8UAAAAYAAJ&dq on August 22, 2011; When the block was finally subdivided, the addition was named Gillett, Forward and Smith's addition.

10. In 1888, for example, the young Cass Gilbert and his partner, James Knox Taylor, were hired to design the Athletic Park in St. Paul. Within a decade, Gilbert's portfolio would include the design for the third (and present) Minnesota State Capitol, built to replace the relatively new but deeply disliked Buffington building. *Minneapolis Tribune*, "A Successful Architect," January 13, 1884; *Minneapolis Journal*, "Sporting," April 15, 1884; Muriel B. Christisson, "LeRoy S. Buffington and the Minneapolis Boom of the 1880's," *Minnesota History* 23:3 (September 1942), 219-232; *St. Paul Daily Globe*, "The Falling Capitol: Architect Buffington Trying to Hang It to Its Roof," August 13, 1884; R. S. Fender vs. Minneapolis Base Ball Association, Hennepin County Lien Book F, 242–245.

11. R. S. Fender vs. Minneapolis Base Ball Association; *Pioneer Press*, "The New Minneapolis Base Ball Park," May 19, 1884.

12. Charles S. Bardwell, et al., vs. The Minneapolis Base Ball Association, 18870, 4th Judicial District, Hennepin County (1884); *St. Paul Daily Globe*, "Minneapolis Globelets," July 2, 1884; *Minneapolis Journal*, "The Courts," July 7, 1884; *St. Paul Daily Globe*, "Enjoining Base Ballists," July 8, 1884; *Minneapolis Tribune*, "They Don't Like Base Ball, and, Therefore, Petition for an Injunction Restraining the Ball Club," July 8, 1884.

13. See, for example, Larry Millett, *Once There Were Castles: Lost Mansions and Estates of the Twin Cities* (Minneapolis: University of Minnesota Press, 2011).

14. *Minneapolis Tribune*, "An Imposing Array of Buildings Erected in Minneapolis in 1882," January 1, 1883; *Minneapolis Tribune*, "The Court Records," July 8, 1884; Charles S. Bardwell, et al., vs. The Minneapolis Base Ball Association.

15. Affidavits from A. C. Lanphere and H. R. Porter, in Charles S. Bardwell, et al, vs. The Minneapolis Base Ball Association.

16. Charles S. Bardwell, et al., vs. The Minneapolis Base Ball Association.

17. Charles S. Bardwell, et al., vs. The Minneapolis Base Ball Association.

18. Charles S. Bardwell, et al., vs. The Minneapolis Base Ball Association.

19. John Rea, letter to the editor, *Minneapolis Tribune*, May 23, 1880, quoted in Theodore Wirth, *Retrospective Glimpses into the History of the Board of Park Commissioners of Minneapolis, Minnesota and the City's Park, Parkway, and Playground System: Minneapolis Park System 1883–1944* (Minneapolis: Minneapolis Parks Legacy Society, 2006), 17–18; Charles S. Bardwell, et al, vs. The Minneapolis Base Ball Association.

20. Charles S. Bardwell, et al., vs. The Minneapolis Base Ball Association.

21. J. H. Murch and F. W. Partridge deposition, in Charles S. Bardwell, et al., vs. The Minneapolis Base Ball Association.

22. *Saturday Evening Spectator*, "Spectator About Town," July 26, 1884, and August 23, 1884; *Minneapolis Journal*, "Sporting: Base Ball," August 21, 1884; *Minneapolis Tribune*, "The City," August 21, 1884; Judgment Rule, Charles S. Bardwell, et al., vs. The Minneapolis Base Ball Association.

23. R. S. Fender vs. Minneapolis Base Ball Association; *St. Paul Daily Globe*, "The Courts," December 28, 1884.

24. Farnham & Lovejoy vs. Minneapolis Base Ball Association, Hennepin County Lien Book F, 204–207; *St. Paul Daily Globe*, "The Close of the Term," November 26, 1885; *St. Paul Daily Globe*, "Left on Third Base," December 24, 1885; *Minneapolis Tribune*, "Court Notes," December 25, 1885; Farnham & Lovejoy v. Murch, 36 Minn. 328; 31 N. W. 453 (1887); *St. Paul Daily Globe*, "A Relic of Base Ball," January 5, 1888; *St. Paul Daily Globe*, "Joe Wins It," January 6, 1888.

25. *St. Paul Daily Globe*, "Field Sports," October 15, 1884; *St. Paul Daily Globe*, "Scraps of Sport," May 30, 1885; *St. Paul Daily Globe*, "Division Drill," June 30, 1885; "Football at Minnesota: The Story of Thirty Years' Contests on the Gridiron," *The Minnesota Alumni Weekly* 14/9 (1914), 12. *Minneapolis Tribune*, "A Season of Tennis," May 7, 1894; *Minneapolis Journal*, "The Park Av. Tennis Courts," June 6, 1896.

Dames in the Dirt

Women's Baseball Before 1945

Anne Aronson

Despite the fact that the great American pastime has been almost exclusively identified as a male sport, women have played baseball in Minnesota for over 100 years. In the early years, from the late nineteenth century through the 1920s, women played baseball in Minnesota on college campuses, in industrial leagues, through local church and community groups, and on barnstorming teams. In 1944, Minnesota was home to a professional women's baseball team, the Minneapolis Millerettes, one of six teams in the All-American Girls Professional Baseball League, made famous through the film *A League of Their Own*. In more recent years, left-handed pitcher Ila Borders played on the St. Paul Saints and Duluth Dukes independent league baseball teams, while numerous girls across the state have played Little League and high school baseball. This article focuses on women's baseball in Minnesota from the 1890s through World War II.

EARLY YEARS

The earliest evidence that women played baseball in Minnesota is a photo from Thief River Falls, dated 1893, of ten female players with two male player-managers. The note accompanying the photo reads, "Thief River Falls Ladies Baseball Team Champions of Northern League, 1893."[1] This note suggests that there were multiple women's teams playing competitively at this time. Baseball historians Gai Berlage, Harold Seymour,[2] and others have documented that women played baseball as early as 1865 at Vassar College. In the Thief River Falls photo, the women are wearing the same type of long dresses with long sleeves worn by women in the early pictures of Vassar baseball teams, adhering to the Victorian standard of feminine modesty.

Women not only played hardball at elite women's colleges on the East Coast in the early twentieth century,

but also at coeducational institutions in the Midwest. *The Minneapolis Journal* of March 17, 1906 announced the start of the women's baseball season at the University of Minnesota: "Girls Will Indulge in National Game." The article highlights the fact that the women would play behind screens, typically used for secret football practices, so that the men could not see them. "If it is found impossible to play the game on Northrop field safe from masculine observation, the girls plan to introduce indoor baseball in the girls' gymnasium."[3]

Baseball was also played by women at Carleton College in Northfield, starting around 1915. In 1916, there were four baseball teams, each representing a class, from freshman through senior. By 1922, the intramural women's baseball program was well established. A May 17, 1922 article in *The Carletonia* listed the lineups for the four teams as they headed into the end-of-year tournament. The teams consisted of ten players, including two shortstops. Surprisingly, the freshman team won the championship by defeating the juniors in the final game by a score of 25–24.

Baseball at Carleton was typical of the women's game in this time period. It was played indoors at least part of the time, although there are references to out-

Thief River Falls Ladies Baseball Team Champions of Northern Minnesota 1893.

COURTESY MINNESOTA HISTORICAL SOCIETY

Ball Playing Nuns, c.1931.

door play as well. Indoor baseball, a precursor to softball, was a popular sport for girls and women in the 1920s. Women's baseball at Carleton was also typical in that it featured intramural, not intercollegiate play. According to Jenny Ring, intercollegiate play was off limits for women because "too much competition was regarded as unhealthy for girls," and "travel was also believed to be too strenuous and unsuitable for the health and morality of the young women."[4] Finally, by 1922, Carleton women were playing in bloomers rather than long skirts, an evolution that was typical of women's baseball during this time period.

Women also played baseball on Minnesota soil when, starting in the late nineteenth century, barnstorming teams visited the state. These teams were called "Bloomer Girls," and they went from town to town all over the country, challenging men's amateur, minor league, or semi-professional teams to games. The bloomer teams usually had two or more men as members, and sometimes the men dressed as women. The term "bloomer" is derived from the name of the mid-nineteenth century advocate for women's rights, Amelia Jenks Bloomer, who argued that women should have the option of wearing less restrictive clothing.

Bloomer Girls teams came from Chicago, Boston, Canada, and elsewhere to play games in Minnesota communities. An early appearance by a women's barnstorming team occurred in 1895, when the Ladies Champion Baseball Club of Chicago visited Duluth. In 1909, the Chicago Bloomer Girls came to Bemidji to play a game against the town team. The article in the *Bemidji Daily Pioneer* previewing the game notes that a "record-breaking crowd" was expected.[5] The captain and proprietor of the team was Miss Bernie Carleton. Carleton was among several women who managed and owned barnstorming teams, an unusually powerful role for women during this time period.

The Bemidji press was relatively respectful toward the women's team, although the reporter expressed typical attitudes of the time when noting that "the members of the ladies' team are well-behaved and conduct themselves in an unapproachable [sic] manner at all times."[6] The restrained tone of the Bemidji paper, however, was not shared by the *Minneapolis Morning Tribune*, which contained this July 30, 1916, headline about a visit by the Western Bloomer Girls: "Comedy for Fans When Bloomer Girls Lose to Minneapolis Athletics." This game, with a final score of 11–8, was played in Nicollet Park before a crowd of 600 "curiosity seekers."[7] The game was unusual in that the bloomer team consisted entirely of women. One of those women, Maud Nelson, was one of the most accomplished and famous women baseball players of all time. Nelson was well known for her exceptional pitching, as well as her hitting and her fielding skills at third base. According to Barbara Gregorich, Nelson was a "world renowned Bloomer Girl pitcher, a third baseman, a scout, a manager, and an owner of the best teams of her era. . . For forty years she was always there."[8]

Women's baseball was not confined to college campuses and bloomer girl barnstorming visits. For example, on April 21, 1911, the *Minneapolis Morning Tribune* reports on a game between the staffs of two hotels—the Dyckman and the Radisson.[9] The pitcher for the Dyckman was Alma Wyness, formerly a player on the Rochester, New York Bloomer Girls. More significantly, an industrial women's baseball league was established in Duluth in 1919. The league consisted of eight teams from local businesses such as the Rust-Parker Grocery Company and the Marshall-Wells Hardware Company. A headline in the July 20, 1919, *Duluth News Tribune* announced the new league: "Duluth Has the Honor of Having 'Something New'/City is One of Few in Country Who Have a Girls' Baseball League."[10] Coordinated by the YWCA, the eight teams played twice a week in various parks throughout the city; the Duluth daily paper covered the games closely and with admiration for the quality of play. The women's league in Duluth was part of a national movement to bring women's sports to the "employed girl." According to the *1918 Cleveland Recreation Survey*, 44 percent of female employees in the city of Cleveland played baseball. The industrial clubs for women that sprung up in Duluth and elsewhere in the early twentieth century were an outgrowth of the social reform movement that sought to improve conditions for American workers.[11]

Several photographs from the Minnesota Historical Society suggest other venues for women's baseball in the state. A series of photographs from 1931 taken by Father Robert E. Russell in Leavenworth, Minnesota, capture nuns in full habit playing baseball and posing for a team photo with a bat. Another photo dated 1926 features 10 young African American diamond ball players from the Phyllis Wheatley Settlement House, a community center that still exists in North Minneapolis and is the oldest organization in Minnesota with continuous service to the African American community. One of the women in the photo is Ethel Ray Nance, daughter of the president of the Duluth chapter of the NAACP. Nance became the first African American policewoman in Minnesota, and later worked for civil rights activist and author W.E.B. Du Bois. She is considered an important figure in the Harlem Renaissance.

The diamond ball played by the young women at the Phyllis Wheatley Settlement House in 1926 probably resembled modern day softball more than it resembled hardball. That's because softball, sometimes called "kittenball" or "mush ball," emerged in the 1920s as the preferred diamond sport for girls and women. The 1929 book, *Baseball for Girls and Women* by Gladys Palmer, professor of physical education at Ohio State University, details the transition from baseball to softball during this period. The book focuses on a sport that featured underhand pitching and smaller base paths, but it also identifies four different versions of the sport, one of which used a nine-inch ball and overhand pitching.

THE MILLERETTES

By the 1940s, the transition from baseball to softball was complete, and the newer sport became wildly popular among both women and men across the U.S. and Canada. In 1943, Philip K. Wrigley, fearing that the manpower shortage caused by World War II would harm major league baseball and his own fortunes as owner of the Chicago Cubs and Wrigley Field, capitalized on the abundance of female softball talent by establishing the All American Girls Professional Baseball League (AAGPBL). In this early phase of the league, the game was a hybrid of softball and baseball. It featured underhand pitching, for example, but it also allowed leading off and stealing bases, forbidden in

Phyllis Wheatley intermediate diamond ball team, Minneapolis, 1926.

regulation softball. League managers felt that base stealing would make the game more attractive to fans.

The AAGPBL, made famous in the movie *A League of Their Own*, began with four teams, located in midsize Midwestern cities: Kenosha, Wisconsin; Racine, Wisconsin; Rockford, Illinois; and South Bend, Indiana. In 1944, Wrigley added two more teams to the league, this time in the much larger cities of Minneapolis and Milwaukee. The Minneapolis Millerettes played their first home game at Nicollet Park on May 27, 1944, against the Rockford Peaches. In anticipation of the game, a United Press story did more to stereotype the players than report on their skills and previous athletic accomplishments: "Quick, Millie, my mask and mascara, for there's a powder puff plot under way at 3 P.M. Saturday at Nicollet park, which threatens the foundation of the national pastime, a conspiracy aimed at virtual extinction of the perspiring, swearing, tobacco-chewing baseball player."[12] After the home opener, which the Millerettes lost 5–4, sports reporter Halsey Hall reported on the game and was a bit more respectful of the women as players: "In a welter of flaring skirts, headlong and feet-first slides into base, bodily contact, good pitching and really brilliant outfielding, Jack Kloza's Amazons won by great defensive work."[13]

The Millerettes were chock full of rookies who brought outstanding softball and other athletic credentials to the team. According to Barbara Gregorich, some of the rookies from California had played softball in front of crowds as large as 30,000.[14] The Millerettes' manager was Clarence "Bubber" Jonnard, who had been a catcher for a number of major league teams and a coach for the New York Giants and Phillies.

COURTESY NORTHERN INDIANA HISTORICAL SOCIETY

The Minneapolis Millerettes pitching staff in 1944. On the far left is Dorothy Wiltse, who won 20 games in each of her first four seasons with the AAGPBL. In the center is Annabelle Lee, who, as a Millerette, pitched the first perfect game in the AAGPBL on July 29, 1944.

Not much is known about how Jonnard managed the team, although one player, Faye Dancer, did express her lack of enthusiasm for the Millerettes' manager: "I loved the sport. I wanted to play to win. Jonnard was always negative. . . we California girls made up our own signals and played our own game."[15]

The season got off to a robust start. By the end of the second week, the Millerettes were in second place in the six-team league, with a record of nine wins and six losses. Fans were particularly interested in hometown players Lorraine Borg and Peggy Torrison, who had excelled on Twin Cities softball teams before trying out for the AAGPBL. The Millerettes were still drawing positive attention on June 16–17 when they hosted a weekend series against the Racine Belles. The June 16 game lasted 15 innings, with the Millerettes' star pitcher, Dorothy Wiltse, tossing 10⅔ no-hit innings. The home team ended up losing the game, 3–2, but took their revenge the next day when they faced the Belles again. With a tie game in the bottom of the ninth, Helen Callaghan and Judy Dusano were on second and third. Pep Paire stepped up to the plate and "slashed a hard one at third sacker English. Maddy came up with a good stop, but the flying Helen beat her throw to the plate in a split-hair play."[16] The Millerettes won, 7–6.

Despite some early successes, by July 5 the Mille–rettes were in last place, and by July 23 they had played their last game in Minnesota. Concerned about the cost of bringing teams to Minneapolis from as far away as South Bend and the low attendance at Nicollet Park, the league decided to reschedule the Millerettes home games to the road. For the remainder of the 1944 season, the team became the "Minneapolis Orphans." The *Minneapolis Tribune* quoted league president Ken Sells, who said that the other teams "objected to making the trip to Minneapolis because of the heavy traveling expenses with such small crowds attending the games."[17] The Millerettes ended the year in last place, although there were some bright spots. One was the league's first perfect game, pitched by Millerette Annabelle Lee on July 29. This shining moment, however, could not stave off the demise of the team. For the 1945 season, the team was moved to Indiana, where they remained for ten years as the much-appreciated and very successful Fort Wayne Daisies.

Why was attendance so poor at Millerette games compared to that of cities like Racine and Rockford? Some might argue that the Millerettes failed because of their poor play later in the season, but this seems unlikely because the Milwaukee Chicks, the other team that met its demise at the end of the 1944 season, won the league championship. In addition, many of the players on the Millerettes went on to become standouts on other teams.

Merrie Fidler, the leading historian of the AAGPBL, argues that there are a number of possible reasons for the Millerettes' struggles.[18] First, the two expansion teams, the Millerettes and the Milwaukee Chicks, played on fields built for American Association minor league teams, which was not the case for the original four teams of the AAGPBL. The sharing of Nicollet Park with the Minneapolis Millers may have invited a direct comparison between the two teams, one that did not favor the Millerettes. Even ticket prices were an issue. A telephone poll in Milwaukee suggested that fans were dissatisfied with the ticket prices for the AAGPBL games compared to the prices for the American Association games. Beyond the competition with men's minor league ball, the big cities of Minneapolis and Milwaukee offered numerous other sports and entertainment options that might have undermined the success of the Millerettes.

The other reason for the failure of the Millerettes, according to Fidler, was a lack of local support from businesses and the press. While the four original teams of the AAGPBL received financial backing from local businesses, this was not the case for the Minneapolis and Milwaukee teams. The expansion teams were likely subsidized by Wrigley himself. In addition, Fidler argues that the press in Minneapolis and Milwaukee was less supportive of the teams than the press in the smaller cities like South Bend. "A comparison of all league city newspapers, from May to July 1944, revealed that the Minneapolis and Milwaukee papers printed shorter stories, less frequently, with a more marked chauvinistic attitude than the other papers."[19] Sharon Roepke and Danielle Barber went so far as to say the press was "antagonistic" in Minneapolis compared to other cities.[20]

The Millerettes may have run aground at the end of the 1944 season, but they left a solid legacy through an outstanding set of players who spent their rookie years in Minneapolis. Here are a few of the most notable players on the 1944 team:

Dorothy Wiltse Collins was one of the best pitchers in the history of the league. A *New York Times* obituary described her hurling prowess: "She pitched underhand, sidearm and overhand; she threw curveballs, fastballs and changeups."[21] During her rookie season with the Millerettes, she won 20 games with a 1.88 ERA. In 1945, pitching for the Fort Wayne Daisies, she pitched two games of a doubleheader and won them both. If that weren't enough, she repeated this feat eight days later, giving up a total of two runs over all four games. Wiltse had a career record of 117–76 and an ERA of 1.83. She won 20 games or more during each of her first four seasons.

Faye Dancer was an exceptional athlete, an entertainer on the field, and a prankster off it. During her year on the Millerettes, she batted .274, the third highest average in the league. She also hit two grand slam home runs, knocked in 48 runs, and stole 63 bases. In 1948, she stole 102 bases. She was well known for her base running panache and her superb skills in catching fly balls. Halsey Hall referred to the "ground-covering, fly-catching genius" of Dancer in center field.[22] She also made her mark through her antics

on and off the field. Out in center field she would do cartwheels, splits and handstands; off the field, she played tricks on other players and especially on new chaperones—for example, replacing the cream in their Oreos with toothpaste. Given her abundance of chutzpah and personality, it is not surprising that Dancer was the inspiration for Madonna's "All the Way Mae" character in *A League of Their Own*.

Helen Callaghan St. Aubin, from Vancouver, Canada, played on the Millerettes alongside her sister, Margaret. Callaghan was a star batter and base stealer. Her .287 batting average was second in the league in 1944. In 1945, at 5-foot-1 and 115 pounds, she the paced the league in doubles and tied for the lead in home runs. One of her sons, Casey Candaele, played for nine seasons in the major leagues. While Candaele swung a bat that was 33 inches long and 32 ounces, his mother's bat was 36 inches long and 36 ounces.[23] Another of Callaghan's sons, Kelly Candaele, made the documentary, *A League of Their Own*, which led to the 1992 film by the same name.

Annabelle Lee Harmon grew up in California and was recruited for the AAGPBL in 1944 by Bill Allington, who managed teams in the AAGPBL every season from 1944 until the league folded in 1954 (except 1947). She distinguished herself as a left-handed pitcher for the Millerettes by throwing the league's first perfect game on July 29, 1944, against the Kenosha Comets. The next year, as a member of the Fort Wayne Daisies, she threw a no-hitter. Lee's career ERA was 2.25, and she was known for throwing a wicked knuckleball. Like Dorothy Wiltse Collins, she was one of the few pitchers who adjusted to the transition from underhand pitching in 1944, to sidearm pitching in 1946, and then to overhand pitching in 1948. Her nephew, Bill "Spaceman" Lee, pitched for the Montreal Expos and Boston Red Sox in the 1970s and 1980s.

Albert G. Spalding, baseball player, baseball writer, and founder of the sporting goods company reflected on women and hardball in 1911:

But neither our wives, our sisters, our daughters, nor our sweethearts, may play Base Ball on the field. . . They may play Lawn Tennis, and win championships; they may play Basket Ball, and achieve laurels, they may play Golf, and receive trophies; but Base Ball is too strenuous for womankind, except as she may take part in grandstand, with applause for the brilliant play.[24]

Fortunately, numerous women ignored Spalding's declaration that baseball was off limits for women. Starting in the late nineteenth century, they grabbed bats, balls, and mitts and played the game hard throughout the state of Minnesota. Refusing to remain in the grandstand, they defied stereotypes, resisted sexism, and asserted their right to take part in the beloved American pastime. ■

Notes

1. Courtesy of the Pennington County Historical Society.
2. While Harold Seymour is the author of record for *The People" Game*, which includes five detailed chapters on women's baseball, Dorothy Jane Mills, Seymour's wife at the time, convincingly describes how she was the main researcher and writer for these chapters. See Dorothy Jane Mills, *A Woman's Work: Writing Baseball History with Harold Seymour,* (Jefferson, NC: McFarland, 2004).
3. *Minneapolis Journal*, March 17, 1906, 2.
4. Jennifer Ring. *Stolen Bases: Why American Girls Don't Play Baseball.* (Urbana, IL: University of Illinois Press, 2009) 35.
5. *Bemidji Daily Pioneer*, August 7, 1909, 1.
6. *Bemidji Daily Pioneer*, August 9, 1909, 1.
7. *Minneapolis Morning Tribune*, July 30, 1916, B1.
8. Barbara Gregorich. *Women at Play: The Story of Women in Baseball.* (San Diego: Harcourt Brace, 1993) 6.
9. *Minneapolis Morning Tribune*, April 21, 1911, 4.
10. *Duluth News Tribune*, July 20, 1919, Section 2, 1.
11. Merrie Fidler. *The Origins and History of the All-American Girls Professional Baseball League.* (Jefferson, NC: McFarland, 2006) 21.
12. *Minneapolis Tribune*, May 27, 1944, 61.
13. Halsey Hall. "Millerettes 'Uncurled' 5–4." *Minneapolis Tribune*, May 28, 1944. *Sports*, 1.
14. Gregorich, op cit. 108.
15. Margot Galt, "The Girls of Summer." *Minnesota Monthly*, May 1991, 52.
16. *Minneapolis Tribune*, June 18, 1944, Sports, 1.
17. *Minneapolis Tribune*, July 23, 1944, Sports, 1.
18. Fidler, op. cit. 46–48.
19. Fidler, op. cit. 46 (2).
20. Quoted in *Stew Thornley, Baseball in Minnesota: The Definitive History.* (St. Paul: Minnesota Historical Society Press, 2006) 169.
21. Richard Goldsteing "Dottie Collins, 84, Star Pitcher of Women's Baseball League, Dies." *New York Times*, August 17, 2008, A22.
22. Hall, op. cit. *Sports* 1.
23. Peter Barrouquere. "Mom Was Provider, Hero, Role Model to Candaele." *Times-Picayune*, August 30, 1998, C1.
24. Spalding, quoted in *Gladys Palmer, Baseball for Girls and Women.* (New York: A.S. Barnes and Company, 1929) 10.

Sources

Barrouquere, Peter. "Mom Was Provider, Hero, Role Model to Candaele." *Times-Picayune*, August 30, 1998.

"Baseball for 'U' Co-Eds," *Minneapolis Journal*, March 17, 1906.

Berlage, Gai. *Women in Baseball: The Forgotten History.* Westport, CT: Praeger, 1994.

"Bloomer Ladies Will Play Here on Sunday," *Bemidji Daily Pioneer*, August 7, 1909.

"Comedy for Fans When Bloomer Girls Lose to Minneapolis Athletics." *Minneapolis Morning Tribune*, July 30, 1916.

"Duluth Has the Honor of Having 'Something New': City is One of Few in Country Who Have a Girls' Baseball League." *Duluth News Tribune*, July 20, 1919.

Fidler, Merrie. *The Origins and History of the All-American Girls Professional Baseball League.* Jefferson, NC: McFarland, 2006.

Galt, Margot. "The Girls of Summer." *Minnesota Monthly*, May 1991.

Goldstein, Richard. "Dottie Collins, 84, Star Pitcher of Women's Baseball League, Dies." *New York Times*, Aug. 17, 2008.

Gregorich, Barbara. *Women at Play: The Story of Women in Baseball.* San Diego: Harcourt Brace, 1993.

Hall, Halsey. "Millerettes 'Uncurled' 5–4." *Minneapolis Tribune*, May 28, 1944.

"Local Baseball Team Decidedly Ungallant," *Bemidji Daily Pioneer*, August 9, 1909.

Palmer, Gladys. *Baseball for Girls and Women.* New York: A.S. Barnes and Company, 1929.

Ring, Jennifer. *Stolen Bases: Why American Girls Don't Play Baseball.* Urbana, IL: University of Illinois Press, 2009.

Seymour, Harold. *Baseball: The People's Game.* New York: Oxford, 1990.

Thornley, Stew. *Baseball in Minnesota: The Definitive History.* St. Paul: Minnesota Historical Society Press, 2006.

United Press. "It's Powder Puff Baseball in Nicollet Opener Today." *Minneapolis Tribune*, May 27, 1944.

John Donaldson and Black Baseball in Minnesota

Steven R. Hoffbeck and Peter Gorton

The problem of the twentieth century is the problem of the color line.
— W.E.B. DuBois.[1]

For sixty years, professional baseball was as segregated as the Deep South. From 1887—when the unspoken national agreement prohibited African Americans from major league baseball—to 1947, when Jackie Robinson broke the color line, black ballplayers were shut out of the highest levels of the organized game.[2] How could black players, in Minnesota and in other states, respond to being banned from baseball? Well, they could have just given up and accepted segregation as grim reality. Or, young black men could resolve to integrate the sport, town by town, city by city, one baseball diamond at a time. That's what happened in Minnesota.

Renowned author Sinclair Lewis, a native Minnesotan, once said: "To understand America, it is merely necessary to understand Minnesota."[3] Let's look at the state's story.

In 1858, Minnesota joined the U.S. and its constitution declared that there would be no slavery in the state.[4] In 1868, Minnesota extended voting rights to African Americans.

The Minnesota Constitutional Rights Law of 1899 prohibited discrimination in hotels, theaters and restaurants, and other public places, but such a law did not apply to professional baseball. Still, the black population of Minnesota yearned for full social equality because they faced a haphazard maze of discrimination against their best efforts, a denial of rights and opportunities, of narrow-mindedness at best and unreasoning hatred at worst.

Minnesota's black ballplayers, therefore, worked to dismantle baseball's color line themselves.

In the 1890s, pitcher Walter Ball integrated the St. Paul city public-school baseball teams and youth teams. In 1897, Ball and the Young Cyclones ballclub won the St. Paul City Amateur Championship—he was the lone black player on an all-white team.[5]

After the turn of the century, Minnesota towns began to import some black players for their formerly all-white teams. In 1900 the small-town Waseca ball-club secured black pitchers George Wilson and Billy Holland—two men who had played for the best Chicago-area African American teams of the late 1890s. Waseca's EACO Flour team brought the first black ballplayers to the ball-diamonds of southern Minnesota, and they won the state semi-professional championship.[6]

In 1902, Walter Ball became the first black player on St. Cloud's formerly white semipro ballclub. Similarly, Billy Williams, also from St. Paul, integrated his high school team and other area teams.[7]

Minnesota's own Bobby Marshall gained entry onto the Minneapolis Central High School baseball team in the late 1890s and then broke the color line on the University of Minnesota's baseball squad in 1904.[8]

Black businessman Phil "Daddy" Reid established Minnesota's first all-black professional ball club, the St. Paul Colored Gophers, in 1907, gathering top talent from Chicago and elsewhere. Home-grown Bobby Marshall became the "star slugger" on the Colored Gophers team in 1909, when the Colored Gophers claimed the championship of black baseball by defeating Rube Foster's Chicago Leland Giants three games to two. The Colored Gophers barnstormed throughout the Upper Midwest for five years, 1907–1911, bringing a fast and colorful brand of black baseball to towns that had never before seen an African American ballplayer on their local diamonds.[9]

*   *   *

The decade from 1910 to 1919 brought a new wave of black barnstorming teams to Minnesota from other locales. Premiere among these was the All Nations ballclub, a multi-racial team founded in 1912 by James Leslie (J.L.) Wilkinson (1878–1964). Wilkinson was a genius in marketing and publicity, as well as a true baseball man. Although Wilkinson was white, he believed that baseball fans in Minnesota and throughout the Midwest would pay to see the very best and en-

Walter Ball (1880–1946), one of St. Paul's best amateur pitchers in 1898, became a premier hurler among Minnesota semiprofessionals by 1902. In 1903 Ball moved to Chicago where he became one of the greatest pitchers in black baseball through 1921.

thusiastically embrace the skills of a truly professional touring team brought in from the top ranks of black baseball and a world that was learning to play America's game.

The All Nations team in 1913 looked like the face of modern baseball with players coming from all over the world. It was comprised of "men from all nations, including Chinese, Japanese, Cubans, Indians, Hawaiians…and the Great John Donaldson, the best colored pitcher in the United States today, also the famous [Jose] Mendez, the Cuban."[10] The All Nations squad competed against anyone who would play them— white semipro teams, regional all-star teams, and professional all-black teams.

The key player on the team, John Donaldson (1891–1970), received top billing through 1918 and would spend many years barnstorming through Minnesota. Known as a power pitcher, Donaldson was lauded as "the "greatest colored pitcher" of the decade."[11] Newspapers printed a quotation from New York Giants manager John McGraw: "If I could change the color of his skin I would give twenty thousand dollars for Donaldson and pennants would come easy."[12] When Donaldson fanned 29 batters in a 16-inning game, the *St. Paul Pioneer Press* judged the contest to have been "one of the best games ever played in the state."[13]

Jose Mendez (1887–1928), dubbed Cuba's "Black Diamond," was the team's second top star. He beat the

Philadelphia Athletics in 1910, struck out Ty Cobb on three swinging strikes, and was labeled the "Black Mathewson" after subduing Christy Mathewson and the New York Giants in 1911 by throwing four innings of scoreless relief.[14]

Donaldson, Mendez, and the All Nations brought interracial baseball to a host of Minnesota's cities, from International Falls in the north to Sleepy Eye and Blue Earth in the south. What began as a novelty ballclub quickly became a great team, and by 1916, the All Nations vied for supremacy among the best professional teams in America outside of major and minor league ball.[15]

In 1920, Rube Foster, supported by others, organized the eight-team Negro National League. John Donaldson, who had pitched so many times in Minnesota, re-joined Jose Mendez as a ballplayer on Wilkinson's new Kansas City Monarchs team.

Minnesota had several all-black teams in the 1920s, including the Askin and Marine Colored Red Sox and the Uptown Sanitary ballclub, but the state was not awarded a Negro League franchise. Racial attitudes seemed to harden in the Twenties as southern blacks migrated north, Minnesotans began to fear Reds and foreigners, and the Ku Klux Klan stirred up hate in the "Jazz Age." Donaldson again toured Minnesota in 1922–1923 because K.C. Monarchs owner Wilkinson needed barnstorming cash to prop up his franchise.

In the mid-1920s, as Rube Foster's mental health deteriorated and disharmony between the Eastern Colored League and the Negro National League brought turmoil to black baseball, John Donaldson jumped from the Monarchs back to Minnesota.[16] By this time he had pitched almost everywhere in the nation, including a number of occasions on the national stage. He had battled Rube Foster's Chicago American Giants in 1916, and in 1918, Donaldson went head-to-head against the great Smoky Joe Williams of the New York Lincoln Giants.[17]

No longer a young man, John Donaldson accepted an offer to play semi-professional ball in Minnesota for the 1924 season, when he was 32 years old. He joined the Bertha Fishermen, a ballclub based in the small central Minnesota town of Bertha. Money was the chief reason—he was offered $325 per month, more than Negro Leaguers were making at the time. What's more, Donaldson's wife, Eleanor, was from the Twin Cities, and the couple could visit family members easily.[18] In any case, when Donaldson led the squad to the Minnesota State Semi-Professional Championship in his first season, he brought instant statewide recognition to his new club.

Nineteen-twenty-seven was a momentous year. The major league season was spectacular: Babe Ruth, the magnificent slugging Bambino, set a home-run record with 60 circuit clouts. The New York Yankees, led by its "Murderer's Row" of superstars—Lou Gehrig, Babe Ruth, Earle Combs, and Tony Lazzeri—earned recognition as one of the greatest baseball teams of all time.[19]

It was also the year that a Minnesotan, Charles Lindbergh Jr., made world headlines when he successfully crossed the Atlantic in a solo flight. Lindbergh's hometown was Little Falls, a thriving community located along the Mississippi River, smack-dab in the central part of Minnesota,

Accordingly, Little Falls gave its favorite son a true hero's welcome-home event on August 25, 1927. The Lindbergh Homecoming Committee arranged for a morning parade, a noon baseball game between the House of David barnstorming ballclub and Bertha, an afternoon motorcade, and an evening banquet.[20] Lindbergh was scheduled to arrive at 2:00 that afternoon, so the parade and baseball game were warm-up activities for the estimated crowd of fifty-thousand adoring Lindbergh fans.

The House of David ballclub amazed spectators with its dazzling skills. The bewhiskered ballplayers of this spiritual sect from Benton Harbor, Michigan, never knew a razor or scissors for beard or hair, but they knew baseball, having practiced their skills religiously. They had been touring the countryside since the 1910s and had a dominant reputation, although none of the men were Goliaths or Samsons in power.[21]

The Bertha Fishermen ballclub featured a black battery of pitcher John Donaldson and catcher Sylvester "Hooks" Foreman. Foreman had been a mainstay with the Kansas City Monarchs and had a long-standing connection with Donaldson.[22] The pitcher had faced the House of David previously, and his Bertha team had beaten the longhaired team by a score of 2–0.

Game day featured the morning parade through the streets of Little Falls, with bands playing, kids smiling, and dignitaries waving. Six thousand fans packed the grandstands and bleachers, while thousands more watched from behind wire fencing that surrounded the ballpark.[23]

At high noon the mayor of Little Falls, Austin Grimes, threw out the ceremonial first pitch and then handed the ball to Donaldson. The pitcher proceeded to throw two shutout innings, allowing no hits, and then switched to center field because he had thrown too many innings in his previous start.

Wisely, the management of Bertha's ballclub had arranged for the mysterious Lefty Wilson as a "ringer" to lend assistance to Donaldson. The two knew each other well, having been opponents in Negro League games several years earlier.

Lefty Wilson was not his real name. He was a fugitive from justice, hiding in the hinterlands of Minnesota's semipro ball and his real name was Dave Brown. Under his real name he had become famous as one of the best left-handed pitchers in the Negro

COURTESY MINNESOTA HISTORICAL SOCIETY

Waseca Baseball Club, 1901 Minnesota state champions, sponsored by the Everett and Aughenbaugh Flour Milling Company. Pitcher George Wilson (back, far left); Billy Holland, pitcher (front row, far right); and Catcher Robert Footes (front, second from right) were the solid foundation of the semi-pro EACO Flour team.

Bobby Marshall (second row, left) integrated the 1900 Minneapolis Central High School baseball team and then broke the color line on the University of Minnesota baseball nine. Marshall (1880–1958) played first base for the St. Paul Colored Gophers and other teams, and the multi-sports star became the first black player in the National Football League (1920).

League and a key player on Rube Foster's Chicago American Giants from 1920 to 1922.

In 1923 Brown jumped ship, signing with the New York Lincoln Giants of the upstart Eastern Colored League. On May 1, 1925, Brown won a ballgame in New York, allowing just one run. After the game, however, policemen came to arrest Brown and two of his teammates for their involvement in a street brawl outside a nightclub in which one of the brawlers ended up dead. Brown fled from the ballpark that night and escaped from the city and a national manhunt.[24]

The authorities never found Brown. He had seemingly disappeared, slipping away into the deepest rural areas of southwestern Minnesota. There, amidst cornfields and cow pastures, Brown became "Lefty" Wilson, performing in ignominy in towns like Pipestone and Ivanhoe and Wanda. Donaldson, no doubt, assisted Bertha in securing Wilson from the Wanda team to pitch in the Lindbergh homecoming game.

In the game itself Wilson allowed only two hits to the House of David barnstormers, combining with Donaldson in a 1–0 shutout. Donaldson scored the game's only run.[25]

As for Charles Lindbergh, he basked in the adulation of his fellow Minnesotans. The aviation hero landed the "Spirit of St. Louis" monoplane outside of town at about 2 P.M., and the townspeople paraded him through his old hometown.

Aviator Lindbergh had arrived after the ballgame had ended, and this perfectly symbolized a segregated America. Donaldson and Lefty Wilson were on the wrong side of the color line, toiling on the mound in relative obscurity. The international hero never saw them, and they likely caught little more than a glimpse of Lindbergh from afar. While the white Lindbergh was naturally feted for his historic flight, he clearly had opportunities unavailable to black Americans. For black men like Donaldson and Lefty Wilson, they could experience fame, but no matter how well they performed, their recognition would always be restricted by the limited nationwide interest in black baseball.

After Lindbergh's celebrated homecoming, Wilson pitched in Minnesota for several more years and then moved away, falling off the map and the historical record. Donaldson continued as he always had, pitching wherever he got the largest paycheck, a growing necessity as the Twenties melted into the 1930s and the Great Depression.

The Negro Leagues crumpled into disarray after 1929 as the Depression clipped spending power, and the players scattered to cities where they could hope to earn a meager living playing ball. Barnstorming baseball teams continued to traverse Minnesota and the rest of the country, earning dimes and nickels for the players. The *Chicago Defender* claimed that the black ballplayers who played for Minnesota teams in the later 1920s and into the 1930s earned the highest pay of any African American baseball stars in the nation. Donaldson stayed in the game, gathering former Negro League players in 1932 for his own team in Fairmont, Minnesota, calling it the Donaldson's All-Stars.[26]

Minnesota finally got a Negro League team in

1942—the Minneapolis-St. Paul Gophers—although baseball historians don't even bother to call it a franchise. The league they joined, the Negro Major Baseball League of America, was a flimsy patchwork that existed merely to provide opponents for the Cincinnati Clowns, which had been denied entry into the Negro American League.

After the Second World War, in 1946, Jackie Robinson broke the minor league color line in Montreal; a year later, under the tutelage of Branch Rickey, he broke the major league color barrier. Donaldson had retired from baseball in 1943 at age 52. With the integration of baseball, Donaldson finally joined major league baseball in one of few capacities then open, becoming the first black major league scout for the Chicago White Sox.[27]

Donaldson had begun his career in Missouri in 1908 and pitched just about everywhere over the next 35 years. Despite the many stops, Donaldson had a stellar reputation in knowledgeable baseball circles. Former Negro League ballplayers selected him as their first-team left-handed pitcher in the definitive 1952 *Pittsburgh Courier* newspaper poll. Modern research over the past decade has only enhanced that reputation. Intense combing of North American newspapers, both in newly-digitized and old microfilm versions, has shown that John Donaldson earned 378 wins in his career, the most by any left-handed pitcher in black baseball history. Documented strikeout totals for Donaldson are equally impressive as he accumulated 4,416 in his lifetime—again, the most strikeouts for an African American left-handed pitcher in all of baseball history.[28] We consider John Donaldson the best left-handed barnstorming pitcher in black baseball history.

*   *   *

It might be argued that the black ballplayers from 1887 to 1947 sought to rectify social injustice by developing their individual talent, so that they would be a credit to the "Negro race." This was the accomplishment of the "talented tenth" of black Americans, as called forth by early civil rights leader W.E.B. DuBois—to rise and pull others up with them "to their vantage ground." While the talent level was wildly uneven and the organization often chaotic, there can be little doubt that black ball hosted some of the finest individuals to ever play baseball.[29]

In 2006, Major League Baseball sought to correct some of the errors of the past when a select list of Negro League and pre-Negro League players, managers, and owners gained posthumous entry into the National Baseball Hall of Fame. Included in this group were two who had barnstormed through Minnesota: J.L. Wilkinson, the white owner of the All Nations (1912–1918) and the Kansas City Monarchs, who guided the Monarchs to become among the most successful franchises in black baseball history, and Jose Mendez, whose early career in Cuba and his accomplishments with the Monarchs, including leading the team to three consecutive Negro League pennants (1923–25) as player-manager, gave him a reputation

THE DONALDSON NETWORK

World's All Nations, 1912, barnstorming club sponsored by the Hopkins Brothers sporting goods company of Des Moines, Iowa. John Donaldson, pitcher, (front, third from right) was known as "The World's Greatest Colored Pitcher" throughout his 30-plus years on the mound. After his playing career Donaldson was hired as the first black scout in the major leagues.

as a premier black pitcher of his generation.[30] Regrettably, John Donaldson was bypassed despite the support of Fay Vincent, the former baseball commissioner and chairman of the special election committee, who believed Donaldson would make the final list. Vincent had become well-versed regarding Donaldson's reputation and statistics.[31]

The contributions of black ballplayers in Minnesota are better known now because SABR researchers have worked together to document and preserve the history of black baseball in the state since the 1970s. What is significant about this story is that black baseball players in Minnesota, such as John Donaldson, Jose Mendez, Bobby Marshall, and Walter Ball, as a microcosm of baseball in America, played the national game in order to integrate baseball, and they succeeded, ultimately, in breaking the color line—one diamond at a time, team by team, town by town. ■

Notes

1. "Worlds of Color," *Foreign Affairs 20*, (April, 1925): 423, in Herbert Aptheker, *Writings by W.E.B. DuBois in Periodicals Edited by Others* (Millwood, NY: Kraus-Thomson Organization Limited, 1982), Vol. 2, 1910–1934, 241.
2. The color line was not fully entrenched in minor league baseball until 1895.
3. Sinclair Lewis, *The Minnesota Stories of Sinclair Lewis* (St. Paul: Borealis Books, 2005), 15.
4. "150 Years of Human Rights in Minnesota," Minnesota Department of Human Rights, www.humanrights.state.mn.us/education/video/sesq.html, accessed on August 26, 2011.
5. *St. Paul Pioneer Press*, August 12, 1897, 7; Jim Karn, "Drawing the Color Line on Walter Ball, 1890–1908," in *Swinging for the Fences: Black Baseball in Minnesota* (St. Paul: Minnesota Historical Society Press, 2005), 34–36.
6. Jim Karn, "Drawing the Color Line on Walter Ball, 1890-1908," in *Swinging for the Fences: Black Baseball in Minnesota* (St. Paul: Minnesota Historical Society Press, 2005), 44–45.
7. Todd Peterson, *Early Black Baseball In Minnesota* (Jefferson, NC: McFarland & Company, 2010), 10–13.
8. "Opening of the Baseball Season," *Minneapolis Tribune*, April 7, 1900, 9; "Baseball at Varsity," *Minneapolis Tribune*, April 3, 1904, 30; Steven R. Hoffbeck, "Bobby Marshall: Pioneering African-American Athlete," *Minnesota History* (Winter 2004–2005), 159, 163.
9. Steven R. Hoffbeck, "Bobby Marshall, the Legendary First Baseman," in *Swinging for the Fences: Black Baseball in Minnesota* (St. Paul: MHS Press, 2005), 62–73.
10. Advertisement for All Nations in *Blue Earth* [MN] *Post*, September 2, 1913, 4.
11. Advertisement in *LeMars* [IA] *Globe Post*, May 22, 1913, n.p.; ad in *Rock County* [Luverne, MN] *Herald*, May 23, 1913, 11, col. 4.
12. "Marshall After Championship," *Marshall News Messenger*, August 1, 1913, 1.
13. "Play a 16-Inning Game," *St. Paul Pioneer Press*, August 25, 1913, 7.
14. "Cuban Nine Defeats Athletics," *New York Times*, December 14, 1910, 14; "Joy In Cuba When Cobb Strikes Out," *New York Times*, December 18, 1910, C6; "Bliss in Cuba," *Washington Post*, December 23, 1910, 11.
15. *Minneapolis Tribune*, July 29, 1914, p. 12; *Blue Earth Post*, September 2, 1913, 4; *Sleepy Eye Herald Dispatch*, August 8, 1913, 4.
16. Leslie A. Heaphy, *The Negro Leagues: 1869–1960* (Jefferson, NC: McFarland & Company), 56–59; James A. Riley, *The Biographical Encyclopedia of the Negro Baseball Leagues* (New York: Carroll & Graf Publishers, Inc., 1994), 290–292.
17. "All Nations Tackle the American Giants," *Chicago Defender*, September 23, 1916, 25: "World's Champions Break Even, *Chicago Defender*, October 7, 1916, 7; "Donaldson Again Bows," *Chicago Defender*, July 13, 1918, 9.
18. Peter Gorton, "John Donaldson, a Great Mound Artist," in *Swinging for the Fences: Black Baseball in Minnesota*, 2005.
19. "New York Yankees," Baseball Library.Com, www.baseballlibrary.com/teams/team.php?team=new_york_yankees, accessed on August 25, 2011.
20. "Colonel Lindbergh Home Thursday," *Little Falls Herald*, August 19, 1927, 1.
21. "Bertha To Play House of David Team This Noon," *Little Falls Daily Transcript*, August 25, 1927, 5; "Ball Team Keeps Beard Monopoly," *New York Times*, May 24, 1934, 25.
22. John Holway, *The Complete Book of Baseball's Negro Leagues* (Fern Park, FL: Hastings House Publishers, 2001), 141, 155, 167; Dick Clark and Larry Lester, eds., *The Negro Leagues Book* (Cleveland: Society for American Baseball Research, 1994), 188.
23. "Bertha Wins, 1–0, From House of David Team," *Little Falls Daily Transcript*, August 26, 1927, 5.
24. "Local Baseball Players Alleged to be Mixed in Shooting of Benj. Adair," *New York Age*, May 2, 1925, 1.
25. "Bertha Wins, 1–0, From House of David Team," *Little Falls Daily Transcript*, August 26, 1927, 5.
26. Highest pay extrapolated from "Webster McDonald Will Quit Baseball In 1936," *Chicago Defender*, April 20, 1935, p. 17; from 1928 to 1932, McDonald was "the highest paid Race player in the country" when he played for the Little Falls, MN, white team.
27. "Chi Sox Sign Donaldson As Talent Scout," *Chicago Defender*, July 9, 1949, p. 16; "Majors In New Search For Negro Ball Players," *Chicago Defender*, July 9, 1949, 1.
28. John Donaldson statistics from www.johndonaldson.bravehost.com/, accessed on August 29, 2011; Spahn and Johnson stats, Baseball Library.com, and BaseballReference.com.
29. Tim Marchman, "Squeeze Play," *Wall Street Journal*, March 11, 2011, A13; W.E.B. Du Bois, "The Talented Tenth," from *The Negro Problem: A Series of Articles by Representative Negroes of To-day* (New York, 1903), www.yale.edu/glc/archive/1148.htm, accessed on August 30, 2011.
30. "J. Leslie Wilkinson," Hall of Fame plaque, National Baseball Hall of Fame, www.mlb.com/mlb/photogallery/hof_2006/year_2006/month_07/day_27/cf1578670.html, accessed on August 25, 2006; "Jose Mendez," Hall of Fame plaque, http://baseballhall.org/hof/mendez-jose, accessed on August 29, 2011.
31. Murray Chass, "A Special Election for Rediscovered Players," *New York Times*, February 26, 2006, 8, 12.

A Perfect Right To Play

Billy Williams, Dick Brookins, and the Color Line

Todd Peterson

After Bill Galloway appeared in 20 games for the Woodstock (Ontario) Bains during the summer of 1899, it would be nearly half a century before another black man was permitted to play Organized Baseball. Three years before the outfielder's brief tenure in the Canadian League, the United States Supreme Court ruling in Plessy vs. Ferguson had essentially legalized the segregation of whites and blacks in American society.[1]

Jim Crow's progress was slowed however, in the relatively progressive state of Minnesota, where African Americans were still able to participate on integrated amateur and semi-professional ball teams. Two such men, slugger Billy Williams and crack infielder Dick Brookins, figured prominently on the Midwestern diamonds of the early twentieth century, although their experiences with the color line took radically different turns.

William Frank Williams, Minnesota's first great black slugger, was born in St. Paul in October 1877, the son of an African American father and a mother of German descent. He first gained notice as a baseball, football, and basketball star at St. Paul's Mechanic Arts High School, while also setting the state shot put record. While still in high school in 1894, the tall, 182-pound youngster began his professional baseball career with the St. Paul Spaldings, the Twin Cities' leading semipro squad.[2]

Billy, as he was commonly known, soon became one of the area's top amateur players. Whether manning first base or roaming the outfield, the "local favorite" could be counted on for at least couple of hits and tracked down pop flies "like the wind." Although barred from Organized Baseball, Williams gained a reputation for playing well against top flight competition. In April 1898, with Western League and future American League president Ban Johnson looking on, the 20-year-old Williams went 3-for-5 with a double and a run batted in during the Hamm's Exports 13–3 loss to the St. Paul Saints at Lexington Park.[3]

Billy Williams was the only African American on the Hamm's Exports, as he was with most of the semi-pro outfits for which he played. In September 1900 the young first baseman was in the lineup for Red Wing during their big game with the Chicago Unions, one of the premier African American teams in the country. The southeastern Minnesota nine dropped a hard fought 7–6 contest, but not before Billy singled and scored a run off Will Horn, compelling the future St. Paul Gophers twirler to force "Williams to take his base on balls." The Unions were impressed enough to offer the slick-fielding Williams a contract for the following year, but he opted instead to remain in St. Paul and keep his position as assistant athletic director and gymnastic instructor at the local Y.M.C.A.[4]

As perhaps the best ballplayer in the state, Williams had little trouble finding teams to pay for his services. In April 1901 he took the field for a Twin Cities squad called the Prairie Leaguers when they met up with the St. Paul Saints in a pre-season contest. Williams collected a single in four at bats, but was overshadowed by tiny Saints second baseman Miller Huggins. The future Hall of Famer laid down a bunt single, stole two bases, and slammed a home run in the Apostles 9–5 win. In June Williams got another crack at the Saints when the Litchfield club of central Minnesota hired him before their big game with the Capital City nine. Billy rapped out two singles, one double, stole a base, scored a run, and registered ten putouts without an error during the independent squad's improbable 4–0 whitewash of the Western League outfit.[5]

Two months later Litchfield took on the fabled Waseca EACOs, one of the era's most fully integrated baseball teams, for the state championship. The EACOs, which went on to defeat the Western League champion Kansas City Blues in September, had four of the nation's best black ballplayers on their roster: third baseman Harry Hyde, catcher Robert Footes, pitcher and outfielder Billy Holland, and legendary fireballer George Wilson. Perhaps because there was "bad blood between the rival organizations," 9,270 fans, the largest Twin City crowd in years, crammed into Lexington Park on August 11 to witness the showdown.[6]

DULUTH NEWS TRIBUNE, SEPTEMBER 11, 1910. MINNESOTA HISTORICAL SOCIETY.

Was he or wasn't he? Dick Brookins (kneeling at far right in the first row) and the 1910 Hibbing Colts. After several unsuccessful attempts to crack organized baseball's color line, the indefatigable third baseman played 12 seasons for Judge Tom Brady's legendary Iron Range outfit.

With Waseca leading 2–0 in the top of the third inning, Williams drove two men home with a booming triple off of George Wilson to tie the score, but things went distinctly south for the overmatched Litchfield side thereafter, as they committed several errors and the EACOs rolled to a 9–2 victory. Wilson struck out nine Litchfield batters, and scattered eight hits to nail down the victory. The big left hander also singled, stole a base and smashed a home run to aid his cause. Billy Holland added two hits to the Waseca attack including a double, and likewise pilfered a base, while Harry Hyde singled twice, scored three runs, and stole two bases, including a swipe of home.[7]

The following April Williams was again manning first base for the Prairie Leaguers when they took on the Minneapolis Millers at Lexington Park. According to the game account in the *St. Paul Pioneer Press*, the Millers were clinging to a 3–1 lead in the eighth inning when Williams, who had twice flown out to deep right field, "sorted out a bat and came in to win the game." He did just that, sparking the busher's three-run rally by ripping a single just inside the right field line, before eventually coming all the way around to tie the contest.[8]

The Prairie Leaguers eked out a stunning 4–3 victory, and after the game a scout reportedly offered Williams a contract to play first base for Ned Hanlon, then manager of the National League's Brooklyn Superbas. A year earlier, John McGraw, one of Hanlon's former players, had attempted to pass off the outstanding black second baseman Charlie Grant as a Cherokee Indian in order to sneak him on his American League's Baltimore Orioles squad—for whatever reason, Native Americans were deemed acceptable by Organized Baseball, while Africans Americans were decidedly not. Unfortunately McGraw's ruse was soon discovered and Grant returned in ignominy to the Chicago Columbia Giants.[9]

Hanlon assured Williams that it would easy to for him to impersonate an Indian because he was "light complexioned, has an aquiline nose, and straight hair." Williams nevertheless declined Hanlon's offer. In 1904 John McGraw also asked Williams to pose as a Native American in order to join the New York Giants, but again he refused, saying, "I am a Negro. I am proud of my race and wouldn't masquerade as an Indian for all the money in the world." Williams held on to Hanlon's contract however, and it long remained one of his most prized possessions.[10]

*   *   *

While Billy Williams was extremely proud of his heritage, Dick Brookins spent much of his life obscuring his—over a century later it is still unclear what the talented infielder's racial makeup actually was, although several Organized Baseball officials had a very definite opinion.

Richard Clarence Brookins was born in St. Louis in July 1879. His father, Richard Sr., was a railroad porter from Germany who later operated a coal yard. Although his mother Louisa's heritage was listed in the 1880 Census as white, a Missouri teammate, Jack Sheridan, recalled that the infielder's mother was a "Sioux Indian." Curiously, when Brookins' younger brother James applied for a marriage license in St. Louis in 1908, he was initially rejected until Louisa "swore" James was a Native American.[11]

In 1903 Brookins was recruited to play third base for the strong semipro Moberly Signals of northern Missouri. From the onset, the "question of his race

DULUTH NEWS TRIBUNE, SEPTEMBER 11, 1910, MINNESOTA HISTORICAL SOCIETY.

In 1907 Dick Brookins batted .307 for the minor league Houghton (MI) Giants. The longtime Hibbing infielder also boasted a .286 average against the mighty St. Paul Gophers and Minneapolis Keystones.

was raised," and Captain Sheridan had to assure the local fans that Brookins was native born. Brookins won over the Moberly faithful by playing "professional ball," earning a reputation as one of the best all-around performers the team ever had and "one of the fastest ball players in the state."[12] Brookins could "run like a deer," never failed to steal a base if he could, and even pitched a game or two. On the mound he did not depend on his "wide curves" to win games, instead preferring to "make his in and out-fields work."[13]

After spending three seasons with Moberly, Brookins made the jump to Organized Ball in 1906 with Green Bay in the Wisconsin Association. Even though the 26-year old infielder posted only a .225 batting average for the middle of the pack Colts, he usually batted in the second, third, or fifth spot in the order. Brookins was hitting .260 for Green Bay in July 1907, when he was sold to Houghton (Michigan) Giants of the Northern Copper County League, a squad desperately in need of an infielder.[14]

At Houghton, the "clever third baseman," batted .307 in 48 games and was also used as a long reliever. Brookins' "phenomenal" hitting and fielding were said to be the best of any third sacker in the league, including recent New York Giants acquisition John Sundheim. Controversy arose late in the season, however. As Houghton started gaining ground in the standings, players from the Duluth White Sox accused Brookins of being "a member of the negro race and not an Indian."[15]

The Duluth owners started to dig into the infielder's background, and it was reported that a man from St. Louis would soon arrive with "birth records and other data," proving Brookins was black. The sports editor for *Duluth News Tribune*, who had instigated the investigation, opined: "If he is an Indian he has a perfect

right to play league baseball. If he is a Negro he will be forever barred from taking part in games played under the supervision of the National Association." The *Tribune* editor also observed that Brookins was perhaps the fastest man ever to play in the Northern League, adding he was "a very gentlemanly fellow and is well thought of by all the Houghton boys." For his part, Brookins stated that, "he was not a negro, but an Indian." After a Giants losing streak put them out of the money, the matter was dropped.[16]

In October Brookins was drafted by Indianapolis of the American Association for the sum of $400, and that fall it was reported he played a few games for the Indians under the name of "Brooks." Elated Indians owner W.H. Watkins announced the discovery of "a star of exceptional quality," and that major league scouts "believed the dark skinned boy will prove a wonder." His skin color soon became an issue, however. A few American Association veterans wintering in Chicago believed Brookins was too dark-complexioned and announced that they would not play with him.[17]

A rumor soon surfaced that the real reason Green Bay had dumped Brookins was because of his race. In January American Association officials announced they were forming a committee to look into the matter, and shortly thereafter it was reported that Brookins' African American heritage had been firmly established. Watkins defiantly vowed he was going to play Brookins anyway, but in the end the "swarthy skinned" infielder failed to report to the Hoosier team that spring.[18]

Instead, Brookins headed back to the Northern League and signed with Fargo. Unfortunately, the infielder, described as the "real star of the team," twisted his knee early in the season and was out of action for several games. The issue of his ethnicity again popped up in early June, when a rival club, attempting to sign the great black pitcher George Wilson, was informed by circuit officials that "negroes would not be allowed to play on Northern League teams." The accusation was then made that Brookins was also black and that if he was allowed to play, the other squads should be able to employ African Americans as well. The *Duluth News Tribune* warned "the league cannot afford to stand for Negro performers and that if it does it will simply sound its own death knell."[19] In any event, Brookins was still manning third base and batting cleanup for the Browns when the league broke up in mid-August.

Following the collapse of the Northern League, Brookins signed with the Hibbing Colts, the "independent champs of the Northwest," beginning a decade-long relationship with the semipro club. Hibbing was a booming mining community of 8,000 located on north-

Billy Williams, the first of the great Minnesota black sluggers, pictured with the Phil Dellar All-Stars in 1910. Williams reportedly twice turned down offers to break into organized baseball as a Native American, saying, "I am a Negro. I am proud of my race and wouldn't masquerade as an Indian for all the money in the world."

eastern Minnesota's Iron Range, and Municipal Judge Thomas Brady heavily bankrolled the city's crack team of former professionals. After Brookins joined the squad, the Colts took five out of six games from the Northern League's Duluth White Sox. Hibbing later traveled to St. Paul for a big showdown with the mighty St. Paul Gophers, where they were no-hit by future Hall of Fame twirler Rube Foster.[20]

During the offseason Brookins, along with fellow Hibbing teammate and future major leaguer Jack Gilligan, signed to play with the Vancouver Beavers of the Class B Northwestern League. In early April it was related that Brookins was "very ill" at his home in St. Louis and probably wouldn't report that year, although at the same time the infielder informed Judge Brady he was in "the best of condition." Brookins soon arrived at the Beavers camp and made the squad as a utility infielder. Despite reports that he created a "great impression," the "full blooded Cherokee Indian," as he was then described, failed to appear in any of Vancouver's first 11 games. He pinch-hit unsuccessfully for the Beavers in the ninth inning of their April 29 contest with the Aberdeen Black Cats but left the squad soon thereafter when questions about his heritage were raised once more. Brookins returned to Hibbing and spent the rest of the summer with the Colts, back in the prestigious third spot in the order.[21]

The indefatigable Brookins next showed up in the spring of 1910 playing third base and batting third for the Regina Bone Pilers of the Western Canada League. Regina was managed by Louis "Roxey" Walters, whom Brookins had played with in Green Bay, and ex-Hibbing pitchers William Gilchrist and George Sage were also on the squad.[22]

Although Brookins was initially described by his manager as being of "Puerto Rican and French ancestry," the Regina press asserted that the slick-fielding infielder was "one of the noble red men." By mid-May however, a few rival clubs yet again accused Brookins of being an African American. Several members of one of the protesting teams, the Calgary Bronchos, had also played in the Northwestern League during Brookins brief sojourn there in 1909.[23]

Further pressure came from the Moose Jaw club, whose fans had been particularly abusive in their treatment of the controversial third baseman, and in early June circuit president C.J. Eckstrom formally expelled Brookins from the Western Canada League. Eckstrom took this extreme action despite Brookins' claims that he possessed a diploma from a Native American University and a report from Organized Baseball's National Association reportedly clearing Brookins to play. To his everlasting credit, Roxey Walters pulled his team off the field before a game against Medicine Hat in protest, thereby forfeiting the contest and earning himself a $50 fine. But it was to no avail. Brookins never returned to the Regina lineup, and the dispirited Bone Pilers wound up disbanding before the end of the season—dead last and bankrupt.[24]

Brookins' Canadian stint was his last foray into Organized Ball. The 31-year-old infielder quietly drifted back to Hibbing where he capably held down the third base bag for the next nine seasons while also working as a fireman in one of the local mines. In September 1917 Brookins keyed a 3–2, 14-inning win over archrival Chisholm by singling, doubling, and scoring a run. During his final go around with the Colts the following summer, the grizzled veteran could still be found batting as high as fifth in the order. Brookins eventually moved his wife and five children to San Leandro, California where he found employment as a railroad carpenter.[25]

* * *

During the summer of 1903 Billy Williams hooked up with the Chippewa Falls club of western Wisconsin and powered them to a 30–2 start and a state championship. That August at Lexington Park, the Badger nine beat Fargo of Organized Baseball's Northern League 4–2. A Milwaukee reporter asserted that "more men of Mr. Williams' stamp would bring better days for the Negro race." In the spring of 1904 Williams was unanimously elected captain of the otherwise white St. Paul Amateur Baseball Association team because of "his knowledge of the game."[26]

In 1905 Minnesota Governor John Johnson was so captivated by the big 27-year-old ballplayer that he hired him as his clerk. Williams, who had worked in a similar capacity with a previous governor, "Happy John" Lind, wowed the Governor-elect by re-designing a vault to store his important documents. According to one report, "When the contractors arrived to construct the vault it was discovered that Williams' specifications did not vary an eighth of an inch from the true dimensions." Billy and Johnson, a big sports fan, were often found discussing "the prospects in the leagues." State officials looking to protect their wagers, were likewise known to approach the former gridiron star "for consul" before a big football game, after he picked the winner of the Minnesota-Wisconsin border war five years running.[27]

By using his allotted vacation time during the summer, the "Governor's messenger" kept playing ball for several years, finally retiring after a 22-year career. When he signed with the newly organized Austin Western outfit in 1908, the team's owner presented him with a "new bat, which is about as long as Billy is." Before a game in May against the St. Paul Gophers, Williams, now known as "the most popular player in Minnesota," was given a large ovation before his first plate appearance. In a June contest against Winona, Williams collected three hits, including two home runs, stole a base, and made a great one-handed catch over his head 30 feet behind first base.[28]

In 1910 "hitting as well as ever," Williams held down first base for the Sauk Rapids, Minnesota squad and toured the Dakotas with the Twin City All-Stars. Said to "be known all over the country as a great batter and fielder," he once so awed a touring party from Japan's Waseda University that they asked him to "teach and coach a team in American baseball," but Williams politely turned down their offer.[29]

Billy Williams retained his executive clerk position even after Governor Johnson's death in 1909. Both Democrat and Republican Governors reportedly "became so used to him, that they never thought of [not] reappointing him." Originally hired at the then respectable sum of $900 a year, the "Prince of Personality" was voted $300 pay raises by the Minnesota Legislature in both 1911 and 1917, leading the *Duluth News Tribune* to muse that "Williams is one of the few people in public office who is next to indispensable."[30]

The Minnesota Legislature always consulted with Billy Williams "before any actual procedure takes place," concerning the black community, and in 1923 a local African American paper declared that his presence, "means so much in the safe guarding of our interest against possible adversaries." In 1945 however, the *Minneapolis Spokesman* claimed Williams was only a glorified receptionist and griped that, "had he been white, we believe he would have long ago have been elected to important posts in the state government."[31]

In November 1963 Billy Williams passed away following a long illness, and the flags on all Minnesota State buildings were flown at half-mast in his honor. He had retired in 1957 after a spending 52 years as the executive aide to 14 consecutive governors. Renowned for his ability to make "friends wherever he goes," Williams had personally met every U.S. President from William Howard Taft to Harry S. Truman. He had truly been, as the combined houses of the Minnesota Legislature once shouted in unison, "Good Bill, good Bill, good Billy Williams."[32]

*   *   *

Billy Williams of the 1907 Chaska White Diamonds. With the big first baseman leading the way, the small town Minnesota squad nearly upset the great St. Paul Gophers.

Neither Billy Williams nor Dick Brookins played for the St. Paul Gophers or Minneapolis Keystones, Minnesota's two premier blackball teams of the era, but they competed against them several times. During the summer of 1907 Williams captained the Chaska White Diamonds in two matches with the Gophers. The St. Paul nine took the first contest 9–3 at a baseball tournament in Lester Prairie, as their ace, Johnny Davis, deliberately pitched around Williams all day. In their next meeting at Chaska, the "Professor of Applied Swatology," ripped two "sky scraping fouls over the right field fence" off of Davis before knocking in two teammates with a "grass cutting" single. Williams also stole a base and scored a run, but the professionals still prevailed, 5–4.[33] Dick Brookins was a particular thorn in the side of the Gophers, clubbing five home runs and five doubles while scoring 18 times against them in 25 games over a four year period (1908–1911). In one 1910 contest against the reigning black ball champions, Brookins singled off Johnny Davis, stole second, and scored on a wild pitch to tie the game at two. In the bottom of the ninth inning, Brookins was walked with the bases loaded, giving Hibbing a 3–2 triumph. A year later Brookins took to the mound and threw an 8–4 complete game victory over the St. Paul squad, striking out four batters while walking none, and hitting a double in his own behalf. The win came with a back story: a few days prior, Brookins, lauded as "one of the most gentlemanly little ball players that stepped on the field" became so unglued that he intentionally spiked a sliding Gophers runner.[34]

Among the many injustices of baseball's color line was the marginalization of African American players' legacies. Although he made the most of his limited opportunities, Billy Williams received very few shots to compete against clubs from Organized Baseball. Dick Brookins did manage to muster over 1,000 at bats in Organized Ball, but the continued animosity he encountered along the way no doubt hindered his performance. Certainly his .250 minor league average does not reflect the high regard in which he was held. Ironically, a better gauge of the crack third baseman's abilities might be his record against African American clubs. In 33 recorded games against the Gophers and the Keystones, Brookins batted .286 while facing major league quality pitchers such as Johnny Davis, "Big" Bill Gatewood, and Louis "Dicta" Johnson. Late in his career Brookins also got the opportunity to face the legendary John Donaldson, then on the famed All Nations team. He only managed two safeties in 11 at bats but drove in two runs and laced a triple against the great southpaw.[35]

The Jim Crow phenomena of blacks attempting to pass as members of other ethnic groups was certainly not unique to baseball, and it was a dilemma many light-skinned African Americans faced. Unfortunately for Dick Brookins, who adamantly denied being a black man, just appearing to be an African American was enough to derail his pro career. Billy Williams was on record that he "never found his color a bar to his recognition for what he is worth." Dick Brookins certainly did, although as the *Regina Morning Leader* once noted without irony, "the Indian has accepted the situation in the stoical manner natural to his race."[36] ∎

Notes

1. Phil Dixon with Patrick J. Hannigan, *The Negro Baseball Leagues: A Photographic History* (Mattituck, New York: Amereon House, 1992), 75–76.
2. *Twin City Star*, July 22, 1911; *National Advocate*, December 12, 1918; United States Government World War I Registration Card, Roll 1682638, serial number 232, September 12, 1918; *Minneapolis Spokesman*, November 21, 1963.
3. *National Advocate*, December 12, 1918; *St. Paul Pioneer Press*, April 11, 1898, June 27, July 11, August 12, 15, 1898; *Shakopee Scott Country Argus*, September 1, 1898.
4. *Red Wing Republican*, September 8, 1900; *Goodhue County News*, September 13, 1900; *Twin City Star*, July 22, 1911; *Wisconsin Weekly Advocate* (Milwaukee, Wisconsin), December 10, 1903.
5. *St. Paul Globe*, April 29, 1901; *Litchfield News Ledger*, June 20, 1901.
6. *Waseca Radical*, October 2, 1901; *St. Paul Globe*, August 11, 1901; *St. Paul Pioneer Press*, August 12, 1901; *Aberdeen Daily News* (South Dakota), August 21, 1901.
7. *St. Paul Pioneer Press*, August 12, 1901.
8. *St. Paul Pioneer Press*, April 21, 1902.
9. *St. Paul Pioneer Press*, April 21, 1902; *National Advocate*, December 12, 1918; James A. Riley, *The Biographical Encyclopedia of the Negro Baseball Leagues* (New York: Carroll & Graf Publishers, 2002), 330; *Minneapolis Tribune*, August 5, 1942.
10. *National Advocate*, December 12, 1918; *Minnesota Messenger*, June 16, 1923; *Minneapolis Tribune*, August 5, 1942.
11. *1880 United States Census*, St. Louis, Missouri; *Moberly Weekly Monitor* (Missouri), January 10, October 2, 1908.
12. *Moberly Evening Democrat* (Missouri), July 7, 20, 1903, August 18, 1904; *Moberly Weekly Monitor* (Missouri), January 10, 1908.
13. *Moberly Evening Democrat* (Missouri), July 7, 1903; *Moberly Sunday Morning Monitor* (Missouri), September 23, 1906; *Moberly Weekly Monitor* (Missouri), January 10, 1908.
14. Baseball-Reference.com, "Dick Brookins," www.baseball- reference.com/minors/player.cgi?id=brooki001ric, December 7, 2010; *Oshkosh Daily Northwestern* (Wisconsin), June 16, August 28, 1906; *Eau Claire Leader* (Wisconsin), August 14, 1908; *Duluth News Tribune*, July 10, 1907.
15. *Duluth News Tribune*, September 3, 1907, August 17, 1908, March 26, 1910; *La Crosse Tribune* (Wisconsin), October 17, 1907; Baseball-Reference.com, "Dick Brookins," www.baseball- reference.com/minors/player.cgi?id=brooki001ric, December 7, 2010.
16. *Duluth News Tribune*, September 3, 1907, January 4, June 10, 1908, March 26, 1910.
17. *La Crosse Tribune* (Wisconsin), October 17, 1907; *Duluth News Tribune*, December 29, 1907, March 26, 1910; *Moberly Weekly Monitor* (Missouri), January 10, 1908.
18. *Duluth News Tribune*, January 4, 19, 1908, March 26, 1910; *Moberly Weekly Monitor* (Missouri), January 10, 1908.
19. *Moberly Weekly Monitor* (Missouri), June 4, 1908; *Grand Forks Evening Times* (North Dakota), May 19, 1908; *Duluth News Tribune*, June 10, 1908.
20. *Duluth News Tribune*, August 14, 17, 1908; *St. Paul Pioneer Press*, August 26, 29,1908; *Hibbing Tribune Daily*, October 13, 1908; William Watts Folwell, *A History Of Minnesota; Volume IV*, (St. Paul, Minnesota: Minnesota Historical Society, [1929] 1969 edition), 50–53; Hibbing Chamber of Commerce, www.hibbing.org/visitor_info.html, January 1, 2006.
21. *St. Paul Pioneer Press*, August 29,1908; *The Oregonian* (Portland, Oregon), April 11, 30, 1909; *Duluth News Tribune*, April 2, 1909; Rich Necker, "The Brookins Banishment—a stain on the reputation of the W.C.B.L.," Western Canada Baseball www.attheplate.com/wcbl/profile_brookins_ dick.html, November 30, 2010.

22. Rich Necker, "The Brookins Banishment—a stain on the reputation of the W.C.B.L.," Western Canada Baseball www.attheplate.com/wcbl/profile_brookins_dick.html, November 30, 2010; *Winona Republican Herald*, April 27, May 2, 1910.

23. Rich Necker, "The Brookins Banishment—a stain on the reputation of the W.C.B.L.," Western Canada Baseball www.attheplate.com/wcbl/profile_brookins_dick.html, November 30, 2010; *Moberly Evening Monitor* (Missouri), May 29, 1910.

24. Rich Necker, "The Brookins Banishment—a stain on the reputation of the W.C.B.L.," Western Canada Baseball www.attheplate.com/wcbl/profile_brookins_dick.html, November 30, 2010.

25. *1930 United States Census.* Alameda County, California; *Duluth News Tribune*, July 20, 1910, March 31, 1912, June 11, 1915, August 28, 1916, September 10, 1917, July 9, 1918; *Hibbing Daily Tribune*, July 14, 1911, June 22, 1912, July 29, 1913, August 10, 1914; *United States Government World War I Registration Card*, Roll 1675891, serial number 2510, September 12, 1918.

26. *St. Paul Globe*, August 7, 10, 1903, March 14, 1904; *Wisconsin Weekly Advocate* (Milwaukee, Wisconsin), December 10, 1903; *St. Paul Appeal*, March 19, 1904.

27. *St. Paul Appeal*, December 30, 1905; *Minnesota Messenger*, June 16, 1923.

28. *St. Paul Pioneer Press*, May 24, 31, 1908; *St. Paul Dispatch*, June 27, 1908; *Minnesota Messenger*, June 16, 1923.

29. *Minneapolis Tribune*, July 31, 1910; *Winona Republican Herald*, June 19, 1908; *National Advocate*, December 12, 1918; *Minnesota Messenger*, June 16, 1923.

30. *Twin City Star*, July 22, 1911; *Duluth New Tribune*, December 31, 1915, April 19, 1917; *Minnesota Messenger*, June 16, 1923.

31. *Northwestern Bulletin*, April 28, 1923; *Minneapolis Spokesman*, January 12, 1945.

32. *Minneapolis Spokesman*, November 21, 1963; *Minneapolis Tribune*, August 7, 1910; *Minneapolis Star-Tribune*, February 23, 2000; *Duluth News Tribune*, April 13, 1917.

33. *Lester Prairie News*, August 8, 1907; *Chaska Weekly Valley Herald*, September 12, 1907.

34. *Duluth News Tribune*, July 18, 1910; *Hibbing Daily Tribune*, July 14, 19, 1911; Rich Necker, "The Brookins Banishment—a stain on the reputation of the W.C.B.L.," Western Canada Baseball www.attheplate.com/wcbl/profile_brookins_dick.html, November 30, 2010; *Regina Morning Leader* (Saskatchewan, Canada), May 17, 1910.

35. Baseball-Reference.com, "Dick Brookins," www.baseball-reference.com/minors/player.cgi?id=brooki001ric, December 7, 2010; *Hibbing Daily Tribune*, June 22, 24, 1912, July 24, 1914.

36. *Wisconsin Weekly Advocate* (Milwaukee, Wisconsin), December 10, 1903; Rich Necker, "The Brookins Banishment—a stain on the reputation of the W.C.B.L.," Western Canada Baseball www.attheplate.com/wcbl/profile_brookins_dick.html, November 30, 2010; *Regina Morning Leader* (Saskatchewan, Canada), June 7, 1910.

Sources
Newspapers
Aberdeen Daily News (South Dakota)
Chaska Weekly Valley Herald
Duluth News Tribune
Eau Claire Leader (Wisconsin)
Goodhue County News
Grand Forks Evening Times (North Dakota)
Hibbing Daily Tribune
La Crosse Tribune (Wisconsin)
Lester Prairie News
Litchfield News Ledger
Minneapolis Spokesman
Minneapolis Star-Tribune
Minneapolis Tribune
Minnesota Messenger
Moberly Evening Democrat (Missouri)
Moberly Evening Monitor (Missouri)
Moberly Sunday Morning Monitor (Missouri)
Moberly Weekly Monitor (Missouri)
National Advocate
Northwestern Bulletin
Oshkosh Daily Northwestern (Wisconsin)
Red Wing Republican
Regina Morning Leader (Saskatchewan, Canada)
St. Paul Appeal
St. Paul Dispatch
St. Paul Globe
St. Paul Pioneer Press
Winona Newspaper Project (www.winona.edu/library)

Note: All newspapers listed were published in Minnesota unless otherwise noted.

Books and Articles
Dixon, Phil with Hannigan, Patrick J. *The Negro Baseball Leagues: A Photographic History.* Mattituck, New York: Amereon House, 1992.

Folwell, William Watts. *A History Of Minnesota; Volume IV.* St. Paul, Minnesota: Minnesota Historical Society (1929), 1969 edition.

Necker, Rich. "The Brookins Banishment—a stain on the reputation of the W.C.B.L." www.attheplate.com/wcbl/profile_brookins_dick.html.

Riley, James A. *The Biographical Encyclopedia of the Negro Baseball Leagues.* New York: Carroll & Graf Publishers, 2002.

Websites
Websites consulted include Ancestry.com, Baseball-Reference.com, GenealogyBank.com, Hibbing.org, www.mcpl.lib.mo.us (Mid-Continent Public Library), and NewspaperArchive.com.

University of Minnesota Baseball

Doug Skipper

In a sport now dominated by teams from sunnier climates, the University of Minnesota baseball program has generated its share of warm memories in the Upper Midwest. The Golden Gophers have captured three College World Series (CWS) championships, finished third once and placed sixth once in 30 National Collegiate Athletic Association (NCAA) Tournament appearances, the most by any Big Ten Conference school. Minnesota has captured 22 Big Ten Conference championships and eight Big Ten Tournament titles through 2011.

More than 30 former Golden Gophers have played major league baseball, including Hall of Famers Dave Winfield and Paul Molitor. The Gophers have also boasted first-team All-Americas 27 times.

Three coaching legends, Frank McCormick, Dick Siebert, and current manager John Anderson, all members of the American Baseball Coaches Association (ABCA) Hall of Fame, have driven the program forward, primarily with home-grown talent. McCormick built the foundation in the 1930s, Siebert made Minnesota a national power for three decades, and Anderson implemented creative measures to maintain the quality of play and to carry on the tradition of a nationally competitive Minnesota baseball program.

Two other coaching legends launched their careers after playing baseball for the Golden Gophers: National Football League Hall of Famer Bud Grant, and Jerry Kindall, elected to the ABCA Hall of Fame after winning three CWS titles at the University of Arizona.

Among the other notable Maroon and Gold alumni are Heisman Trophy runner-up Paul Giel, who served as the University of Minnesota's athletic director after a stint in the major leagues, and Bobby Marshall, one of the first two African Americans to play in the NFL.

THE PIONEER YEARS (1876–1905)

While citizens of the United States were preparing to celebrate the nation's Centennial in the spring of 1876, a baseball team represented the University of Minnesota for the first time. The overmatched college team suffered a 91–39 setback at the hands of the St. Paul Saxons, a club that had successfully represented the Lowertown area of St. Paul for a decade. Two years later, the University nine won two of three games from the Minneapolis Millers, a squad made up of men who worked in the nearby flour mills along the Mississippi River (the city's minor league team would later appropriate the nickname). Minnesota played at least one game a year through the 1880s against local colleges, high schools, and town teams, and hosted a nine from Omaha, Nebraska. In 1891, the Minnesota baseball team traveled out of the state for the first time to play at Beloit, Wisconsin, and at the University of Wisconsin in Madison.

Minnesota fielded a team on a regular basis through the 1890s, and by the end of the 1899 season, had posted a 51–42–2 record in games where the outcome is known. Minnesota posted three straight winning seasons between 1900 and 1902, but then failed to field varsity teams in two of the next three seasons.

THE BIG NINE YEARS (1905–1921)

The squad returned in 1906 and competed in the Big Nine, the forerunner of the Big Ten, for the first time (though a charter member of the conference, Minnesota did not compete in baseball the first 10 seasons). For two seasons, the Gophers were led by first baseman Bobby Marshall, a talented athlete who also who also boxed, played ice hockey, and competed in track, but was best known for his feats on the gridiron.

A Milwaukee, Wisconsin native, Marshall was the first African American to play football in the Big Nine. In Marshall's three football seasons, the Gophers posted a 27–2 record and shared two conference titles under legendary head coach Henry L. Williams. Marshall starred at end, and in his senior season, drop-kicked a 60-yard field goal to beat a powerhouse University of Chicago team. He earned all-conference and All-America honors, and in 1971, was inducted into the College Football Hall of Fame.

After he graduated, Marshall played professional baseball and football. Blocked from Organized Baseball by the color barrier, Marshall starred for regional

One of the University of Minnesota's great all-around athletes, Bobby Marshall, shown here in 1933, starred in both baseball and football, breaking the color barrier in the latter sport as the first black player in the Big Nine (now Big Ten).

teams, and in 1909, played a key role when the St. Paul Colored Gophers knocked off Rube Foster's Chicago Leland Giants in a matchup of the nation's top African American teams. Marshall also played for several regional football teams, and when the league now known as the National Football League was formed (for two seasons it was known as the American Professional Football Association) in 1920, he and Fritz Pollard became the league's first two African American players. Marshall played for the Rock Island (Illinois) Independents that year, the Minneapolis Marines for three seasons, and the Duluth (Minnesota) Kelleys for a year, before he left the NFL after the 1925 season.

Meanwhile, in 1908, a year after Marshall played his final season at Minnesota, Walter Wilmot became the program's first official baseball coach, the first of five men to hold the position over the next seven seasons. Two members of the 1911 freshman squad, Ralph Capron and Henry "Heinie" Elder, were the first Gophers to make it to the major leagues, but there was no team in 1912, and the program shut down after the 1915 season

RESURRECTION (1922–30)

After a six-year hiatus, University of Minnesota baseball was reborn in 1922, and the Gophers resumed play in the conference that had become the Big Ten. Lee Watrous Jr. served as the program's first full-time coach in 1923, but managed just a 32–39 record over the next four seasons. In 1924, the Gophers embarked on their first early spring southern road trip, playing in Arkansas, Louisiana, and Texas. The Minnesota nine

played in Texas the next two springs, but when Watrous was replaced by George "Potsy" Clark in 1927, the Gophers started three straight seasons with swings to Ohio and Kentucky. In 1929, Minnesota hosted its first international competition and defeated the Meiji team from Japan. Arthur Bergman coached the squad through the 1930 season, when the Gophers made an early season trip to Mississippi and New Orleans before they returned home to register wins over Minneapolis Shoe Service and Bohn Refrigeration, in a schedule sprinkled with games against local amateur teams.

THE McCORMICK YEARS (1931–1941)

After more than a half century of a coaching carousel and sporadic play, the University of Minnesota finally achieved prominence in college baseball with the arrival of its first baseball coaching legend, Frank McCormick. A South Dakota native who had played pro football, McCormick served as head coach of the baseball program and as assistant coach for the Gopher football team from 1930 to 1941. McCormick, who was elected to the ABCA Hall of Fame in 1967, built up the program and guided the Gophers to a 140–89 overall record and their first two Big Ten conference titles.

McCormick's first squad started the season with games at Mississippi and Louisiana State, then returned to take on an assortment of squads sponsored by area merchants, a team from Japan, and then a tough Big Ten and regional schedule. Minnesota finished with as many losses as wins that year and again in 1932, but in 1933, playing a schedule that included only college teams, the Gophers posted a 12–2 record

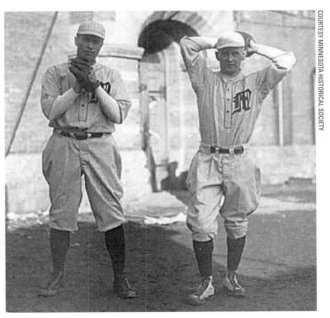

University of Minnesota players at the Memorial Stadium gate, 1926.

and won their first Big Ten title with a 6–1 mark. McCormick's charges captured the conference flag again two years later, and posted a winning record each year for the rest of his reign, with the exception of the 1938 campaign, when the squad posted an 11–11 mark. The Gophers opened each season between 1936 and 1941 with a swing through Mississippi and Louisiana.

THE MACMILLAN YEARS (1942–47)

Named full-time athletic director after the 1941 season, McCormick picked David MacMillan as his successor. MacMillan had coached Minnesota's basketball team from 1927 to 1942 and won the 1937 Big Ten championship behind All-America Martin Rolek and John Kundla, who would later coach the Minneapolis Lakers to six titles. MacMillan managed the Gopher baseball program for six seasons, posting a 66–36 record, and topping out with a second-place Big Ten finish in 1943.

THE SIEBERT YEARS (1948–1978)

In the summer of 1947, McCormick launched a legendary coaching career when he hired former major league All-Star Dick Siebert to take over the program, still considered a "minor" sport at Minnesota. Later known as "The Chief," Siebert had played first base for the Brooklyn Dodgers (1932, 1936), St. Louis Cardinals (1937–1938), and Philadelphia Athletics (1938–1945). Siebert coached the Gophers for the next three decades, posted a 753–361–7 record (a winning percentage of .676), captured 11 Big Ten titles, and led Minnesota to five College World Series and three national titles.

The Gophers opened Siebert's first season in Texas, their first southern road trip since the outbreak of World War II. They would make the early season journey to the Lone Star State in each of Siebert's 31 seasons. Outfielder Harry Elliott, a junior from Watertown, and center fielder Bud Grant from Superior, Wisconsin, led the team to a 14–12 mark, but Minnesota finished with a losing record the next two years.[1] Grant went on to play pro basketball with the Minneapolis Lakers, and pro football with the NFL's Philadelphia Eagles and played and coached the Canadian Football League's Winnipeg Blue Bombers before embarking on a legendary coaching career with the NFL's Minnesota Vikings.

Siebert began a string of 11 straight winning seasons in 1951, and the following year coached his first All-America, second baseman Gene Elder. That same year he welcomed Paul Giel, a great all-around athlete from Winona, Minnesota. Giel earned All-America honors in 1953 and 1954. He was also spectacular as the quarterback of the Golden Gopher football team. He was a first team All-America in 1952 and 1953, earned the *Chicago Tribune* Silver Football Award as the Big Ten Most Valuable Player twice, and finished second in the Heisman Trophy Award voting. Giel, who was elected to the College Football Hall of Fame in 1975, chose baseball over football, and jumped directly to the major leagues. After his playing days were over, Giel was a radio broadcaster, and then served as the University of Minnesota athletic director.

A year after Giel's departure, the 1955 Gophers, led by infielder Jerry Kindall from St. Paul, posted a 23–9 record, and finished second in the Big Ten. In 1956, Kindall led the Golden Gophers to a 33-9 mark, a Big Ten title with an 11–2 conference record, and Minnesota's first appearance in the NCAA Baseball Tournament. After they dropped the first of a three-game series to Notre Dame in the opening round at home, the Gophers bounced back to win the next two games. They swept two games from Ohio University in the second round at Athens, Ohio, to earn their first College World Series berth. Fielding a roster with 16 of 18 players from Minnesota, the Golden Gophers opened with a win over Wyoming, then defeated Arizona, Mississippi, and Bradley to land in the finals of the double-elimination tournament at Omaha. Minnesota, which needed to win one of two games to earn the title, suffered a 10–4 setback in the first game with Arizona, which had come back through the loser's bracket, but won the second game 12–1 behind New Ulm's Jerry Thomas, who pitched a five-hitter to secure CWS Most Valuable Player honors. Thomas and Kindall earned first team

The 1960 Minnesota Gophers baseball team celebrating their College World Series championship.

All-America honors. A month later, Kindall joined the Chicago Cubs. After his major league career, he served as an assistant to Siebert, and later became the coach for the University of Arizona baseball program, where he won three CWS titles. Kindall remains the only man to have won the CWS as both a player and head coach. Like Siebert, he is enshrined in the ABCA Hall of Fame.

The Gophers posted a winning season in 1957 behind George Thomas, Jerry's brother, and then won three straight Big Ten titles from 1958 to 1960 and advance to the NCAA Tournament each year. Fred Bruckbauer, born in New Ulm, raised in Sleepy Eye, posted a 16–5 record for the Gophers in 1958 and 1959 and outfielder Ron Causton earned first team All-America honors.

In 1960, Siebert guided a Gopher team made up of 18 Minnesota natives to the school's second CWS championship. Minnesota opened NCAA Tournament play at Midway Stadium in St. Paul with a win over Notre Dame in the first round, and then swept the University of Detroit to qualify for a second trip to Omaha. At the CWS, Minnesota defeated North Carolina, Arizona, rallied from an 11–2 deficit to defeat USC, 12–11, and topped Oklahoma to reach the championship round against USC, which had advanced through the loser's bracket. Minnesota needed just one win in the final round, and again lost the opener but bounced back to win the second game and the NCAA title. Jim Rantz, who went on to become the director of the Minnesota Twins' farm season for more than 25 seasons, tossed a four-hitter in the 2–1, 10-inning win. Two Gophers, pitcher Larry Bertelsen and pitcher-first baseman Wayne Knapp, were first team All-Americas.

In 1964, Minnesota finished 31–12 overall, won its seventh Big Ten title with an 11–3 mark and captured the school's third CWS. The Golden Gophers opened NCAA Tournament play with a sweep of host Kent State in the NCAA District 4 playoffs, to advance to Omaha, and then made another impressive run through the tournament field, defeating Texas A&M, Maine, and USC. Once again Minnesota met the winner of the loser's bracket, and needed just one more win. Once again, Minnesota lost the first game of the finals, then bounced back to beat Missouri in the second contest, 5–1. Catcher Ron Wojciak was named a first team All-America, and captain Dewey Markus and first baseman Bill Davis also played key roles.

Siebert's next three squads posted winning records behind future major leaguers Frank Brosseau, a Drayton, North Dakota, native, Bobby Fenwick, who was born in Okinawa but attended Anoka High School, and Richfield High product Mike Sadek. First baseman

Dennis Zacho from White Bear Lake earned 1967 All-America honors.

Minnesota posted a 105–37 record between 1968 and 1970, won three more Big Ten titles, and played in the NCAA District 4 Tournament each year. First baseman Mike Walseth of St. Paul Park and outfielder Noel Jenke earned All-America honors. Jenke, from Owatanna, also earned letters in hockey and football, was drafted in all three sports and went on to play four years in the NFL.

Before the 1968 season, Delta Field, the Gophers' ancient home park, was renamed Bernie Bierman Field in honor of the legendary coach who led Minnesota to five football national championships between 1934 and 1941. In 1971, the Golden Gophers moved to an adjacent new 1,500-seat facility, which was also named Bierman Field.

All-America Dave Winfield of St. Paul, who also starred in basketball, guided Minnesota to a 31–16–2 overall record, a Big Ten title, and a third place finish at the CWS in 1973. Minnesota defeated Miami of Ohio in the opening game of the NCAA District 4 playoffs, at Carbondale, Illinois, and then swept Southern Illinois to advance to the CWS. At Omaha, Minnesota upended Oklahoma, lost to Arizona State, and defeated Georgia Southern to advance to the semifinal round. Minnesota led defending champion USC 7–0 through eight innings behind Winfield, who had allowed only an infield single and had struck out 15. But he had thrown more than 160 pitches. Winfield finally tired in the ninth, the Gophers stumbled in the field, and the Trojans rallied for eight runs to win. Winfield was selected fourth overall in the in the baseball draft and in the later rounds of the NBA, ABA and NFL drafts (though he had not played college football). Winfield signed with the San Diego Padres, jumping straight to the major leagues. In his 22-year big league career Winfield became the nineteenth player in to collect 3,000 hits (he finished with 3110), hit 465 home runs, and was enshrined in the National Baseball Hall of Fame in 2001.

The Golden Gophers captured a share of the Big Ten title and defeated Southern Illinois and Miami (Ohio) to open the double-elimination 1974 Mideast Regional in Minneapolis, and needed just one more win to eliminate SIU to earn another trip to Omaha. The Salukis won the first game of the final round to force a deciding game, which they also won.

Minnesota returned to the playoffs in 1976, and won two games, but was eliminated by Arizona State at the NCAA Rocky Mountain Regional at Tempe, Arizona. St. Paul native Paul Molitor earned All-America honors. Led by Molitor and pitcher Dan Morgan, both of whom earned All-America honors, Minnesota won the Big Ten title outright in 1977 and finished sixth in the CWS. Minnesota defeated Central Michigan and Florida twice to win the Mideast Regional in Minneapolis, lost to Cal State Los Angeles in the first game at Omaha, then defeated Baylor before Arizona State put an end to the Gopher season. Molitor went on to play 21 years in the big leagues, became the twenty-first player to collect 3,000 hits (3,319 total), and was elected to the Baseball Hall of Fame in 2004. Duluth's Jerry Udjur and Richfield's Brian Denman, both future major leaguers, also played key roles.

Minnesota posted its 16th straight winning record in 1978, Siebert's final season. On December 9 The Chief passed away at the age of 66. Bierman Field was officially renamed "Siebert Field" on April 21, 1979.

THE THOMAS YEARS (1979–81)

University of Minnesota Athletic Director Paul Giel promoted assistant coach George Thomas to replace Siebert. Thomas led the Gophers to a 95–43 record over the next three years. In 1981, Minnesota won the Big Ten title, split four games in the first ever Big Ten Tournament, then lost to Miami and Florida State at the NCAA Southern Regional at Coral Gables, Florida. After the season, Thomas stepped down to re-enter private business.

THE ANDERSON YEARS (1982–PRESENT)

When Thomas resigned, Giel turned to 26-year old John Anderson. Anderson had come to Minnesota from Hibbing State Junior College (now known as Hibbing Community College) as a pitcher but did not make the Gopher squad. Instead he was named student manager by Siebert, a role in which he became so highly regarded that in his senior season in 1977, he was voted the team's Most Valuable Player. Although Anderson himself was sheepish about the award, Molitor, the team's best player, told biographer Stuart Broomer that the student manager deserved the honor: "John Anderson embodied what we had in mind that season. He did everything except play. He was a groundskeeper, equipment man, assistant coach, and even a confidant for many of the players. He was very exceptional, so we decided he should get the award."

Known as Walt, a high-school nickname, by the players, Anderson earned his degree that spring and joined Siebert's staff as an unpaid graduate assistant. The next season he became a full-time assistant when Thomas was hired as head coach. Three years later, Thomas endorsed the 26-year-old Anderson to be his replacement. "I saw in John an ability to get along with players," Thomas said. "He was good at the public relations end of it [coaching] and the practice part of it. One time, I just said to myself, 'Hey, this fella keeps getting better every year.'"[2]

Despite his youth, Anderson earned Big Ten Coach of the Year honors his first season. The Golden Gophers posted a 33–22–1 record in 1982, finished second in the Big Ten West Division (The league was split into East and West Divisions between 1981 and 1987), won the Big Ten Tournament with four straight victories, defeated Oral Roberts, but fell to host Oklahoma State and Middle Tennessee State at the NCAA Midwest Regional in Stillwater, Oklahoma. Minnesota was led by first team All-America catcher Greg Olson, an Edina High School product, and the Steinbach brothers from New Ulm, Terry, Tom, and Tim.

Terry Steinbach was the 1983 Big Ten Player of the Year, and the Gophers won the West that year and again in 1984. In 1985, Minnesota won the Big Ten Tournament and advanced to the NCAA Midwest Regional at Stillwater, Oklahoma. The Golden Gophers captured the Big Ten West title in 1986 and again in 1987, and played in the NCAA West 1 Regional at Palo Alto. They won the conference tournament in 1988 to earn another NCAA appearance, this time at the West Regional in Fresno, California.

In earlier years, the Golden Gophers had won with homegrown talent, but by the mid-to-late 1980s, Anderson and his staff needed to recruit nationwide to stay competitive. While players from Minnesota like Minneapolis product Tim McIntosh and Bemidji's Bryan Hickerson, continued to form the backbone of the team, the coaching staff also brought in future

University of Minnesota Head Coach Dick Siebert, shown here with Dave Winfield, led the Gophers to three CWS titles.

major leaguers Denny Neagle from Gambrillis, Maryland, and J.T. Bruett from Oconomowoc, Wisconsin. By the mid-1980s, the Gophers were using both Siebert Field and the Hubert H. Humphrey Metrodome, which had opened in 1982, for home games.

Minnesota missed out on NCAA play in 1989 and 1990, but posted 67 wins in two seasons behind two All-Americas, catcher Dan Wilson, a Chicago-area product, and second baseman Brian Raabe, from New Ulm.

After the two-year absence, the Gophers made four consecutive NCAA appearances between 1991 and 1994, led by a pair of All-America infielders, Brent Gates, a shortstop from Milwaukee, Wisconsin, who was the 1991 Big Ten Player of the Year, and Mark Merila, a second baseman from Litchfield who was the 1994 Big Ten Player of the Year and later served as the San Diego Padres bullpen catcher. Several future major leaguers also contributed to the run, including Northfield's Jeff Schmidt, Park Cottage Grove High School product Kerry Ligtenberg, and Minnetonka's Jim Brower.

Minnesota made four straight NCAA regional appearances between 1998 and 2001, and returned again in 2003 and 2004. Among the standouts for Anderson's teams in the late 1990s and early 2000s were Rob Quinlan, the 1999 Big Ten Player of the Year from Maplewood's Hill-Murray School, Jack Hannahan, the 2001 Big Ten Player of the Year, from St. Paul's Cretin-Derham Hall, Stillwater's Glen Perkins, who was Big Ten Pitcher of the Year and earned All-America honors in 2004, and South St. Paul's John Gaub. (Gaub went on to become the 32nd Golden Gopher to play in the major leagues late in the 2011 season).

The Golden Gophers played in the Big Ten Tournament championship game for the seventh straight year in 2007 and returned to the NCAA Tournament, where they scored a victory over the host team, fourth-ranked San Diego.

On May 14, 2009, Anderson became the thirty-ninth Division I coach to win 1,000 games and the twentieth to do so with one program when Minnesota won at Penn State 7–6. All-America second baseman Derek McCallum from Shoreview and outfielder Eric Decker from Cold Spring led the Gophers to NCAA regional play at Baton Rouge, Louisiana, where they split a pair of games with Baylor and beat Southern before eventual national champion Louisiana State ended their season. Decker went on to become a starting wide receiver for the NFL's Denver Broncos.

Minnesota captured the 2010 conference regular season title, won the Big Ten Tournament at Columbus, Ohio, and the first two games of the NCAA Regional at Fullerton, California. The Golden Gophers downed Cal State Fullerton and New Mexico, but lost the next two to the host Titans. The NCAA appearance was their ninth in 13 years and 17th under Anderson.

Minnesota played the first ever game at Target Field, the new home of the Minnesota Twins, on March 27, 2010. After heavy winter snows caused the Metrodome roof to collapse, the Gophers split their 2011 home games between Target Field and Siebert Field. The roof collapse also played havoc with a tradition established during Anderson's tenure. Since 1985, Minnesota has hosted an early March tournament, generally with ranked and highly regarded teams. With the Metrodome unavailable, the 2011 tourney had to move to Tucson, Arizona.

Minnesota's Pro and Legends Alumni game was played at the Metrodome each year between 1992 and 2007. Over the years, the game featured a number of major leaguers, including Hall of Famers Dave Winfield and Paul Molitor, who returned to their alma mater to take on the varsity team in an exhibition game before Spring Training. The event, which benefitted the Dick Siebert Scholarship Endowment Fund, was discontinued after the 2007 season because of an NCAA rule change that mandated that the college baseball season could not start until the last Friday in February, by which time the professionals were at Spring Training. When the rules changed again, Minnesota resumed the Pros and Legends Alumni game in 2010, and though the 2011 game was cancelled because of the Metrodome roof collapse, the game returned as a Minnesota tradition in 2012.

Both the early season tournament and the pro-alumni game were implemented under Anderson, who joined McCormick and Siebert in the ABCA Hall of Fame in 2008. Anderson entered the 2012 campaign with an overall record of 1063–699–3 over 30 seasons, and ranked first among all Big Ten coaches in conference wins with a 482–276 record in Big Ten play. The Golden Gophers had made 26 Big Ten Tournament appearances, won nine championships, and finished second 11 times under Anderson through the 2011 season. He led Minnesota to 40 wins in a season nine times, and at least 30 victories in 27 of his first 30 seasons. ∎

Notes

1. Armand Peterson and Tom Tomashek. *Town Ball, The Glory Days of Minnesota Amateur Baseball*. (Minneapolis: University of Minnesota Press, 2006).
2. Rich Arpi, "John Anderson." In *Minnesotans in Baseball*, edited by Stew Thornley. (Minneapolis: Nodin Press, 2008).

Sources

Anderson, David. *Before the Dome, Baseball in Minnesota When the Grass Was Real, Minneapolis*, MN: Nodin Press, 1993.

Arpi, Rich. "Dick Siebert." In *Minnesotans in Baseball*, edited by Stew Thornley. Minneapolis, MN: Nodin Press, 2008.

Arpi ,Rich. "John Anderson." In *Minnesotans in Baseball*, edited by Stew Thornley. Minneapolis, MN: Nodin Press, 2008.

Geller, Steve, ed. *The 2008 Minnesota Men's Baseball Yearbook*. Minneapolis, MN: University of Minnesota Printing Services, 2008.

Geller, Steve, ed. *The 2011 Minnesota Men's Baseball Yearbook*. Minneapolis, MN: University of Minnesota Printing Services, 2011.

Johnson, Scot. "Jerry Terrell." In *Minnesotans in Baseball*, edited by Stew Thornley. Minneapolis, MN: Nodin Press, 2008.

Levitt, Dan. "Bill Davis." In *Minnesotans in Baseball*, edited by Stew Thornley. Minneapolis, MN: Nodin Press, 2008.

Levitt, Dan and Doug Skipper. "Paul Molitor." In *Minnesotans in Baseball*, edited by Stew Thornley. Minneapolis, MN: Nodin Press, 2008.

Peterson, Armand and Tom Tomashek. *Town Ball, The Glory Days of Minnesota Amateur Baseball*. Minneapolis, MN: University of Minnesota Press, 2006.

Rippel, Joel. "Greg Olson." In *Minnesotans in Baseball*, edited by Stew Thornley. Minneapolis, MN: Nodin Press, 2008.

Rippel, Joel. "Rob Quinlan." In *Minnesotans in Baseball*, edited by Stew Thornley. Minneapolis, MN: Nodin Press, 2008.

Schaper, Herb. "Terry Steinbach." In *Minnesotans in Baseball*, edited by Stew Thornley. Minneapolis, MN: Nodin Press, 2008.

Shepard, Nat. "Steve Comer." In *Minnesotans in Baseball*, edited by Stew Thornley. Minneapolis, MN: Nodin Press, 2008.

Skipper, Doug. "Dave Winfield." In *Minnesotans in Baseball*, edited by Stew Thornley. Minneapolis, MN: Nodin Press, 2008.

Smith, Cary. "Paul Giel." In *Minnesotans in Baseball*, edited by Stew Thornley. Minneapolis, MN: Nodin Press, 2008.

Thornley, Stew. *Baseball in Minnesota: The Definitive History*. St. Paul, MN: Minnesota Historical Society Press, 2006.

Thornley, Stew. "George Thomas." In *Minnesotans in Baseball*, edited by Stew Thornley. Minneapolis, MN: Nodin Press, 2008.

Thornley, Stew. "How I Helped the Gophers Win the Big Ten Title…and How I Almost Helped Them Lose It." In *Before the Dome, Baseball in Minnesota When the Grass Was Real*, edited by David Anderson, Minneapolis, MN: Nodin Press, 1993.

Thornley, Stew. "Jim Rantz." In *Minnesotans in Baseball*, edited by Stew Thornley. Minneapolis, MN: Nodin Press, 2008.

Thornley, Stew, ed. *Minnesotans in Baseball*. Minneapolis, MN: Nodin Press, 2008.

Tomashek, Tom. "Jerry Kindall." In *Minnesotans in Baseball*, edited by Stew Thornley. Minneapolis, MN: Nodin Press, 2008.

Websites

www.baseball-almanac.com
www.gophersports.com
www.baseballhalloffame.org
www.bigten.org
www.bigtensports.com
www.okstate.com
www.ballparkreviews.com/minn/siebert.htm
www.lowertownlanding.com/Lowertown/History.html
http://stewthornley.net/batboy.html
http://conservancy.umn.edu/bitstream/51850/1/1967September-October-PressReleases.pdf

Small College Baseball in Minnesota

Doug Skipper

Some of the finest small college baseball in the country is played in the Upper Midwest. Here's a look at the conferences which are home to college programs in Minnesota.

NORTHERN SUN INTERCOLLEGIATE CONFERENCE (NSIC)

The Northern Sun Intercollegiate Conference (NSIC) was formed when the men's Northern Intercollegiate Conference (NIC) and the women's Northern Sun Conference (NSC) merged in 1992. The NIC, incorporated in 1932, was a highly competitive small college conference that competed in the National Association of Intercollegiate Athletics (NAIA). In 1995, the NSIC transitioned to NCAA Division II play, and now includes 14 members, with two more on the way.

Minnesota State University, Mankato, was known as the Mankato State Teachers College when the NIC was formed in 1932, as Minnesota State College when it jumped to the North Central Conference (NCC) in 1968, as Mankato State University when Dean Bowyer became head baseball coach in 1977, and as Minnesota State University, Mankato 31 years later, when Bowyer retired with a 990–487–7 record. The Mavericks, who joined the NSIC after the NCC disbanded in 2008, won 28 conference championships and made 29 NCAA tournament appearances between 1960 and 2011. Four former Mavericks have played in the major leagues: Bob Will, Jerry Terrell, Gary Mielke, and Todd Revenig.

St. Cloud State University was called the St. Cloud State Teachers College when it began baseball play in 1924 in the Minnesota State League. The Huskies joined the NIC as one of six charter members in 1932, moved to the NCC in 1942, and entered the NSIC in 2008. By 2011, the Huskies had won 17 conference championships, made three NAIA World Series appearances, finishing third twice, and more recently, made three NCAA Division II playoff appearances. Head Coach Denny Lorsung posted more than 500 career wins between 1979 and 2007 and seven former Huskies have played in the major leagues: Eldon "Rip" Repulski, Greg Thayer, Jim Eisenrich, Dana Kiecker, Gary Serum, Bob Hegman and Mike Poepping.

Bemidji (MN) State University, a NIC charter member, was known in 1932 as Bemidji State Teachers College. The Beavers played in the NAIA World Series in 1982, and have made five NCAA playoff appearances.

Minnesota State University, Moorhead was known as Moorhead State Teachers College in 1932 when the Dragons joined the NIC for its initial year, and later became Moorhead State College before becoming a Minnesota State University.

University of Minnesota–Duluth was the Duluth State Teachers College in 1932, one of the six NIC charter members. The Bulldogs left the NIC, then returned in 1972, moved to the NCC in 2004, and joined the NSIC when the NCC disbanded in 2008.

Winona (MN) State University began baseball play in 1919 and joined the NIC at its inception. The Warriors made six NAIA World Series appearances and had won 31 conference championships prior to the 2012 season. Legendary coach Gary Grob won 1,020 games in 35 seasons, and current coach Kyle Poock led his team to the 2011 Central Region championship and second place in the NCAA Division II finals.

Southwest Minnesota State (Marshall) University joined the NSIC in 1969. Jim Denevan coached the Mustangs for 21 years, and Paul Blanchard led the Mustangs to an NCAA tourney appearance in 2009. Blanchard is the son of Johnny Blanchard, a schoolboy legend at Minneapolis Central High School, who went on to play for the New York Yankees.

Two other Minnesota schools joined the Northern Sun in 1999: the University of Minnesota Crookston Golden Eagles, and the Concordia University (St. Paul) Golden Bears. Three former Concordia players have made it to the major leagues, including Dick Siebert, an All-Star first baseman in 1943 who later coached the University of Minnesota to three College World Series titles.

The conference has also expanded beyond Minnesota. The Northern State University (Aberdeen, SD) Wolves joined the NSIC in 1978 and the Wayne (NE) State College Wildcats entered in 1998. The University of Mary (Bismarck, ND) joined the NSIC in 2006. The

Marauders had won one Dakota Athletic Conference championship and had made three NAIA playoff regional appearances. The Upper Iowa (Fayetteville, IA) Peacocks also joined the NSIC in 2006, and the Augustana College (Sioux Falls, SD) Vikings were a longtime North Central Conference member before entering the NSIC in 2008.

Two teams joined the NSIC in 2012, the University of Sioux Falls (SD) Cougars from the South Dakota Intercollegiate Athletic Conference, and the Minot (ND) State Beavers, who were North Dakota Athletic Conference champions five times.

THE MINNESOTA INTERCOLLEGIATE ATHLETIC CONFERENCE

The Minnesota Intercollegiate Athletic Conference (MIAC) consists of 13 private colleges from around the state, including 11 that play a highly competitive level of Division III baseball. One of the oldest and most stable conferences in the country, the MIAC was formed in 1920. All seven original members of the conference are members today: the Carleton College (Northfield) Knights, The Gustavus Adolphus College (St. Peter) Gusties, the Hamline University (St. Paul) Pipers, the Macalester College (St. Paul) Scots, the St. John's University (Collegeville) Johnnies, the St. Olaf College (Northfield) Oles, and the University of St. Thomas (St. Paul) Tommies. The Concordia College (Moorhead) Cobbers have been members since 1921, the Augsburg College (Minneapolis) Auggies since 1924, and the St. Mary's University (Winona) Cardinals since 1926.

There has little turnover among the league's members. Both Carleton and St. Olaf left, but rejoined, Minnesota–Duluth was a member for 25 years, and the Bethel University (St. Paul) Royals are relative newcomers, having joined the conference in 1978. Two women's colleges also are MIAC members, St. Catherine University (St. Paul) and the College of St. Benedict (St. Joseph).

The league has boasted its share of outstanding players and coaches. Dennis Denning led St. Thomas to seven straight MIAC titles and 11 in 15 seasons. (He also coached 17 seasons at St. Paul's Cretin–Derham High.) He compiled a 522–157 record, and led the Tommies to 14 NCAA playoff appearances. His teams made four Division III World Series appearances, finished second twice and won national championships in 2001 and 2009. He ranks first among Division III coaches with a .769 winning percentage. In earlier years Angelo Giuliani of St. Paul, Francis "Red" Hardy, a Marmath, North Dakota native, Larry Miggins, Johnny Rigney, Rip Conway, and Chuck Hiller went on to play in the major leagues. Hamline's Howie "The Steeple" Schultz

also played in the majors and enjoyed a career in the National Basketball Association. Lew Drill, another former Piper, also was a major leaguer, back in the first decade of the twentieth century. Three-time MIAC Most Valuable Player Chris Coste, a former Concordia Cobber, played in the 2008 World Series with the Phillies before returning to his alma mater as an assistant to head coach Bucky Burgau. Burgau has more than 600 wins to his credit and four MIAC Coach of the Year Awards. Former major leaguer Brian Raabe coaches Bethel. Jim Dimick served as head coach at St. Olaf for 26 seasons between 1967 and 1994, and Matt McDonald posted 428 wins in 17 seasons for the Oles through 2011. Augsburg's Mike Davison, Concordia's Arlo Brunsberg, and St. Mary's Lefty Bertrand and Dave Thies all played in the major leagues.

THE UPPER MIDWEST ATHLETIC CONFERENCE

Known as the Upper Midwest Athletic Conference (UMAC) since 1983, the league was founded in 1972 as the Twin Rivers Conference, and consists of eight Minnesota, South Dakota, and Wisconsin schools that play NCAA Division III baseball. The Northwestern College (Roseville, MN) Eagles are the league's lone remaining charter member, but have been joined by the Bethany Lutheran College (Mankato) Vikings, the Crown College (St. Bonifacius) Storm, the Martin Luther College (New Ulm) Knights, the University of Minnesota, Morris Cougars, the Northland College (Ashland, WI) Lumberjacks, the Presentation College (Aberdeen, SD) Saints, and the College of St. Scholastica (Duluth, MN) Saints. Kerry Ligtenberg played at UM Morris before moving on to the University of Minnesota and later the major leagues.

JUNIOR COLLEGES

There are also 17 Minnesota colleges that play National Junior College Athletic Association Baseball. ∎

Sources

Johnson, Scot. "Jim Eisenreich." In *Minnesotans in Baseball*, edited by Stew Thornley. Minneapolis, MN: Nodin Press, 2008.

Hamman, Rex. "Angelo Giuliani." In *Minnesotans in Baseball*, edited by Stew Thornley. Minneapolis, MN: Nodin Press, 2008.

Peterson, Armand and Tom Tomashek, *Town Ball, The Glory Days of Minnesota Amateur Baseball*. Minneapolis, MN: University of Minnesota Press, 2006

Rekela, George. "Rip Repulski." In *Minnesotans in Baseball*, edited by Stew Thornley. Minneapolis, MN: Nodin Press, 2008.

Thornley, Stew, ed, *Minnesotans in Baseball*. Minneapolis, MN: Nodin Press, 2008.

Thornley, Stew, *Baseball in Minnesota: The Definitive History*. St. Paul, MN: Minnesota Historical Society Press, 2006.

One or more of the media guides, yearbooks, and websites for each of the colleges mentioned in this article were consulted.

Hamline University baseball team, 1912.

A close play during a Macalaster College game.

Minnesota State University, Mankato's Jerry Terrell played eight years in the majors, including five with the Twins.

St. John's University baseball team, 1907.

St. Cloud State Head Coach Denny Lorsung posted more than 500 career wins between 1979 and 2007.

College of St. Thomas, winners of the Intercollegiate Pennant in 1903.

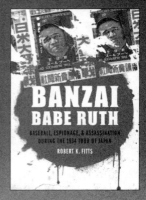
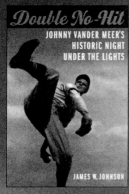

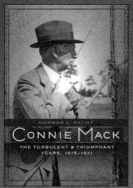
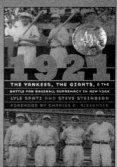
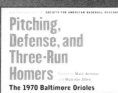

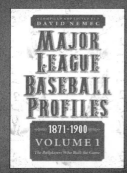

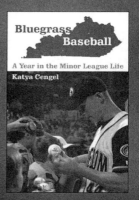
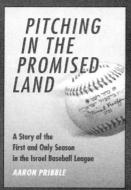

Play Ball

Minnesota Baseball Litigation Lore

Marshall H. Tanick

The State of Minnesota has had its share of high-lights and lowlights on the baseball diamonds throughout the state. They range from the ecstasy of the World Series victories in 1987 and 1991 to the nadir of the Twins agonizing 99-loss season last year, its second-worst ever since moving from Washington.

Baseball has also been a recurring subject in the courtrooms of this state. For more than a century, Minnesota jurisprudence has addressed issues relating to the national pastime with cases ranging from injuries to Little Leaguers and spectators to the travails of major league owners, stadiums, teams, and players.

Many of the cases concern topics that are unique to baseball while others raise issues that cut a broad contemporary swath. Here's look at some of the more notable cases that have contributed to the litigation lore of baseball in Minnesota.

MANAGERIAL MATTER

Minnesota's earliest baseball-related litigation was fought over an issue that is as contemporary as today's troubled economy: job security. In *Egan v. Winnipeg Baseball Club*, baseball manager Ned Egan sued his team for unpaid salary after he was fired in mid-season.[1]

The case was unusual because the ball club he sued was centered some 60 miles north of the border in Winnipeg, Manitoba. The manager, who also doubled as a player, was ousted with 2½ months to go in the season, ostensibly because he was too ill to continue managing.

In 1905 the State Supreme Court affirmed a jury verdict for the manager, noting that the contract was "something more than the ordinary contract for personal services." The early twentieth century jurists exhibited familiarity with baseball terminology in reaching this conclusion, observing that a term in the contract proscribing the team from giving the manager a "release" was equivalent "in baseball circles" to barring a "discharge."

SPECTATOR INJURY RISKS

Fast forward nearly a century to Midway Stadium, home of the minor league St. Paul Saints of the independent American Association, where in 2010 a spectator was hit by a foul ball while returning to the stands from the restroom. The Minnesota Court of Appeals applied an age-old doctrine of assumption of risk to bar the fan from pursuing a claim for his injuries. The ruling in *Alwin v. St. Paul Saints Baseball Club, Inc.*[2] is instructive not only about baseball, but offers some lessons about tort law in general. In affirming the Ramsey County trial judge's decision, the court held that the claimant's claim was precluded by the "well established" principle of assumption of risk.

Returning from a bathroom break late in the game, the claimant was walking near a concession stand, which blocked his view of the field. He was struck in the mouth by a foul ball, knocking out a tooth and requiring extensive dental procedures. He sued the Saints, claiming negligence for failing to provide some type of protective netting around the concession area.

The Court of Appeals first pondered whether the team owed the spectator a "duty," concluding that the ballpark has only a "limited duty to offer the spectator the choice between screened in seats and seats without protective netting" and refused to extend this obligation to non-seating areas of the ballpark. The spectator's claim that the restroom and concession areas should be protected because "he could not see the batter or game from that area" raised the issue whether he "assumed a risk inherent to the game of baseball," even though he was not seated in the bleachers when he was struck by the foul ball.

The court reasoned that the doctrine of primary assumption of risk barred that claim, although it recognized the "difficulty at times" in applying the principle in tort cases. Because sporting events necessarily "present inherent risks that are well known to the public," anyone who attends those events assumes the risk of injury. Citing numerous cases from Minnesota and elsewhere involving injuries to spectators at baseball games, as well as those attending other sporting events, the court refused to follow the rationale of the Pennsylvania Supreme Court in *Jones v. Three Rivers Mgmt. Corp.*, which permitted a spectator to sue after he was hit by a batted ball during batting practice while standing in an interior walkway rather than seated in the stadium.[3] The Pennsylvania case was distinguishable because the ballpark's duty was premised on the "specific architectural feature of the stadium." Midway Stadium, where the Saints play, does not have such a "distinctive architectural feature." The Court feared that following the Jones case would lead to a "slippery slope of drawing a line between risk and protected areas" of a stadium.

"CONTRACTION" CASES

The most significant baseball related litigation in Minnesota was unquestionably the Metrodome lease case which guaranteed the Twins' existence after the club was tottering on the brink of extinction at the beginning of this millennium. In late 2001, to bolster its financial condition and leverage with the players union, Major League Baseball was considering eliminating at least two teams under the rubric of "contraction." Litigation brought by the Metropolitan Sports Facilities Commission, which owns and operates the Metrodome, however, prevented the Twins from this fate. The Commission sued the Twins and Major League Baseball for an injunction to require the team to honor the remaining year of its lease. Hennepin County District Court Judge Harry Crump granted the injunction because of the "irreparable harm" which would have resulted if the Twins exited early and the "public interest" in assuring that the team play out the final year of its lease. The Minnesota Court of Appeals affirmed the decision, in *Metropolitan*

Sports Facilities Commission v. the Twins Partnership.[4] It held that Judge Crump properly applied the "five-factors" test under *Dahlberg Bros. v. Ford Motor Company.*[5]

In its decision, the Appellate tribunal held that the trial judge correctly found that there was a "substantial likelihood that the Commission would prevail on the merits." Specific performance, requiring the Twins to play at the Metrodome, was supported by the "plain language" of the lease, which authorized "any remedy allowed by law or equity." The contention by the Twins that the law does not favor "a government mandate for continued operation of a private enterprise" was outweighed by the public financing that went into the Metrodome, which is "operated for the benefit of the public." The Supreme Court declined to reverse the ruling, leaving the injunction intact indefinitely. As a result, Major League Baseball agreed not to eliminate the Twins for three years. This delay, along with increased profitability in baseball coming out of the 2001 recession, effectively ended the contraction scheme. The club played in the Metrodome for the rest of the decade, giving its ownership enough time to work out the necessary arrangements for a new baseball stadium. The ruling by the Appellate Court, upholding the lower court injunction, however, did not end all the litigation. An ancillary case brought by the *Star Tribune* newspaper and other media seeking to intervene and modify a protective order seeking access to various documents produced in the case was rejected in *Star Tribune v. Minnesota Twins Partnership.*[6]

The effort to obtain access to discovery documents exchanged by the parties in the litigation was rebuffed under the Minnesota Government Data Practices Act, common law, and the First Amendment. Affirming

Hennepin County District Court Judge Harry Crump helped prevent the contraction of the Twins when he granted an injunction because of the "irreparable harm" that would have resulted if the Twins exited their lease early and the "public interest" in assuring that the team play out the final year of its lease.

another ruling of Judge Crump, the Appellate Court held that because the media "did not have an interest" relating to the discovery materials in the case or the financial information filed under seal, they were not allowed to intervene in the underlying proceeding.

The contraction calumny followed short-lived litigation brought by the Minnesota Attorney General, looking into potential antitrust implications of the Twins' arrangement with Major League Baseball. The Attorney General's inquiry into antitrust issues was squelched by the state Supreme Court in *Minnesota Twins Partnership v. State of Minnesota*.[7] The court, with one recusal, unanimously ruled that the Twins did not have to respond to the investigation because the sport is not subject to federal and state antitrust laws. It relied upon the oft-criticized, but never repudiated, rulings of the U.S. Supreme Court holding the game to be exempt from antitrust litigation.

STADIUM SUITS

Long before the Metrodome was ever conceived, a big league ballpark was envisioned, but never constructed, a few miles outside of downtown Minneapolis at the intersection of then US Highway 12 (now Highway I-394) and Minnesota Highway 100 in St. Louis Park in the mid-1950s in an attempt to lure the then New York Giants to relocate to the Twin Cities. The land was set aside for a proposed stadium and contained a covenant restricting the sale of food or liquor on the property except in connection with baseball games or other recreational events.

Two decades later, long after the Giants had bypassed Minnesota and moved to San Francisco, a successor owner of the property sought to remove the restriction on the sale of food and liquor in order to construct restaurants and bars in the area, where they now proliferate. In *Matter of Turners Crossroad Development Co.*, the Minnesota Supreme Court struck the restraints on grounds that the "covenant has no further value and cannot be enforced" by the original purpose.[8] It noted that the original restaurant which imposed the restriction as a noncompete clause was no longer in business. Thus, the covenant is of no further value to and cannot be enforced by the original vendor. Further, the limitation was invalid under Minn. Stat. §500.020, subd. 2, which renders restrictive covenants inoperative after 30 years.

The Metrodome itself, which the Twins left after 2009, was the source of its share of litigation. Prior to its construction in 1981, in *Lifteau v. Metropolitan Sports Facilities Commission*,[9] a Washington County bar and restaurant owner challenged the statute creating the

Ted Uhlaender, shown here in 1967, led the legal challenge in which a federal judge agreed that a player's "name, likeness, statistics, and other personal characteristics, is the fruit of his labors and is a type of property" entitled to protection from unauthorized commercial use by others.

Metropolitan Sports Facilities Commission, which was empowered to select, design, and construct a new or remodeled sports facility in the Twin Cities. The authorizing legislation provided that the stadium was to be funded by bonds issued by the Metropolitan Council. The bonds would be paid off, in part, by a 2% on-sale liquor tax throughout most of the seven-county metropolitan area. The Ramsey County District Court deemed the legislation invalid, but the Minnesota Supreme Court reversed, rejecting the plaintiffs various claims: that the title of the law did not properly express its subject; that the anticipated stadium was not a "public purpose;" that the statute improperly singled out the Twin Cities metropolitan area for imposition of the liquor tax, while impermissibly exempting three municipalities; and that the law was not adopted by the requisite three-fifths vote of the Legislature required for public debt.

The Court rejected the challenge to the law's title because the "broad coverage" the news media gave to the law was sufficient "to alert legislators and the public" to its contents. Construction of a sports stadium was regarded as a "public purpose," even though a 1923 Minnesota case held to the contrary. Observing that the overwhelming weight of modern authority in other jurisdictions regard athletic facilities as proper subjects of public financing, the Court took judicial notice of "the important part that professional sports plays in our social life." The Court also upheld the Legislatures' determination that the tax should be imposed on the metropolitan area because "the benefits [of the stadium] would be primarily metropolitan" and sustained the exclusion of three small communities as "a reasonable exercise of legislative discretion." Finally, the Court approved the issuance of bonds by less than a three-fifths vote of the Legislature because they were "more closely related to revenue bonds" than to general obligation bonds, which trigger the 60 percent requirement.

Another attempt to doom the Dome failed the following year. In *Eakman v. Brutger*, the Court affirmed a decision of the Hennepin County District Court denying an injunction against constructing the Dome.[10]

Raising issues concerning the legality of nearly every aspect of the stadium project, two subsequent actions were brought regarding construction of the Dome. One was a declaratory judgment action by the Minnesota Vikings in Hennepin County and the other was a challenge in Ramsey County to the determination to build the stadium in downtown Minneapolis. The two cases were consolidated for trial and eventually reached the Supreme Court in *Minnesota Vikings Football Club v. Metropolitan Council*.[11] The trial court, in an extensive ruling, upheld the validity of the project, including the Stadium Commission's lease with the Minnesota Twins which included an escape clause permitting the baseball club to move the franchise if the Twins did not have an average attendance of 1.4 million for three consecutive years. None of these substantive issues came before the Supreme Court. Instead, it upheld the lower court's decision on the grounds that the challengers failed to file a timely appeal after their counsel stipulated that an appeal would be brought within three days of the trial court's ruling.

Having withstood challenges to its construction and leasing, on the eve of its opening the Dome next had to confront yet another challenge to its financing mechanism by a group of Minneapolis taxpayers seeking a referendum on a proposed amendment to the Minneapolis City Charter. The amendment, if approved by the voters, would have repealed a hotel-motel liquor tax passed by the city in 1979 to finance construction of the stadium.

The Hennepin County District Court ruled against the taxpayers. The Supreme Court affirmed in early 1982, declaring in *Davies v. City of Minneapolis* the proposal a "manifestly unconstitutional" impairment of the contract rights of those who in 1979 had purchased the $55 million in revenue bonds used to finance the stadium. 12 These bonds were issued after the Court's decision in the Lifteau case. The Court in Davies reasoned that the liquor tax was "an important security provision in the bondholder's contracts," and elimination of it, as envisioned by the proposed

charter amendment, would infringe the prohibition against impairment of contracts of the U.S. Constitution, Article 1, 10.

ADVERTISING AND RIGHTS ISSUES

Even the scoreboard had to overcome a financial challenge. To finance its construction, the Stadium Commission permitted the scoreboard manufacturer to negotiate the exclusive right to advertise on it in exchange for providing the scoreboard at no cost. As part of the deal, the Commission also excluded any competitor of scoreboard advertisers from advertising in the stadium. WCCO obtained the exclusive arrangement; rival television station KSTP then challenged the procedure and advertising ban on several grounds, including violation of the Minnesota public bidding laws and infringement of its constitutional rights of freedom of speech and equal protection.

The issues were decided in to separate proceedings, with KSTP losing both ends of the judicial doubleheader. The Eight Circuit Court of Appeals certified the public bidding issue to the Minnesota Supreme Court under Minn. Stat. § 480.061, which ruled that the scoreboard arrangement was not subject to public bidding requirements, nor was it an unlawful delegation of the Commission's powers. A few months later, the Eight Circuit rejected KSTP's constitutional claims in *Hubbard Broadcasting, Inc. v. Metropolitan Sports Facilities Commission*.[13] The Court determined the exclusivity provisions to be "reasonable and content-neutral" and that the policy did not "discriminate against either" WCCO or KSTP.

More significant than the amount of advertising in the Metrodome was the advertising on television and radio broadcasts. Watching baseball on television is probably the most prevalent way in which Minnesotans become involved with the professional game. In *Midwest Communications, Inc. v. Minnesota Twins, Inc.*, the corporate owner of WCCO television challenged an arrangement between the Twins and the NHL's Minnesota North Stars to market their telecast rights jointly.[14] WCCO alleged a number of federal and state antitrust claims as well as breach of contract and tortious interference with contract assertions. The jury ruled in favor of WCCO on the antitrust issues, but notwithstanding the verdict, Judge Robert Renner granted a judgment for the Twins, and the Eight Circuit Court of Appeals affirmed. The Eighth Circuit held that WCCO lacked standing to assert antitrust claims because "WCCO has not identified any threatened injury to itself, much less an antitrust injury." It also upheld the lower court's determination that a right of first refusal claimed by WCCO as assignee was invalid because the contract creating the right was not assignable. The moguls are not the only ones who litigate over the finances of baseball.

DOME DEFECTS

The collapse of the Metrodome in the fall of 2010 (after the Twins had moved out but when the stadium was still used by the Minnesota Vikings of the National Football League) following two prior deflations did not precipitate major litigation. But the earlier deflations did, spurring claims by the Commission and its insurers against parties involved in constructing the Dome, including the company that provided management services. The Hennepin County District Court ruled in favor of the construction management company regarding the two roof collapses and ordered the Commission to reimburse the legal expenses incurred in litigation, pursuant to a contractual indemnification provision. With respect to reimbursement of the legal fees, The Minnesota Court of Appeals reversed in *Century Indemnity Co. v. Metropolitan Sports Facilities Commission*, ruling that the trial court erred in finding the indemnification agreement to be unambiguous. The provision of the contract requiring the Commission to reimburse the construction manager "for legal expenses and suits relating to the Project" did not constitute a "sweeping indemnity clause."[15]

Another defect, leading to the death of a utility repair worker at the Dome, ended unfavorably for the decedent's widow. In *Graves v. McConnell*, the widow of an employee of the company that supplied steam for heating buildings in downtown Minneapolis brought suit after high-pressure steam, released into a connecting facility where employees were working near the Dome, burned and killed two crew members, one of them her husband.[16] The widow sued the plant operator on grounds that he was grossly negligent in checking the whereabouts of the crew after they had serviced a steam outage at the Metrodome. The plant operator had authorized the release of steam into an interconnection because he had thought the crew had left the area after completing repairs on the Metrodome when, in fact, they were still in the vicinity.

Affirming the ruling of the Hennepin County District Court, the appellate court upheld dismissal of the lawsuit. The claimant had recovered benefits under the worker's compensation law and was now suing a co-employee. Co-employees are generally "immune from liability" unless the co-employee had a "personal duty toward the employee and acted with gross negligence." The plant operator was engaged in "general adminis-

trative responsibility," which did not "translate into a personal duty" owed to the deceased member of the repair crew.

TAX TOPICS

Tax topics also have been litigated in baseball-related lawsuits in Minnesota. In *Metropolitan Sports Facilities Commission v. County of Hennepin*, the State Supreme Court held that a state statute exempting the space in the Metrodome leased by the Commission to the Twins and Vikings from property taxes did not violate Equal Protection or the "single subject" clause of the Minnesota State constitution.[17] The court deemed the use of the facility "inherently and functionally limited to two major occupants," the Twins and Vikings.

In 1993, the Twins failed to convince the tax court that its novelty items should be exempt from the Minnesota sales and use tax. In *Minnesota Twins Partnership v. Commissioner of Revenue*, the Tax Court rejected the Twins' contention that novelty items that are distributed to fans who pay taxable admission charges (a cost included in the standard ticket price) constituted "purchase for resale." The Twins argued they were not taxable to the club because they were given without charge to fans who bought tickets for the games.[18] The court held that the items were subject to the sales and use tax because the Twins "did not resell [items] to game attendees, but instead gave the items away."

CRIMINAL CAPERS

The Twins ballparks and their surroundings have also been the source of criminal wrongdoing. In *Schreiber v. Commissioner of Revenue*, the tax court upheld a ruling of the Commissioner of revenue assessing a controlled substance tax and penalty of $440,000 against a man found in possession of 1,100 grams of cocaine.[19]

Initially, the man and his wife had planned to fly to Las Vegas to pick up the cocaine. After making telephone calls from the Metrodome prior to leaving, however, the man indicated to a friend that his wife could not accompany him and asked the friend to do so. The two men picked up the drugs in Las Vegas and brought them back to the Twin Cities where they were apprehended, with the cocaine found in a man's suitcase. The taxpayer—who was the drug dealer and was incarcerated for the offense—was subject to the tax, notwithstanding his claims that it was his companion who was carrying them. Both parties pointed fingers at the other and disclaimed knowledge of the drugs. But most of the items in the suitcase belonged to the taxpayer, who alone had keys to it. Because he was "either in actual or in constructive possession of the drugs," he was liable for the controlled substance tax stemming from the arrangements initially made at the Metrodome.

In another case, the imposition of two concurrent sentences for aggravated robbery and assault stemming from an attack near the Metrodome was disallowed in *State v. Norregaard*. Initially, the defendant was convicted of aggravated robbery and third degree assault.[20] But the State Supreme Court cut back on the sentence, holding that the assailant could not be sentenced for both third degree assault and robbery because they occurred as part of a "single behavioral incident." Therefore, his sentence of 70 months was reduced to 49.

BALLPLAYERS' BROUHAHAS

Twins players have had their share of legal disputes, ranging from manager Billy Martin punching out pitcher Dave Boswell at a hotel bar in Detroit in 1969 to Martin getting into a fight with a marshmallow salesman at a bar along the Bloomington I-494 strip a few years later while managing an opponent of the Twins. But the pugnacious Martin isn't the only Twin personality involved in legal brouhaha's.

Mike Marshall and his wife disputed whether his deferred compensation plan from Major League Baseball constituted marital property for purposes of their marital dissolution.

In *Uhlaender v. Hendricksen*, the Federal Court in Minneapolis upheld the "proprietary interest" of Major League Baseball players in their identities and sporting accomplishments.[21] The case, brought by Twins center fielder Ted Uhlaender, sought to enjoin a manufacturer of a "scientific" baseball board game from using players' names and statistical records without payment of royalty or licensing fees to the players.

A federal judge agreed with the players, holding that a player's "name, likeness, statistics, and other personal characteristics, is the fruit of his labors and is a type of property" entitled to protection from unauthorized commercial use by others. The Court rejected the claim of an unlawful antitrust conspiracy by the ballplayers' trade association in demanding royalty fees for use of the players' names and likenesses. Once a ballplayer, always a ballplayer, in the eyes of the law. The case fueled the development of the now-established "right of publicity" for celebrities, entertainers and other well-known personages.[22]

In *Marshall v. Marshall*, former ace relief pitcher Mike Marshall—whose career included a stint in Minnesota in the 1970s and 1980s—and his wife disputed whether his deferred compensation plan from Major League Baseball constituted marital property for purposes of their marital dissolution.[23] The wife had agreed to waive any rights to the ballplayer's income after their separation early in 1981, and the ex-Twin claimed that this post-separation deferred compensation constituted "income," and thus was covered by the waiver.

The State Court of Appeals agreed with the former reliever's spouse, viewing the deferred compensation as "more analogous to a pension plan than to income," and it affirmed the lower court's equal distribution of the proceeds to the former pitcher and his wife.

LITTLE LEAGUE ISSUES

Little League and sandlot experiences often provide lasting legacies and, occasionally memorable litigation, such as *United States Jaycees v. McClure*, a case that made it all the way to the U.S. Supreme Court.[24] In 1981, the Minnesota Supreme Court relied heavily upon a Little League baseball case in deciding whether the Jaycees is a "public accommodation" which must allow women to join. The Court found an "instructive analogy" in a ruling by a New Jersey appellate court that Little League baseball was a public accommodation under that state's civil rights statute, and thus girls must be allowed to play.

The Minnesota Supreme Court viewed the Little League case as properly focusing upon whether an organization "engages in activities in places to which an unselected public is given an open invitation." Relying on the Little League analogy, the Minnesota Supreme Court concluded that the Jaycees fell within this description and, thus, were subject to suit under the Human Rights Act by women excluded from its chapters in the Twin Cities. In *Roberts v. United States Jaycees*[25] the U.S. Supreme Court subsequently agreed, brushing aside constitutional claims of associational rights and privacy concerns advanced by the Jaycees.

LASTING LEGACY

As the Minnesota Twins club embarks on its sixth decade, its members likely hope that their victories—and even losses—in the national pastime take place on the field, not in the courtroom. But it's probably inevitable that Minnesota's baseball litigation legacy will be long lasting and extended by new cases and controversies.

Lawsuits are a pastime that, like baseball, is not past its time. ■

Notes

1. 96 Minn. 345, 104 N.W. 947 (1905).
2. 2003 WL 22952707 (Minn. Ct. App. December, 16, 2003).
3. 394 A.2d. 546 (Pa. 1978).
4. 638 N.W.2d 214 (Minn. App. 2002), rev. denied (Minn. February. 4, 2002).
5. 272 Minn. 264.137 N.W.2d 314 (1965).
6. 659 N.W. 2d 287 (Minn. App. 2003).
7. 592 N.W.2d 847 (Minn. 1999).
8. E.g. Flood v. Kuhn, 407 U.S. 258 (1972); *Federal Baseball Club v. National League*, 259 U.S. 200 (1922).
9. 277 N.W.2d 364 (Minn. 1979).
10. 285 N.W.2d 95 (Minn. 1979).
11. 289 N.W.2d 426 (1979).
12. 316 N.W.2d 498 (Minn. 1982).
13. 797 F.2d 552 (8th Cir. 1986).
14. 779 F.2d 444 (8th Cir. 1985).
15. 1993 WL 35930 (Minn. App. 1993) rev. denied (Minn. April 7, 1993).
16. 2000 WL 719753 (Minn. App. 2000) (unpublished).
17. 478 N.W.2d 487 (Minn. 1991).
18. 1993 WL 359300 (Minn. App. 1993) (unpublished) rev. denied (Minn. April 17, 1993).
19. 1991 WL 198966 (T.C. 1991).
20. 384 N.W.2d 449 (Minn. 1986).
21. 316 F.Supp. 1277 (D. Minn. 1970).
22. 1991 WL 13728 (D. Minn. 1991); See also M.B. Nimmer, "The Right of Publicity," 19 *Law & Contemp. Probs.* 203 (1954).
23. 350 N.W.2d 463 (Minn. App. 1984).
24. 305 N.W.2d 764 (Minn. 1981).
25. 468 U.S. 609 (1984).

A Saint and a Miller

Doug Ernst

Rutherford "Herman" Hanforth had always loved the taste of raw, sweet onions. It was better than eating a fresh apple, the crunch was the same, but as his teeth sliced through the layers of an onion there was a feeling in his mouth of rings coming away. It reminded him of running the bases after hitting a long ball to the deepest part of the field. Circles of sweet, pungent firmness falling away from his teeth. The grass and loam of the base ball diamond felt the same way under his spiked shoes. He made the comparison at every match he played in over twenty years as a St. Paul Saint.

Over the past month or so, though, every time he smelled the onions carried by the poorest cranks, fans who were usually immigrants by their accents, sitting on the sides of the field, a sour taste would rise in his mouth. These fans would make a day's entertainment of the batting practice, ball match, and mingling after, he always liked to hang close to them. They added a rich dimension to the game he loved all his life. They reminded him of his own family and their struggles. "Herman" identified with their movements, first from Norway, Sweden and Germany; then across their adopted country of 45 states. He had loved everything about their clothing, their accents, their foods. Now he would have to drink down a warm beer to get the acid, metallic taste out of his mouth that gagged him.

Last week, he went behind the bleachers, and threw up half way through the match. He knew there was something seriously wrong. He didn't know what it might be though. He hoped it would go away, and by evening it usually did. It went away to a degree, but not entirely.

Hanforth began to dread the time at the ball field. It was something he had never experienced before, and it dismayed him. The dread made the time surrounded by the rancid onions worse.

The trip to the ball field had started to remind him of the one time, out west, he had seen a hanging, when he was a wild veteran fleeing echoes of the Rebel Yell. He had heard the condemned man had been a hardened criminal. The man had taken horses from a wagon train. He had robbed a small bank, hardly getting enough cash to make the effort worth while. He had killed a cavalry soldier who had been part of a pursuit party. It was for this last offense that he had been condemned to hang. Hanforth thought that such a desperado would continue to thumb his nose at social rules and Christian conviction. But, as the three armed guards pushed him through the crowd of curious onlookers and unchristian thrill seekers, the man kept pushing back against his sentries, forming a human wall between the death walker and the watchers. He cried. He cringed. He pled desperately for clemency. He fell. When he reached the first steps, he went limp and they had to carry him trembling to the platform. As they placed the noose around his neck, the man became hysterical, and could only mouth words. His desperado eyes darted from side to side, looking to be extricated, his soul salvaged. Then in tears, he simply gave up the present and focused on a distant mountain top, he had already died.

His body simply did not know what his brain had done. That was Kansas, 1871.

Over the years, Hanforth's mental toughness had become his guards. But now, what had protected him previously ushered him back and forth from the field for each match. They had become his death sentinel. He could feel himself wrestling emotionally. The ballist felt he knew the battle that the death walker must have struggled with a score and eight years earlier.

He had gotten through this match, so far, by putting bear grease under his nose so that he wouldn't be touched by the smell of fertile onions in the heat and humidity. He spent the whole match in pain. Pain had now become a way of life to him. There was a visible loneliness about him, and he wrapped the pain about him like a blanket. Lately, the blanket had begun to grow tight and cruel.

There were a couple times, once in the fourth frame, after legging out a double; then again in the eighth, after running back, and catching a foul for the third out; Hanforth had been unable to stand the pain, couldn't get his breath, and stood wavering like an oak about to be cut down by the final blow of an ax. He was drunk dizzy.

Outside of the warm beer before the match, he had nothing to drink but tepid water. Even that had the faint taste of onion. He found he could not imagine what he had ever enjoyed about the noxious plant.

Now, in the bottom of the ninth, his last appearance at the bat, Hanforth focused on a spot on the plate just in front of his feet. Catcher Robert Morressey was in his peripheral vision. Hanforth had long ago learned to hate this man. It was far more than hating a Minneapolis Miller player. He had blotted out the fact that they had actually grown up seeing each other across Lexington Avenue in St. Paul and had played together. Outside of Hanforth's view Morressey flashed his signal to the hurler. The catcher used a variation of line commands he had been taught in the Confederate army. They were simple directional cues.

Instantly, Hanforth looked out to second where the runner, Andre LeJure was peering in. The giant runner blinked twice and then licked the left side of his mouth. Years of playing together had brought a sense of unspoken communication. The striker and the runner were not what you would call friends, but they had spent enough time together to know the mind of the other. They had discovered and exploited their own language in signals.

The pitch would be inside and chest high. It would be a brush back pitch. If Hanforth swung, he would be jammed and pop up. If he wasted it, the pitch might brush the inside corner and be a called strike. He could try to let the pitch hit him, but not in the chest or shoulder, those two body parts hurt too much already.

Hanforth's chest had been tight and sore for almost two days, he had played with pain before. It was a near constant companion after twenty-six years of ball. He even had a name for it, Camille. He held conversations with it, and referenced it when talking to other players. While they thought it was odd, they understood. Each of the veterans had referred to their hurt in some manner.

To some the pain was simply "It." Others referenced "The Companion." One even claimed it as "My Lover." There was almost a sense of dignity to the discussion, it was a badge of honor. It never really left them, and while the pain may have been dull at times, almost unnoticeable for moments at a time, it would wake them in the night and sit at their side in the day.

This was different. Camille was warm and familiar. Camille was almost a friend.

This pain was new, cold, indifferent, and clung onto him like a wet shirt. There was almost a "need"

about it, but not an emotional need. That's why it was cold and indifferent.

Hanforth was scared of it. He did not wish to talk to it, or about it. There was a sense of cheating on Camille. There was betrayal this pain. This pain grew with every passing hour. It was tight, controlling. His night thoughts focused on it. His daily actions were centered on it, keeping his left side and chest away from anything that could bump against him.

Hanforth's team mates had already made a few cracks about "the old man being tenderized," and "Hanforth's last season."

Morressey had chided him his previous at bat. "Ya looked like a plowhorse out there, tryin' ta dig a furrow to second. I coulda cut ya down by ten feet, 'cept I almost felt a pity for ya." This insult from the adversary Hanforth swore at regularly. The two had gone from competitors, to adversaries, to enemies, to opposite sides of a stereoview photo card. Two halves molded to the point where each had minute differences, but viewed side by side, they would appear as one fully developed, complex and whole.

Hanforth, without taking his gaze off the pitcher, nor moving a muscle, replied; "If you'd a tried, I woulda kept plowin' round the bags and sheered ya' plum in half as a two share blade would weedy soil. You'd a been turned upside down, an' inside out."

Another in a long series of fights was being instigated. Both men knew it. There was at least one fight with Morressey every match. There had been no brush ups yet in this match.

Hanforth didn't want Morressey's pity. He didn't want the fight to stop. The two men hated one another with childish dedication. It wasn't just that they played for rival teams, there was personal history. Hanforth lost his wife to be to the better looking, wealthier catcher.

In turn, Morressey had lost money when Hanforth had bought out the catcher's share of the Millers team. It didn't matter that he had bought into a rival team. He did it through a front man, and he had been able to watch Morressey's agony without the catcher ever knowing who had bested him, financially. In Morressey's eyes, on a balance scale, money outweighed love. In Hanforth's eyes, love trumped everything else.

Hanforth played for the love of it. Morressey played for the cheers, because it meant a large gate. Hanforth lived to find love. Morressey lived to find a mark he could take advantage of. Hanforth used money to counter anything that would obstruct him from finding love. Morressey spent his whole life creating what he loved—wealth.

"Strike one!"

Hanforth hadn't even seen the ball leave the pitcher's hand because of the pain. But he heard the deep rumbling laugh that came from behind him. The cranks watching the match had started to make light of him. His own personal demon was calling his name.

"Ya like lookin' at first pitches, but ya never seem ta' see 'em delivered, just like the one I gave your wife. Ya' see 'em only as they go past." Morressey tensed for a blow deflected off his hat. None came. Morressey looked up at the batter for the first time. He got great pleasure from the fact that this man seemed old. It bothered him for a second, too. For the first time, he heard the labored breathing. He took satisfaction from the fact, but it also made him reflect back to his childhood for an instant. That labored breathing used to be his, and Hanforth was his protector from bullies trying to take…what, something, anything they wanted from "Baby Bobbie Morressey." The catcher suddenly realized that for all the insults, dust-ups, down and dirty sucker punch fights they had over the years, Hanforth had never stooped to calling him that, out loud, or under his breath. Why had he never thought of that before? Morressey snuck a look at the batter's face in front of him and saw him, for an instant, in a way he hadn't seen him for decades.

The blow never came. In that split second glance Morressey was also shaken—just a bit—because he also only seemed to catch a glance of a shadow. Hanforth seemed hollow for an instant. Morressey focused anew, and the shadow appeared solid again.

Hanforth seemed to wobble momentarily. Then he steadied himself and looked out to the pitcher, then his runner. Morressey called for low and outside, a slow pitch that Hanforth would find irresistible.

Hanforth looked out to second. Right thumb jammed into the pants pocket of the uniform.

Hanforth felt momentarily helpless. The pain he would feel if he turned on it, but it would be a beautiful pitch, in his wheelhouse. A pitch he could drive a mile. Or he could take it and hope that the pitcher's precision would be just off the mark. A precious ball, just outside. Hanforth had never tended to be a gambler. Everything he did was by design, to attain an objective. He knew there was no such thing as a sure bet. Trusting a pitcher, either way was never a sure bet, so he focused on Lucus Grider's face.

The pitcher's nickname was "The Grinder" because he was so good at grinding off the edges of the strike zone. Umpires talked about how every call was an emotional decision. No matter how consistently an umpire might try to call a game, there would be a debate within the crew later about the issue that what looked like "painting the edges of the zone" behind the plate, looked foul from first or third base.

Hanforth had heard of these debates all too often. He decided that he would swing, at whatever cost.

"Strike two!"

"Your swing. Looks like ya got lessons from a newborn, there, loverman." Morressey stopped short because he could hear the rattled breathing and when he looked up, the batsman's face was white, there was sweat coming off him. His hands trembled. Morressey caught himself thinking his enemy looked like a drunk, trying to hold onto a bar rail for support. In this case, the rail was a bat unattached from any support, and suddenly without the power to slice the air swordlike or protect the holder from a final fate.

"You ok, there, Herman," barked the umpire.

No answer.

"Boy'o! You need a replacement?" The umpire barked again, but this time there was some real concern in his voice.

Still no answer, but Hanforth managed to wag his head with some vigor.

Morressey growled out, "Hold yer mouth, ump, this'un's held his own with the best, an' thas' me. I 'spect he's just settin' us all up for his big attempt to be the winnin' hero, an I don't plan to have anyone spoil that joy, 'ceptin' me!" He pounded his fist into his glove so that it sounded like a base drum. Somewhere, deep inside, Morressey wished that he had never split from his childhood friend over "Mr. Lincoln's War."

It was stupid. Somehow, two competitive spirits turned ugly and defined the rest of their two lives. It bound them together by forcing them onto opposite sides of every event. Fate chose an event at Fort Snelling six years before Herman was born that, in a myriad of ways defined life for both Hanforth and Morressey. Hanforth's father was an abolitionist preacher. Morressey's father, Winston, was an army surgeon who knew slave holder Doctor John Emerson. Winston Morressey believed Emerson to be a good, fair and just man. He was a man simply seeking to maintain control of his property.

Even in a free Minnesota, there was a legal question about what Dred Scott was: Property, or a Free Man with a soul.

Each boy was a benefactor of his father's philosophy. Emerson was often asked to see veterans living away from Fort Snelling, Morressey and his father would accompany the surgeon to the clinic/home of a doctor who lived across the street from the Hanforth home. Young Morressey spent afternoons there, playing with neighborhood boys, Hanforth among them. Herman sometimes went to the fort and played base ball with Morressey and the men. As time passed, the street became a barrier, then a wall between the two boys. In early 1864 each stole away and rode the same train, unknown to one another, to opposing camps. Morressey fought for the rebel cause in Missouri. Hanforth took up arms in Kentucky for "Father Abraham". Both left as boys with adventure-lust in their eyes, both returned as angry men, much older than their 16 years would allow the world to see.

After Lincoln's death, Morressey returned to St. Paul, wore bitterness like a shield and played Base Ball at every chance, charging every base with a Rebel yell that either got him booted, fined, or both. He was so antagonistic about it, that long after fining players went by the way, Morressey still generated fines every match. He would show his disdain by throwing coins at either the umpire or manager. Occasionally, other players would imitate Morressey's coin tossing to irritate him, but this only served to fuel his passion.

Hanforth simply came home after following the length of Lincoln's funeral train from Washington to New York, and then west to Illinois. It was as if he were searching for the sign that everything was as it had been. To this day in 1899, Hanforth sought signs. Off the field, he saw signs where none existed. But on the field, he was uncanny about catching movements, repetitive looks, anything that might be a tip-off to a pitcher's next pitch or a runner's intention to go. Some catchers said Hanforth had eyes in the back of his head because he always seemed to know what would be thrown next. But not Morressey.

This time Hanforth didn't make the effort to see the sign off the catcher, he just stared out to second. There LeJure, with a mix of concern and anger in his eyes threw out the same sign as for the second pitch. Hanforth, gazed at his baseman for a very long second and then stood very tall and straight in the box. He smiled at the runner. LeJure found himself thinking, "he looks so small in there," and then shook it off.

He had seen that smile, mixed with that tall comportment from this batter before. It was a totally unconscious signal between the two that LeJure had best be ready to run. Run like shot from a high powered weapon. Run like there was no tomorrow. Run for the cheers of the fans, his mates, for the tie score. Run to get out of the way, because a lightning bolt was going to be trying to charge up his leg.

Run as if unchained by gravity.

The pitcher went into his wind-up. Hanforth was tracking the movement of every muscle of the pitch, by the time "The Grinder" had reached his release point, fifteen years had slid off, Camille, and the new pain, were lost for the instant. Hanforth knew where the pitch would cross the plate, and he could tear the cow hide off of it.

Ball met sword. The missile launched without devastating speed, but with an arc that would carry. The pain came back, stronger. Hanforth could only stand and watch as the ball became light itself, traveling far enough to drive in the tying run, before landing just inches foul.

Panting now, and bent over in pain, Hanforth understood that Morressey would call the same pitch again. The pitcher wouldn't want to put it over in the same place. He wouldn't want do the same thing. Hanforth knew what was Morressey had in mind. Seeing the intensity in Morressey's deep set eyes, the Grinder was hypnotized. He was all but compelled to do Morressey's bidding.

All of a sudden there was a hand on his shoulder, the field captain was standing over Hanforth's bent frame. "Boy, you need to leave now. Go sit it out."

Almost crying, Hanforth struggled and whispered, "This is mine. It's what I have, I'm gonna' give it."

Morressey stood and defiantly stuck a finger in the Saint's field captain's chest, "He's a big boy, it's his decision. I want him to do this. Him and me got history. This ain't between you and him, this is between him and me, you can't fine me, I ain't on your roster, but I'll beat ya' ta' death if ya' take 'im out."

Hanforth, without waiting for the signal, stood so straight and tall that he once again looked like the oak tree people had compared him to when he first came up. He smiled a triumphant smile at LeJure.

LeJure took four steps of the bag. He took another two steps and roared out so that the pitcher and the crowd had to hear, "My man! I'm comin' home, an' there ain't one damn thing you'll do about it, 'cept wish ta hell you never delivered that pitch." With that, he pulled a dollar, a gold eagle, out of his pocket and threw it in the direction of the umpire and proclaimed, "here's you bleedin' fine! Buy four beer on me tonight! But mark my words well, sir—I am coming home on this pitch!" This time, it had Morressey's attention.

Sudden silence. The sun bore down on the scene creating waves of wet heat that radiated off the ground, bounced off the stationery men and created motion where there was none, yet.

LeJure dug in with his left foot, muscle sinew coiling to thrust away on contact.

Morressey cooled into a slab of oven-forged iron, ready for all blows.

Hanforth, for a second time, was lost in the moment. Everything became clear, calm, and very large. Camille was next to him, the new invader was nowhere to be felt.

The broken lace on the ball had created a whistle that the base tenders, and runner, could hear.

History repeated itself. "The Grinder" moved with the same motions. The release point was exactly the same. The path of the ball split the air in the same way. To Hanforth's eye the ball was bigger than big, slower than slow. He could track the broken lace as the ball spun toward him. Half a generation spent swinging at pitches was stored memory in the muscles of his legs, torso, shoulders and arms. Anyone under twenty years of age had not yet been conceived when Hanforth first drove a base ball far over the fielder's heads and he had tallied his first ace.

Then there was this. No ball had seemed larger. No ball had seemed slower. The ball was under a wizard's spell of time, talent, practice and destiny. Even the ball knew what was about to happen, for as the hand polished ash bat cut time and space, that broken lace seemed to give an eagle's screech as it began a head first dive toward a far distant prey.

The shudder went up Hanforth's arms. Ran across his shoulders, down his spine where it finally met the cold, indifferent intruder between his shoulder blades. By then it was far too late. The ball flashed up, out and away. The bat dropped from Hanforth's hands, suddenly cold and cramped.

LeJure let forth an exhortation as he was half way past third, "Move, move, for God's sake move!"

Morressey never moved, just mouthed an expletive.

Hanforth, already almost drained of energy, began plodding, pleading his legs to move faster. His heart felt like there was a hot lead rod pushing in on it.

LeJure completed his run, touching the plate with his hand and he intentionally speared the catcher. He yelled above the roar of the crowd, "Safe! Tie score! Safe! Come home!" At that, his tone changed as he watched the runner flailing toward second base. The look on Hanforth's face was beyond agony, it was moving in the direction of rigor-mortis. Still his arms kept pumping, as if by their own volition. His fingers seemed to stretch out claw like. Still his legs thrashed, one in front of the other, as if by habit. His head was down, staring straight into the ground.

It was as if the ball knew it had an extra mission to accomplish at the end of this war of wills. The ball seemed to hang, going deeper, just out of reach of the fielders converging on it.

One sports writer later fell away from the straightforward prose of the day and wrote, "This ball, this damaged, beleaguered spherical orb that had no reason to do any man a favor, seemed to take pity on old Hanforth. For the pure joy of exacting revenge on those who had used it so badly over the course of nine frames, and for the complete sympathy upon he who would end the game; seemed to play a boy's game of tag with the fielders. That spirit infused cowhide was staying up, and away, and just beyond the grasping, wishing hands of those who would put an end to old Hanforth before he would achieve his final salvation."

Whatever the truth was, the ball seemed to hang as it went deeper and deeper, finally dropping as Hanforth was half way to third. The runner had found some inner strength, and picked up speed. Maybe that is what really occurred, maybe not.

The fielder hurled the ball with a devil's fury that the ball had to give in to. It found the hands of the relay man as Hanforth came off third. Turning, giving a mighty yell, "Coming Home!" the relay man launched the ball.

Morressey covered the plate, still looking dazed, one hand covering his left eye, there wasn't a visible speck to be seen. He was almost actually sitting on the round dish. He spit out two teeth that had broken as LeJure speared him, There was blood coming out his mouth.

And still Hanforth came.

The ball was on target.

Hanforth stumbled about eight feet away from where the plate should have been. His face transformed into a cruel puzzle, and Morressey took a moment to savor the chilling truth. Hanforth could not find the plate. Morressey cleared his head sufficiently enough to form the words silently "I'm sitting on it, it's mine!"

Hanforth seemed to dive. Some would later claim he had merely bobbled on weak legs as he continued the stumble toward the invisible plate. Morressey continued to sit semi-dazed on the plate, the ball bounced once in front of him and to the runner's side. With a crazed flailing Hanforth managed to get two fingers on the ball and brush it off course.

Morressey was forced to react, leaving a piece of the plate exposed. Hanforth fell, and inertia alone carried him forward toward the final stopping point.

Morressey screamed "No, no you don't! Damn it, I won't allow it!"

LeJure pounced and blocked the vision of the umpire for the briefest of moments, but long enough for him to get one hand on Morressey and tip him just away. "He's safe, ump, he touched!"

But, there, laying face down with one arm and hand extended in a disjointed way, as if they had left

Hanforth's body despite the best efforts of the ball, LeJure, and the runner—a two-inch gap spanned like an ocean between the plate and extended fingers.

By then, Morressey had recovered the ball. The umpire had regained perfect vision of the scene. LeJure stood between the catcher and the umpire, suddenly thrust in the role of Protestant preacher arguing for a final salvation. He implored to God and invoked country. He looked deep into Morressey's eyes and told him he owed Hanforth this one, it would make up for the wrongs of the past. He pled, and a tear even began to form. He did something he had never done to another ballist before, he apologized for his actions.

Morressey looked at the ball he now held in his hand. He looked at the prone, motionless form covered in sweat and dirt, little cuts oozing from where he had fallen. He looked at the crowd that had gone from frenzied to funeral quiet. Morressey looked at LeJure.

"Not doin' this for you, nor anything you said. Doin' it for the glory o' the game!"

He dropped the ball about six inches away from the plate, grabbed hold of Hanforth's wet hand and pulled, just a bit. He dropped the hand on the edge of the perfectly round, mostly white iron dish, stood, turned, faced the crowd. "Damned if I didn't try! My enemy is safe at home."

He walked back to the rest of his team, stopping to raise his head in one last, long "Rebel Yell" and never looked back.

A Dakota Indian watching the match turned to his companion, "It is the death chant."

A visiting Chicagoan told his traveling companion, "There's a crazy rumor that 'Old Roman' Comiskey wants the Saints in Chicago. Think it'll happen?" ■

Contributors

KRISTIN ANDERSON is a professor of art at Augsburg College in Minneapolis, where she teaches courses in art history and architectural history. Together with co-author Chris Kimball, she is writing a book on the urban and architectural history of Twin Cities ballparks. In what passes for free time, Dr. Anderson leads tours at Target Field, including special focus tours on architecture, engineering, and sustainability.

ANNE ARONSON is a professor of writing, rhetoric, and communication at Metropolitan State University in Saint Paul, Minnesota, where she coordinates the professional writing program. She has written articles on women's baseball for *Elysian Fields Quarterly*, the *Star Tribune*, and the book *Minnesotans in Baseball*. She recently started teaching a class on gender, sport and the media.

MARK ARMOUR is the author of *Joe Cronin: A Life in Baseball* (Nebraska, 2010) and the director of SABR's Baseball Biography Project. He writes baseball from Oregon, where he resides with Jane, Maya, and Drew.

RICH ARPI is an independent researcher living in suburban St. Paul and has been the editor of the Bibliography Committee's Current Baseball Publications since 1986. He is an active Halsey Hall chapter participant and officer and has attended many national conventions since the mid 1980s. Rich is also a vintage base ball player on the Quicksteps and manager of the Great American Fantasy League's Washington Senator/Minnesota Twins franchise.

CHARLIE BEATTIE is a freelance sportswriter and broadcaster based in Minneapolis. His credits include coverage of Major League Baseball, the NFL, NHL, NCAA Basketball and the Olympic Games. His baseball credits include written and broadcast work for the Wilson (North Carolina) Tobs, Bowie Baysox, St. Paul Saints and the Minnesota Twins. He is new to SABR in 2012.

JOHN BONNES writes at TwinsDaily.com with TwinsCentric. He is also owner/editor GameDay Program and Scorecard, which provides the content for the Minnesota Twins Official Scorecard. You can follow him on Twitter at @TwinsGeek or hear his Gleeman and the Geek show on 100.3 KFAN.

DOUG ERNST grew up in West Central Minnesota on a farm where he and his grandfather listened to Halsey Hall call Twins games on the radio evenings and weekends. As a history teacher Doug often used baseball as a timeline to discuss the social history of the United States. Now, as a historic fiction writer and historic interpreter, Doug uses his experiences playing Vintage Base Ball as a way of helping him better understand the times he writes about, and interprets.

AARON GLEEMAN is a baseball writer at NBCSports.com, a senior editor at Rotoworld, and a lifelong Minnesotan who has written about the Twins on a daily basis at AaronGleeman.com since 2002.

PETE GORTON is the Presentation Services Coordinator for Faegre, Baker & Daniels, an international law firm based in Minneapolis.

He is a former broadcast journalist who has written dozens of articles about John Donaldson, including a chapter in *Swinging for the Fences: Black Baseball in Minnesota* (Minnesota Historical Society Press, 2005). He is the founder of "The Donaldson Network," a group of over 450 researchers, authors, and historians dedicated to the rediscovery of Donaldson's baseball career. Gorton is the co-founder of *johndonaldson.bravehost.com*, a website detailing the career of "The Greatest Colored Pitcher in the World." His efforts on behalf of Donaldson have been honored by the Society of American Baseball Researchers/Negro Leagues Committee with the 2011 Tweed Webb Lifetime Achievement Award, recognizing long-term contributions to the field of Negro League and black baseball research. He resides in Northeast Minneapolis with his wife and two children.

REX HAMANN first became interested in baseball history while teaching in the Milwaukee Public Schools during the 1990s. As part of doing research on the Milwaukee American Association club, he began looking for the graves of players who spent time with Milwaukee. Grave hunting led directly to the formation of the *American Association Almanac*, a baseball history journal devoted to the American Association's first five decades which he has been dedicated to since 2001. He hopes to publish a book on the rivalry between the Minneapolis Millers and St. Paul Saints by early 2013.

KEVIN HENNESSY has been a member of SABR and the Halsey Hall Chapter since 1997. He lives in St. Paul.

STEVE HOFFBECK is a Professor of History at Minnesota State University Moorhead and general editor/author of *Swinging for the Fences: Black Baseball in Minnesota*, which won a Sporting News/SABR Baseball Research Award in 2005. Hoffbeck, his wife and his family reside in Barnesville, Minnesota.

CHRIS KIMBALL is the president of California Lutheran University in Thousand Oaks, California, where he is also a professor of history. Dr. Kimball and his co-author, Kristin Anderson, are writing a book on the ballparks of the Twin Cities. Although a long-term resident of Chicago, the Twin Cities, and now Los Angeles, he remains a steadfast Red Sox fan.

FRANCIS KINLAW has contributed to twelve SABR convention publications and written extensively about baseball, football, and college basketball. He has attended 16 SABR conventions, that number matching the number of doubles hit by Harmon Killebrew during the Twins' pennant-winning season of 1965. A member of SABR since 1983, he resides in Greensboro, North Carolina.

DANIEL R. LEVITT is the author of *The Battle That Forged Modern Baseball: The Federal League Challenge and Its Legacy*, released in the spring of 2012 by Rowman & Littlefield under its Ivan R. Dee imprint. He is also the author of *Ed Barrow: The Bulldog Who Built the Yankees' First Dynasty*, a Seymour Award finalist and co-author of *Paths to Glory: How Great Baseball Teams Got that Way*, winner of The Sporting News/SABR Baseball Research Award. He lives in Minneapolis with his wife and two boys.

BILL NOWLIN has been Vice President of SABR since 2004 and is frequently author and editor of various SABR publications, with over 250 biographies contributed to BioProject. He has written several books on Ted Williams, and many more on the Boston Red Sox.

JOE O'CONNELL has been a member of SABR since 1985 and is a charter member of the Halsey Hall Chapter. He enjoys researching the American Association's St. Paul Saints from before the arrival of the Twins.

TODD PETERSON is a Kansas City based visual artist, historian, and educator. The Twin Cities native has published several articles on the Negro Leagues, and is the author of *Early Black Baseball In Minnesota*, published in 2010 by McFarland and Company.

JOEL RIPPEL is the author of seven books on Minnesota sports history. Rippel, a graduate of the University of Minnesota, is a member of the Society for American Baseball Research and resides in Minneapolis.

DOUG SKIPPER is a marketing research, customer satisfaction, and public opinion consultant from Apple Valley, Minnesota, who reads and writes about baseball and engages in father-daughter dancing. A Colorado product who has resided in Wyoming and North Dakota, he has been a SABR member since 1982. He researched and wrote four biographies for *Deadball Stars of the American League*, and has contributed to several SABR biographical publications. Doug and his wife, Kathy, have two daughters, MacKenzie and Shannon.

STEVE STEINBERG is the co-author with Lyle Spatz of *1921: The Yankees, the Giants, and the Battle for Baseball Supremacy in New York*, winner of the 2011 Seymour Medal. They are currently working on a book on Jacob Ruppert and Miller Huggins. Steve has also written *Baseball in St. Louis, 1900–1925* and many articles revolving around early 20th-century baseball, including a dozen for SABR publications.

MARSHALL H. TANICK is an attorney with the law firm of Mansfield, Tanick & Cohen, P.A. in Minneapolis, St. Paul and St. Louis Park. He has lectured and written extensively on baseball law subjects and has represented amateur and professional baseball players, coaches, managers, executives, and umpires.

BOB THOLKES, a charter member and sometime officer of the Halsey Hall Chapter, has written articles for SABR publications and for the journal *Base Ball*, edits *Originals*, the newsletter of SABR's Origins of Baseball Committee, and operates a vintage base ball team, the Quickstep BBC, in the Twin Cities. He also belongs to the 19th Century Committee and the Biographical Research Committee.

STEW THORNLEY is an author of books on sports history for adults and young readers. He received the SABR-Macmillan Baseball Research Award in 1988 for his first book, *On to Nicollet: The Glory and Fame of the Minneapolis Millers*. He also enjoys visiting graves of notable people and is the author of *Six Feet Under: A Graveyard Guide to Minnesota*. Stew is an official scorer for Minnesota Twins home games and also does the datacasting of games for mlb.com Gameday. He lives in Roseville, Minnesota, with his wife, Brenda Himrich, and their cats, Jeter and Mickey.

Upper Midwest Hall of Honor

Honorees were selected as players unless otherwise noted

John Anderson, coach, Nashwauk and Keewatin, Minnesota

Adrian "Cap" Anson, Marshalltown, Iowa

Dave Bancroft, Sioux City, Iowa

Chief Bender, White Earth Reservation, Minnesota

Johnny Blanchard, Minneapolis, Minnesota

Mike Boddicker, Cedar Rapids, Iowa

Joe Bush, Brainerd, Minnesota

Jim Eisenreich, St. Cloud, Minnesota

Darin Erstad, Jamestown, North Dakota

Urban "Red" Faber, Cascade, Iowa

Angelo Giuliani, player and scout, St. Paul, Minnesota

Dave Goltz, Rothsay, Minnesota

Burleigh Grimes, Clear Lake, Wisconsin

Travis Hafner, Sykeston, North Dakota

Halsey Hall, media, Minneapolis, Minnesota

Sid Hartman, media, Minneapolis, Minnesota

Kent Hrbek, Bloomington, Minnesota

Walt Jocketty, executive, Minneapolis, Minnesota

Jerry Kindall, player and coach, St. Paul, Minnesota

Jerry Koosman, Appleton/Morris, Minnesota

Corey Koskie, Anola, Manitoba, Canada

Roger Maris, Fargo, North Dakota

Joe Mauer, St. Paul, Minnesota

Paul Molitor, St. Paul, Minnesota

Jack Morris, St. Paul, Minnesota

Andy Pafko, Boyceville, Wisconsin

Dick Siebert, player and coach, St. Paul, Minnesota

Terry Steinbach, New Ulm, Minnesota

Toni Stone, St. Paul, Minnesota

Hal Trosky, Norway, Iowa

Rube Walberg, Pine City, Minnesota

Charlie Walters, player and media, St. Paul, Minnesota

Wes Westrum, Clearbrook, Minnesota

Dave Winfield, St. Paul, Minnesota

Notes: In general, the hometown listed is where the person lived during high school. The selections were made by the Halsey Hall Chapter of SABR with people considered from Minnesota, the Dakotas, Manitoba, and portions of Iowa, Wisconsin, and Ontario. Thanks to Kevin Johnson for providing information on the players' high schools.